AIMPOL
NORMANDY
ST. MALO
ES
GEORGES
TEMBAULT
SAINT-BRIEUC
AINT-
BRIEUC
LAMBALLE
MONTFORT
MAINE
RENNES
LOUDEAC
NTIVY
RENNES
ST. MALO
Villaine
River
VITRÉ
ANNES
PLOERMEL
ANNE D'AURAY
ANJOU
VANNES
RIEUX
NANTES
ST. NAZAIRE
River
NANTES
Loire

GOOD FATHER IN BRITTANY

THE LIFE OF
BLESSED JULIEN MAUNOIR, S.J.

GOOD FATHER IN BRITTANY

THE LIFE OF BLESSED JULIEN MAUNOIR

By

MARTIN P. HARNEY, S.J.

ST. PAUL EDITIONS

IMPRIMI POTEST:

JOHN V. O'CONNER, S.J.
December 8, 1963

NIHIL OBSTAT:

MATTHEW P. STAPLETON
Diocesan Censor

IMPRIMATUR:

✠ RICHARD CARDINAL CUSHING
Archbishop of Boston
January 24, 1964

In conformity with the decree of Urban VIII, all expressions regarding the sanctity or holiness of persons not yet canonized or beatified are made without any anticipation of the decision of the ecclesiastical authorities.

Library of Congress Catalog Card Number: 64-19478

Printed by *Daughters of St. Paul*
50 St. Paul's Ave., Jamaica Plain, Boston, Mass. 02130

To the diocesan priests,
my brethren,
in gratitude
for their help
and inspiraton
through all the years

FOREWORD

On the twentieth-first day of May, 1951, Pius XII proclaimed the beatification of Père Julien Maunoir (1606-1683), a Breton Jesuit widely known and loved in the turbulent Brittany of his own seventeenth century and reverently remembered by the Bretons of today as "An Tad Mad", the Good Father. Records from his hand and from other hands reveal that he preached four hundred missions, ten to a year on the average, during a forty-two year missionary crusade. The records reveal further that crowds, sometimes twenty thousand in number, sometimes thirty thousand, attended his missions. He made teaching the catechism so large a part of his labors, employing charts, symbols and tableaus, anticipating the methods of modern visual education, that he might well be considered for a patron for the Confraternity of Christian Doctrine. He furthered the good effects of his instructions by composing in Breton a large number of doctrinal hymns, which have gained for him a unique place in the literature of that Celtic tongue. He had the wisdom to organize the diocesan clergy, one thousand of them, into a closely knit apostolate to assist him in preaching, teaching and bringing sacramental life to the people in their desperate need. He had also the vision to pioneer the movement for laymen's retreats. Through forty-two years Père Maunoir traveled, on foot most of the time, from diocese to diocese, holding aloft his crucifix as a symbol and a challenge. Thus did he become "An Tad Mad", the Good Father. He did not travel alone. A mystic himself he had the assistance of the prayers and penances of mystics under his direction. Blessings, favors, even miracles attest that God Almighty furthered his work. Yet he trod not an easy road; his fight was against frailty, corruption, sin and diabolism. When he came to die, he was Brittany's best loved personage; after three centuries he remains the uniquely revered hero of the Bretons.

The writer of this biography has the very special obligation of thanking the Breton priests and nuns who helped him in its composition. Their whole-hearted generosity has been most touching; one could seek no stronger proof of "Breton Faith". In particular gratitude is due to the late Père Emile Le Provost, S.J., Vice-Postulator, for his assistance, for his gift of two rare books:

Boschet's *Le Parfait Missionnaire, ou Vie du R. P. Julien Maunoir,* and Le Roux's *Recueil des Vertus et des Miracles du R. P. Julien Maunoir, S.J.*, and for his personal gift of a first class relic. Gratitude is also due to the memory of the late Pére P. d'Herouville, S.J., for his excellent works, *La Jeunesse du Vénérable Julien Maunoir* (his own personal and last copy) and *Le Vincent Ferrier du XVII e Siècle, Le Vénérable Julien Maunoir;* to Père R. M. de la Chevasnerie, S.J. for his very interesting, *Le Tad Mad, Vie du Bienheureux Julien Maunoir, S.J.*, and for his *Panégyrique du Bienheureux Julien Maunoir, S.J.*: to Père J. de Tonquedec, S.J. for his study, *Le Bienheureux Père Maunoir et le Clergé Breton*: to M. le chanoine Louis Kerbiriou for the manuscript copy of his conference, *L'attitude du Père Maunoir à l'égard des états mystiques* and his learned book, *Les Missions Bretonnes.* The writer is very happy to express his obligations to Mère Sainte-Armelle, now gone to God, and to the sisters of the Congregation, Les Filles du Saint-Esprit, for their keen and helpful interest. But his best thanks must be reserved for Soeur Marguerite Félicie, F.S.E. for her valuable help and for her numerous encouraging letters. She was most generous in her sacrifice of time although she was carrying a crowded teaching schedule and was in the midst of the publication of her own book, *Revêtus de Force.* May God and the Tad Mad bless these sons and daughters of Brittany!

Acknowledgements are also due to the following publishing firms for their generous permissions to use material from their publications: The Gilmary Society of New York for quotations from the *Catholic Encyclopedia;* Burns, Oates and Washbourne of London for a quotation from Henri Joly's *Life of St. John Eudes*; Librairie Bloud et Gay of Paris for quotations from Henri Bremond's *Histoire littéraire du Sentiment religieux en France*; and the Imprimeries Simon of Rennes for a picture from Marthe Le Berre's *Un Grand Missionnaire Breton.*

Finally the writer must express his sincere gratitude to three colleagues of the Faculty of Boston College: Father Joseph D. Gauthier, S.J., Father Maurice V. Dullea, S.J. and Mr. John F. Norton for their kindly, unfailing patience with a persistent inquirer and for their invaluable assistance in refashioning the manuscript.

Feast of Bl. Julien Maunoir, January 28, 1964

CONTENTS

Chapter I

BRETON BACKGROUND

Brittany, land of ancient monuments, of timeless traditions, and of Celtic speech was the country of Bl. Julien Maunoir, S.J. He was born there and he labored there for the entire forty-two years of his apostolate. What is this Brittany? It is the northwest corner of France, a unique and isolated region, comprising a massive peninsula which thrusts bold headlands far out into the Atlantic. In length it extends 124 miles from east to west. In breadth, at its widest it stretches along Normandy, Maine and the Loire country for 105 miles; and at its narrowest, across the western extremity of Finistère, it reaches but 62 miles.

Washed by the sea on three sides, Brittany possesses the longest coastline in all France, 475 miles from Cancale on the Baie du Saint-Michel, in the north, around to Sainte-Nazaire at the mouth of the Loire, in the south. This coastline is the most varied in France. Wide blue bays framed in yellow salt marshes, like the Baie de Douarnenez, continuously indent a rugged shore, except where great almost landlocked bodies of water, such as the Rade de Brest, stretch out to afford safe fishing and sailing. Several tranquil estuaries wind inland pleasantly through green meadows to reach quiet little brown ports. So the Rance leads to Dinant, and the Odet comes up to Quimper. At the ocean's edge here and there rise up mighty granite promontories, sombre gray sentinels, to hurl back the foaming attacks of the sea's long deep-green swells. So stand Pointe de Saint-Mathieu and Pointe de Raz. Offshore there are numerous rocky islands; best known among them are Batz, Ouessant, Molène and Sein. Guarding both capes and islands are sharp reefs and dangerous shoals through which swirl treacherous currents. Small wonder that Brittany bred bold Jacques Cartiers and sturdy "Pêcheurs d'Island." Today as in the past fishing-towns literally dot the Breton coast. It was along those shores, around those cliffs and into those home-ports that Père Maunoir journeyed for more than forty years to cleanse and to strengthen tough-fibered souls.

From the low-lying coastal plains quickly mount the uplands of the interior. Two lines of high plateaus cross the peninsula, one paralleling the north coast, the other the south coast. They converge in the west in Finistère. The highest peak in the north is Mont Saint-Michel-de-Brasparts, 1,280 ft.; the highest in the south is Menez-Homs, 1,083 ft. This interior is a vast region of grave and melancholy landscapes. Whole districts contain nothing but far extending moors, called locally "landes." Lonely undulating heaths, they are cut by sombre ravines and marked occasionally by remnants of those primeval forests which gave to Brittany the description, "land of granite covered with oak." Long ago the forests were cleared. Today there are only scattered traces such as the Forêt de Paimpomt (23 miles square), the *Brocéliande* of the Welch and Breton romances that told of King Arthur, Merlin and the fairy Vivien, "the lady of the lake". It would be hard to say how much of the forests were standing in Père Maunoir's time. Very likely some dense masses still remained. In them and on the solitary moors was fostered the diabolism which he battled unremittingly. Countless times Père Maunoir climbed those uplands and traversed those desolate moors to bring salvation to the lonely peasants in the scattered tiny hamlets. Towards the eastern border the forests and the *landes* soften, especially on the plateaus surrounding the basin of Rennes. Farming is more extensive and the population is more numerous. It was in the northeast corner, on the plateau of Fougères, that Père Julien was born.

The never-distant sea affects the days and works of all Bretons. The temperature is fairly mild, with neither extreme heat in summer nor great cold in winter. But cloudiness is frequent and rains are numerous and abundant, for the mountains do not rise high enough to bar the sweep of the Atlantic storms. For days on end the weather can be raw and bleak. Père Maunoir encountered some of his severest trials plodding along primitive paths in the cold, rainy hills.

Brittany's history extends far back into megalithic times and begins with the mysterious people who erected her menhirs, cromlechs and dolmens. About the fourth century B.C. invading Gauls made the peninsula completely Celtic. The region came to be known as Armorica. In the middle of the first century B.C. the Roman conquerors appeared. The Celts resisted Caesar's legions with desperate valor, but all in vain. Eventually the Armoricans became completely Latin in speech, dress, customs and outlook. Christianity was established with an hierarchy of bishops dependent on St. Martin's see of Tours in the fourth century A.D. Some scholars believe St. Patrick to have been an Armorican. He was a Romanized Celt; and his birthplace, if not in the island of Britain, might well have been in the Armorican peninsula.

Roman Armorica lasted until the second half of the fifth century when it was Celticized again, this time by British refugees fleeing the sword and slavery of the Anglo-Saxons. Mostly from Devon and Cornwall they crossed the Channel in a constant stream of small boats. First they settled in the southwestern part, which they named Cornouailles after their old home, then they took over the whole coastal region and finally penetrated into the forests and moors of the interior. Though received with kindness by the Gallo-Roman Armoricans, the newcomers before long began a violent conquest of the country. A long and bitter struggle ensued, but in the end the refugees gained the mastery of the greater part of the peninsula. The British imposed their own language on the conquered and made a Celtic tongue once more the speech of Armorica. As it developed variations from the Cornish language it received the designation, "Breton". Similarly the people grew to be known as "Bretons" and the country, as "Brittany". But the absorption of the Gallo-Romans was not everywhere complete. In the eastern areas the fusion was not achieved until the tenth century; indeed the entire eastern frontier, the Frankish March, always remained Latin. Two divisions eventuated: Lower Brittany, Breton-speaking; and Upper Brittany, French-speaking. The traditions of the new-coming Bretons, however, obtained a wider extension; even in modern times they are encountered in all parts of the peninsula. Bl. Julien Maunoir belonged to both divisions; he was born in Upper Brittany, and he labored largely in Lower Brittany.

Numerous Celtic saints, British and Irish, accompanied the refugees or worked among them after the settlement. They laid the foundation of the proverbial Catholic Faith of Brittany. Throughout the new Brittany soon appeared the characteristics of Celtic Christianity: pre-eminence of monasticism, predilection for solitary mysticism and the veneration of a host of local saints. This is evidenced by the frequent occurrence in Breton place-names of the Celtic prefixes, *Lann, Loc,* and *Plou. Lann* meant monastery, as Lanrivoaré, the monastery of St. Rivoaré; *Loc* meant hermitage, as Locronan, the hermitage of St. Ronan; *Plou* meant people, or parish, as Ploucadeuc, the people of St. Cadoc. Missionary monks from Wales founded all the dioceses of Brittany, with one exception. Thus Saint Brioc founded Saint-Brieuc; Saint Paul Aurélian, Saint-Pol-de-Léon; Saint Samson and his successor, Saint Magloire, Dol; Saint Malo, Aleth which later became Saint-Malo; Saint Tugdual, born in Wales of Breton stock, Tréguier. The exception was Saint Corentin, a native Breton, who founded the bishopric of Quimper. [1]

Among the Irish evangelists of their Breton fellow-Celts was the great Saint Columban, who began his

[1] From the first days and through the middle ages it was called Cornouailles.

apostolic career in Brittany and at Locminé built his first monastery. Others included Saints Brendan, Fingar, Briac, Maudez and Vouga. The abbey of Landévennec, celebrated among the early Breton monasteries, revealed a mingling of three Celtic peoples: it was founded by Saint Guénolé, a native Breton, the son of refugees from old Britain; it was much frequented by Irish monks, at least in its beginnings; and its spirit embraced both a very austere asceticism and a wide-spreading apostolic zeal, the two distinctive marks of the monasticism of Ireland.

The history of Brittany in the early Middle Ages is an obscure record of the petty conflicts of shadowy princelings, and of the unrelenting resistance to Frankish attempts at overlordship. In the last part of the ninth century overwhelming disaster swept up from the sea in the incursions of the Norse pirates. In raid after raid, the ruthless heathen massacred and enslaved first along the seaboard and then through the interior. The Vikings' invasions reached tidal-wave proportions from 921 to 936, when they held the whole of Brittany in their savage grasp. The pagan flood receded after a three years' war of deliverance, but it left a legacy of widespread disorders.

As elsewhere the reforms of Pope St. Gregory VII were desperately needed. But in Brittany there was little hope for better things, since the clergy under the domination of a lay aristocracy, indifferent or worse, had become ignorant and corrupt. To remedy the sad conditions the bishops and some noble-hearted counts sought aid from French monasteries. The monks responded and by their new foundations effected a thorough reformation. They also gave a strong impulse to the country's agricultural development by their clearing of large tracts of the forests and by their improvement of the barren soil of the *landes.*

The Bretons successfully opposed William of Normandy's attempt to add their duchy to his conquests. But its independence remained in constant jeopardy, with the aggressive Normans not only all along its eastern frontier but also across the Channel on the English shore. Despite valiant efforts the duchy gradually sank into a position of a subordinate state between the French and the English, and was often the battleground of their rivalries. At the end of the twelfth century the line of native dukes died out. For the next two hundred years Brittany was ruled by dukes backed by France or by England. Their wars sometimes deluged the Breton towns in blood. The last ruler was the beloved Duchess Anne of Brittany (1477-1514). It was her marriage to Louis XII that brought about the union of Brittany with France. Anne maintained her personal rule and Louis XII pledged himself and his heirs to respect the liberties and the customs of the duchy. The Bretons, retaining their parlement at Rennes, guarded their autonomy jealously and fairly successfully in the face of Bourbon absolutism right down to the French Revolution.

Medieval Bretons concerned themselves with much more than dynastic problems. For one thing they preserved their Celticism. "Breton" has a meaning today because a grave yet imaginative people clung tenaciously through centuries to their traditions, customs and language. Of even greater intensity was their dedication to religion. Seven of Brittany's eight cathedrals were erected by them between the thirteenth and the sixteenth century. One has but to view Quimper's imposing medieval structure to appreciate the piety of a people who were neither rich nor numerous. Their religious spirit was continually nourished at the numerous shrines where medieval Bretons loved to venerate the Blessed Mother of God, or Saint Anne, their aunt as they called her, or their own Celtic apostles. No wonder then that vast crowds listened to St. Vincent Ferrer when he preached in Brittany near the end of his life. He died at Vannes in 1418. No wonder that medieval Brittany produced her own great saint, a Breton of Bretons, Saint Yves born at Tréguier in 1253. First as a just and incorruptible lawyer he gained the title "the poor man's advocate;" and later as a parish priest he earned the blessings of his flock by his devotion to them and by his compassion for the afflicted. St. Yves died at Kermartin in 1303.

At the close of the Middle Ages, Brittany in common with the rest of Christendom was grievously affected by the confusion of beliefs and the breakdown of morals resulting from interminable wars, fearsome plagues and the intellectual anarchy of the pagan humanists. Yet in the subsequent religious revolution, Brittany stood firm in her ancient Catholicism. Only in a few places in the east, notably Vitré, did Calvinism obtain even a brief ascendency. Vitré, it may be recalled, was a possession of the Colignys, the powerful family that headed the Huguenots. Through the thirty-five sanguinary years of the Huguenot Wars the Bretons paid dearly for their staunch adherence to Catholicism. At the end of the bitter conflicts they found themselves in the midst of their ruins disordered and demoralized in all save their Faith. It was in Brittany so desolated that Bl. Julien Maunoir began his apostolate.

This apostolate was a part of the brilliant revival French Catholicism made in the seventeenth century. It shared every phase: the extension of faith, the improvement of morals, the rejuvenation of the spirit of the clergy, the flowering of mysticism, and the re-evangelizing of the common people. This last phase associates Bl. Julien Maunoir with the great French missionaries: St. Francis de Sales in Chablais, St. John Francis Régis in Vivarais; St. Peter Fourier in Lorraine; Ven. Michel Le Nobletz, his predecessor, in Brittany; St. Vincent de Paul in Paris, Picardy and all over France; St. John Eudes in Normandy; Jean le Jeune in Limoges and Languedoc; Antoine Yvan in Provence; and, at the end, St. Louis de Montfort in Eastern Brittany and Vendée.

What was the state of religion in Brittany at the beginning of the seventeenth century? Certainly ignorance and neglect were to be encountered in every part of the duchy. [1] Yet sweeping judgments must be avoided. One can concentrate unduly on the darker aspects while trying to bring out the truly great achievements of Bl. Julien. Even the denunciations of abuses made by

[1] Some uncomprehending writers have portrayed the Bretons as a backward people, existing in semi-barbarism. Such they surely were not. The prosperity of the duchy before the Huguenot Wars was renowned in all France. Abundant exports were carried from its ports to many European countries by adventurous Breton sailors. Jacques Cartier, discoverer of Canada, was one of them. Old inventories of the chateaux of the noblesse reveal them as large feudal abodes, surrounded by spacious barns and stables. The chateaux were perhaps not impressive exteriorly, but they were well-known for the wealth of their furniture and decorations. Similar inventories show the homes of the bourgeois, and even of the peasants, to have been substantial structures. The nicely-wrought and beautifully carved tables and chairs from peasants' cottages prove that the arts flourished in humble quarters. But the best art in Brittany was to be found in the churches with their beautifully stained-glass and their imposing statues. The great open-air crucifixion groups of Brittany belong to these years. The much admired Calvary of Guéhenno dates from 1550, and the world-renowned Calvary of Plougastel with its two hundred figures was erected in 1602-1604.

Père Maunoir, as also those made by Dom Le Nobletz, must be accepted cautiously and in their context. Otherwise, how explain the immediate and enthusiastic response of the people to Maunoir's preaching, of the large numbers of the secular priests who joined in the labors of his missions. Such is the opinion of Abbé Brémond, a redoubtable critic surely.

The principal saving element, beside the grace of God, was the religious, even mystical, character of the Breton people themselves. But what of their practise of religion at the beginning of the seventeenth century? Certainly there were abundant evidence of popular piety. They thronged in crowded processions to their numerous and beloved shrines; they generously supported financially the recurring jubilees at Léon; and they joined faithfully the active confraternities of the Blessed Sacrament, of the Rosary, or of the Holy Souls, which were to be found in most of their parishes. More essentially the Bretons were constant in attending their Sunday Masses and Vespers. On the word of Père Maunoir himself they were faithful in the performance of their Easter duty.

It would be gratuitous to assert that this religious practise was largely routine formalism. However unlettered the simple rude folk were, they believed with complete conviction in God, whole-heartedly adored Jesus Christ, and confidently prayed to the Blessed Virgin and to the Saints. The crowds always besieging Père Maunoir's confessional knew that the sacramental absolution washed away their sins. The throngs at the communion rail from the first days of the mission movement certainly venerated and believed unquestionably in the Holy Eucharist. The Breton people characteristically maintained a complete and an abiding loyalty for the

Catholic Church. Amongst them Protestantism never made headway. Philip Le Noir, a Huguenot historian, admits that at the height of the religious revolution the Calvinists had no more than eighteen churches in the peninsula, all near the eastern border. Père Maunoir used to assert that the man was yet to be born who heard a Breton-speaker preaching any other religion than the Catholic. Yves Le Gac, parish priest of Plouvorn in the diocese of Saint-Pol-de-Léon, could say: "It was certain that no person in this diocese had made a profession of heresy."

About the clergy of Brittany, especially from the second half of the sixteenth century, there was much that was admirable. The bishops in the main were zealous shepherds. Prelates like René de Louët, Charles de Rosmadec, François de Visdelou and François Coëtlogon caused Père Maunoir to exclaim: "Be thou a thousand times praised, my God, for having given to your church of Brittany such holy bishops." Among the numerous lower clergy not an inconsiderable number devoted themselves to the religious instruction of the people, a fact amply demonstrated by the people's quick response to the missionary's exhortations. The most striking testimony to the essential soundness of Breton priesthood was the rallying of the secular clergy to Maunoir's appeal for assistants. He was able to organize a body of co-workers that numbered over a thousand priests.

These brighter aspects should be remembered when considering the pictures which Le Nobletz and Maunoir drew of the ignorance of faith and the collapse of morals among the Bretons. Yet these two missionaries were no scandal-hunters. And their strictures were supported by many of their priest-assistants. In the good fields of

Brittany the enemy of God and mankind had been sowing the tares and cockles long and widely. During three centuries the duchy had been the fighting ground for several bitter wars. The last ones, the Huguenot Wars, had entailed forty years of bloody battles, stubborn sieges, agrarian insurrections and fearful massacres of peasants. Peace in 1597 found Brittany, from end to end, a desolated and a prostrate land. To add to its woes bands of ferocious brigands infested the province. Most evil of all was La Fontenelle, "a beast of prey with a human face," "Christian in name but Turk in deed," who terrorized the entire peninsula, levied ransoms on and killed without mercy even his own co-religionists–the terrible massacre of Penmarc'h has been laid to his charge. The undisciplined bands spared not even the Church. They pillaged the Abbey of Landévennec; they extorted large sums from the bishop of Léon; they sacked the parish-church of Mizarnou and carried off its gold chalices and jewelled crosses.

Nor was there an end of misery with the peace. In the years following the wars, the Breton people had to endure widespread calamities: plagues, like that at Quimper, which carried off in a single month 1,700 victims; a long famine, which lasted through a whole year and brought wolves into the streets of the towns. In consequence there was a great diminution of the population, in some places by two-thirds. Overwhelming debts mounted up everywhere. Quimper had to be freed from taxes for fifteen years to meet the burden of 166,000 livres for rebuilding its ruins. In the fearful train of war and calamity, of bloodshed and licence, a wide paralysis of good and a sad decline of morals were inevitable.

In the universal turmoil, it is to be expected that the spirit and morale of the clergy were affected by the collapse of all values in the dreadful wars. Worldly priests, avaricious, ignorant, idle and often vicious were numerous. That there was a crying need for a reform among the clergy of France, the dedicated labors of St. Vincent de Paul, M. Olier and M. Boudoise amply proved. The Breton clergy were perhaps less affected by the evils of the times; still they had their own very distressing problems. There was in the first place a lack of proper episcopal supervision. More than once the bishopric had been bestowed on Italian ecclesiastics, who never set foot in their dioceses. Some of the resident bishops, French and even Breton, lacked all knowledge of the Breton tongue and hence were seriously hampered in dealing with their flocks. Pluralism, absenteeism and the appointment of incapable officials gravely weakened vital discipline. The dioceses of Léon, Tréguier and Quimper suffered from continual changing of bishops. Quimper had not been visited in the regular form by its bishop for two centuries. The presence of worthy bishops, especially after the Council of Trent, does not gainsay the persisting effects of former evils.

Complaints were frequent that the higher clergy, the pastors, canons and prebendaries, were chiefly interested in acquiring benefices, in living grandly, in busying themselves with secular affairs, and in enriching their relatives. Some were blamed for abandoning their pastoral duties to meagerly-paid curates. Others were criticised for being strangers to the specific problems of the country, and especially for being ignorant of the Breton language. Many were charged with ignorance, lack of vocation or spiritual formation. René de Rieux, the reforming bishop of Léon in the second decade of the seventeenth century, was particularly caustic in criticising some of his pastors. In justice, it must be noted that his criticisms have been questioned as exaggerated.

Against the lower clergy, the curates and sub-curates, grave charges of ignorance, neglect and vice were levelled. That large numbers of the priests were ignorant or very poorly educated was only too true. In Brittany as everywhere else, until the Council of Trent, clerical formation was a sadly haphazard affair. The greatest reformatory innovation of Trent was the seminary, the institution devoted to the complete and solid training of future priests. Yet it was well into the seventeenth century before Brittany possessed its first seminary. A common reproach for the Breton priests was their meagre knowledge of Latin. It was probably true, for in the duchy there were no great schools where boys could learn Latin well until the Jesuits opened the Collège of Rennes in 1608 and the Collège of Quimper in 1620.

Critics berated the lower clergy for laziness and lack of zeal. They were portrayed as too little occupied with priestly duties, as neglectful of their flocks, never preaching to them, never even teaching the catechism to the children, as wasters of their vocations in unsacerdotal employments. The truth of the matter was that there were too many priests in Brittany, too many with too little to do. Some were idle because they were waiting for a benefice to be vacated; others, because they had failed to obtain one. Such unemployed priests were often found in the quality of witnesses at baptisms and marriages, or in humble service at chapels-of-ease or wayside shrines. A number lived at home or on small plots which they tilled themselves. Some poverty-stricken priests eked out a livelihood in work incongruous with their priesthood. Truly Brittany had an ecclesiastical proletariat. The Bretons had a name for such a subordinate cleric; they called him "Dom Ian." How numerous the "Dom Ians" were may be judged from the diocese of Léon, where there were 90 parishes and missions with 1,200 priests–an average of 13 to a parish. Bishop de Rieux, attempting to solve the problem of the numbers presenting themselves daily to say their masses, recommended that the pastors arrange the masses successively until 10 in the morning.

Finally there were undisciplined and vicious clerics. Under the conditions obtaining, it was inevitable that some of impecunious and ignorant "Dom Ians" lived unworthily. Among the higher clergy, too, there were the disordered members. The chapters of Léon and of Quimper complained of the irregular lives of some of the canons and severely punished them and other clerics who haunted inns or drew their swords in tavern brawls. The reports of visitations, however, revealed one redeeming feature: there were relatively few failures in chastity. The Breton clergy preserved themselves a pure priesthood. Their special failing was weakness for strong drink. Even First Mass celebrations were occasions for heavy drinking that might last for days. Sobriety for the Breton priests of those days was a heroic virtue, even as it was for their people. In 1651 a sodality of priests for combatting drunkenness among clerics was established at Quimper. One happily notes that by the eighteenth century the evil had decreased to a great extent. Whatever else may have been their deficiencies, the Breton clergy, from the mitred bishops to the humblest "Dom Ians," kept themselves completely free from heresy. Such loyalty to the Faith, maintained through a long era of religious conflicts, was surely of no small merit.

The people of Brittany reflected pretty much the character of their priests. There was a gross ignorance of matters of faith in some areas; the missionaries cite startling instances. Certainly in the orgy and blood of the religious wars many forgot their Baptismal promises. In the upper classes were to be found the libertines and sceptics of the Pagan Renaissance; in the lower classes, the adepts of subversive sects. As everywhere else sensuality had its victims and slaves. Superstition, met at every turn, was a very disturbing evil, especially when with it were involved sorcery or diabolism. In the anarchic disorder old heathen survivals emerged once more. In such sinister forces Père Maunoir encountered his most formidable antagonists. And yet, in spite of all the evils, Brittany did not lapse into a pagan society. The numbers who had gone astray did not lose Christ completely. If many were sluggishly indifferent, and for this they were not wholly responsible, the majority of Bretons loyally held to their Catholic spirit and practices. Brittany was still a good field, even if the tares and the cockle had been widely sown.

Bl. Julien Maunoir worked that field assiduously for more than forty years, eradicating the weeds, refreshing the soil and bringing the good grain to golden harvest. What he accomplished was much more than a reformation; it was a glowing revivification of the Catholic faith in the loyal hearts of the Bretons, something which neither Voltarians, nor Jacobins, nor Secularists have been able to destroy. More than ever he made Breton faith proverbial.

Chapter 2

FIRST YEARS

In the northeast corner of Brittany, among the green hills that border Normandy quietly sits the small village of Saint-Georges-de-Reintembault. There Bl. Julien Maunoir, S.J., the Breton's "Good Father," was born October 1, 1606. He was christened on the day of his birth, as the ancient register of the parish shows. The entry reads: "October, 1606, the first day of the month was baptized Julien, son of Isaac Maunoir and Gabrielle Deloris, his wife. The god-parents were Dom Julien Jamet, priest, and Mathurine Cador. Officiating M.D. Bertin, Pastor." Isaac Maunoir was a small cloth-merchant. With Gabrielle's help he conducted his little shop on the ground floor of their humble dwelling. The house is still standing. It is a solid granite structure, like its neighbors, and with them keeps in perfect alignment along the village's narrow street. Dom Jamet, a family friend was a venerable priest who dwelt in the parish. Of Mathurine Cador nothing is known. Dom Michel Bertin deserved his reputation as the zealous pastor of his simple flock. The baby was the fifth of the seven children of Isaac and Gabrielle. Earlier that year they had suffered a great loss in the death of their eldest son, Julien of whom they had had high hopes as assistant in their little business. A pious couple they looked upon the new son as God's consolation for them in their sorrow. So they named the infant Julien after his deceased brother; and straightway they dedicated their freshly baptized boy to the service of the altar, if such should be the holy will of God.

Somewhat later, it would seem, far in the western extremity of Brittany, the destiny of the child was revealed to Vénérable Michel Le Nobletz, a lonely missionary among the fisherfolk there. He had been begging God for a successor; and now he received the intimation that his petition would be granted. Dom Michel did not keep the revelation hidden. During a mission in Landerneau, in 1613, he foretold that the Jesuits would be established in Quimper, the chief town of the west, and that his successor would be a member of their Society. Also in the same year at Douarnenez the holy priest paused in the middle of his sermon to cry out: "Let us thank God that he has given me a successor. He is seven years of age; he is of the diocese of Rennes and he will be a Jesuit." The distant missionary had no specific knowledge of the child of the Maunoirs. One day, however, he was to become the father-in-God to Julien Maunoir.

The birthplace of Bl. Julien.

Saint-Georges-de-Reintembault.

Dom Michel Le Nobletz was born at Plouguernau in the diocese of Saint-Pol-de Léon in 1577; he belonged to a noble family of the district. He made his classical studies at the Jesuit colleges of Bordeaux and Agen. On their completion he resolved to dedicate himself to the fishermen and peasants of Léon, Tréguier and Cornouailles. After following the theological courses of the Sorbonne the young nobleman was ordained a priest in 1607. In imitation of the ancient apostles of Brittany he spent a year in prayerful and penitential preparation as a solitary on the sea-cliffs and sands of Penmarc'h. He entered the Dominican Order at Morlaix, but left after an unhappy experience. Then Dom Le Nobletz found his true vocation, that of an itinerant missionary in the service of the bishops of the three western dioceses of Brittany. For six years he evangelized the isolated islanders of Ouessant, Molène, Sein and Batz, and the fisherfolk of the adjacent coasts of Léon. Then he moved into the diocese of Cornouailles establishing his headquarters at Douarnenez, out of which he worked for a quarter of a century. Dom Michel preached to his humble listeners the simplest of sermons; but he delivered them with all the fire of a Hebrew prophet. He expanded his message by composing catechetical hymns and devising *enigma* [1] charts, whose strange symbols he explained with his famous white pointer. Both hymns and charts later became characteristic features of the Breton Missions.

Dom Le Nobletz toiled all alone, except on the rare occasion when a Dominican friend, Père Quintin, came to assist him. He had often to struggle against the opposition of dissolute nobles and of indolent priests.

[1] *Enigma* charts will be explained in Chapter VIII.

VENERABLE MICHEL LE NOBLETZ.
1577 - 1652.

From an 18th century statue erected on his tomb in the church of Le Conquet.

Eventually misinformed ecclesiastical authority drove him from Douarnenez. He returned to his native Lèon, where in the coastal village of Le Conquet he found a refuge. There he spent the last six years of his life, for most of the time incapacitated by a severe paralysis. With the fisherfolk caring for his wants, Dom Michel in his small hut on the seashore relived the prayerfulness and austerities of the old Celtic solitaries. Despite his infirmities he plied his pen busily, writing numerous tracts in Breton, French and Latin. He died in 1621 on a borrowed bed, for his own he had given to a beggar-man. All Bretons hope for the day when Dom Michel Le Nobletz will be beatified, and for the day when together with Bl. Julien Maunoir he will be canonized.

The childhood of Julien Maunoir passed peacefully enough in the modest dwelling of his parents. Their training of the children was somewhat austere, but it was founded on their own piety and charity. The last was well known in the countryside since the good couple made it their practice to share the meagre profits of their small trade with the poor. The solid virtues of his father and mother prompted, years later, their missionary son in his sermons and writings to present them as true models of parental duty, instruction and correction. The date of Julien's First Communion is not precisely known; but it must have occurred before his eighth birthday, for in 1615 he received Confirmation from the Bishop of Rennes, François Lochiver. It was indeed appropriate that this learned and holy prelate imparted the gifts of the Holy Ghost to Brittany's future Jesuit apostle. He was a native of Lower Brittany and he was the founder of the Jesuit collège of Rennes. The ceremony took place at Fougères; there the children of the hamlets roundabout had been gathered for the sacrament. The old frontier town lay some thirteen miles of hill-country roads from Saint-Georges-de-Reintembault, a long distance for a little lad on his first journey from home. But what marvels there were for eager eyes! The new fields and the distant uplands seemed never ending. And at long last the wide gray walls of Fougères loomed up, with eight towers rising from the ramparts. Inside were narrow, thronged streets clustering about a high, grim feudal castle. There was too a great church, sparkling with lighted candles and sweet-smelling with clouds of incense. And finally, seated on a glorious throne was a grave, holy bishop with a mitre on his head and a crozier in his hand.

Fénelon's saying of St. Teresa that "the very games of her childhood felt the first fruits of the Holy Ghost," applied to small Julien Maunoir. Up in the loft of his home he loved to play at imitating the priest in the ceremonies he had watched at church. That was not very remarkable; Catholic children in all times have done the same. More prophetic of the future missionary was his leading of processions of his playmates to the Cross of Lac. Many, many years afterwards, during the processes for the beatification of Père Julien, old men, once the little marchers in his processions, delighted to describe the scenes. Little barefooted Julien, calling from house to house, would assemble his comrades in the center of the village and align them in two ranks; then he would lead them, all singing hymns and reciting prayers, just like the big folk in the fêtes-processions, across the Rue de Longuève and off to the Cross of Lac, a distance of a good three miles. On arrival the wee pilgrims would kneel before the ancient cross, recite the Pater, Ave and Creed and sing a familiar hymn. Then small Julien would climb up upon the base and speak vigorously to his childish followers, just as the preachers did. Finally, reforming the ranks he would lead the little lads back in good and pious order.

Sometimes he gathered his comrades in the parish church. From the pulpit he would recite with them their familiar prayers. Then he would lead his small auditors to shrill singing of hymns which they knew so well. They were restless as only small boys can be, but they obeyed Julien's commands promptly. The old men assured the officials of the process of the amiable and joyous goodness of their little leader of those distant days, insisting that in him there was not a trace of priggishness. The village elders, watching the processions, divined the future priest and preacher. They congratulated Isaac and Gabrielle on their blessed child and predicted for him a holy destiny.

The most significant trait of Julien's boyhood was his devotion to the Holy Eucharist; for him the Tabernacle held almost a mystical appeal. A anecdote oft-retold in Brittany illustrates his intense devotion. To each of the Maunoir children was assigned a special task. Julien's charge was tending the family's cow in a small field belonging to his parents. The field was called "the thorn field," from a hedge surrounding it; it is still pointed out to visitors. One can visualize barefooted Julien stepping along the road and guiding the peaceful beast to the grazing plot, like those other small lads, later to be St. Vincent de Paul, St. John Bosco, or St. Joseph Sarto. One half the Thorn Field was a pasture, the other half was a vegetable garden for the family. A few yards away stood the parish church. Julien from the field frequently prayed to his Master dwelling in its tabernacle. On one occasion hearing the mass-bell tolling, the lad forgot his task of keeping the cow in the narrow pasture and hastened to attend the sacrifice. When he came to leave the church the fearsome thought of the cow invading the cabbage rows struck him. What would happen at home when he had to avow his imprudence and the loss of the cabbages? At least a good whipping, as he knew only too well. But no, not this time, for there right in the pasture, just where he had left her, was his cow browsing contentedly. What a relief! But never again did Julien abandon his charge. The result of incident remains vividly at Saint-Georges-de-Reintembault after three hundred and fifty years. Mothers still caution their children, "Above all, guard the cattle well, like the little Maunoir."

A priest of the parish, observing the lad so often at the altar, offered to teach him the elements of Latin. Who was this priest? He might have been Dom Bertin, the pastor. In that case one can picture the small altar-boy at the door of the solid and spacious presbytery (it is still standing), book in hand and nervously repeating a well conned lesson before knocking for admission. But a vague expression of an early biographer suggests another priest. Possibly it was Dom Roussel, or even Dom Jamet, the boy's god-father. In every Breton parish there were unattached priests who devoted their leisure to instructing children. Whoever the generous preceptor was, he did his work well; when Julien entered the collège of Rennes he was admitted into the Fourth Class. All the while Isaac and Gabrielle Maunoir were nourishing the vocation of their son, especially by their own good example. His development in holiness was to their faithful hearts a sure sign of God's acceptance of the dedication of their son to His service. So they worked harder than ever in their little cloth-shop to accumulate the funds for his education.

Julien was fourteen when his parents sent him to the college of the Jesuits at Rennes. Brittany's capital was forty-five miles southwest of Saint-Georges, down the hills and through the Forest of Rennes. The ancient city made a grand sight to the wide eyes of the little country boy when he first beheld its high ramparts and behind them the clusters of towers and belfries of its numerous churches, monasteries, convents and hospitals. No doubt his wonder was tinged with apprehension, for he had never been far from his native village except for his childhood journey to Fougères for his Confirmation. Though born not very far from the Bay of Cancale and its Mont Saint-Michel, it is probable that he had never gazed on the green-blue waters of the sea, he who was to be the apostle of the fishermen of Concarneau and the Isle of Sein. Julien, reared in a rustic hamlet, must have considered Rennes with its 30,000 inhabitants a vast metropolis, truly a world within itself.

Once within the city gates the lad found himself in a maze of narrow streets lined with tall edifices. Timorously he moved through the noisy crowds, the carts and the horses until he stood before the Jesuit's College of Saint Thomas and its church of All Saints. Both buildings were located on an island formed by a branch of the Vilaine River that followed the south rampart. The Collège of Saint Thomas, founded in 1606, the very year of Julien's birth, had become in less than twenty years one of the larger French Jesuit colleges, numbering on its rolls 3,000 students. The Rennois prized the institution both because of the excellent classical education which it afforded their sons and because of their conviction that that education bound their sons closer to the heart and culture of France.

The new pupil, upon examination of the Prefect of Studies, Père Le Meneust, was admitted into the Fourth

Class. The course extended through seven classes. The lowest class, designated the Sixth, introduced the student to the rudiments of Latin and Greek; the next three, the Fifth, the Fourth and the Third, increased his knowledge of grammar and vocabulary. He was then ready for the study of classical literature, which was made in two years: the first, Poetry; the second, Rhetoric. The highest class was called Logic; in it were taught Logic and Physics. Julien was particularly fortunate in having as his master in the Poetry Class, Père Jean Rigoleuc, at the time not yet ordained but later to be renowned as a director of retreats and a writer of ascetical books. An excellent Latinist and an untiring preceptor the young teacher spared neither himself nor his pupils. Julien was an industrious scholar and profited by the pressure. Of a serious bent, more solid than brilliant, his rare quality of work earned him not only scholastic honors but the esteem of his professors and fellow-students.

Since the college did not maintain dormitories Julien took his lodgings in a nearby house, a modest place, no doubt, in keeping with his family's means. The neighborhood was a busy spot, for all the pastry shops were located there. And the Rennois loved good fare. The master pastry-makers were an enterprising lot; each evening they sent out their servants with baskets of biscuits and cakes to meet the hungry scholars returning from classes.

A life without supervision held grave dangers for a country lad. Inns were too plentiful and they were very much frequented by the collegians. The youth of Brittany were strongly addicted to excessive wine-drinking, according to Boschet, Julien's first biographer. Some of the collegians showed little regard for the rights of others. The Benedictines of Saint Melaine's Abbey repeatedly complained of the students loafing in the adjacent Thabor Groves and poaching rabbits in the monastery's precincts. The harum-scarum youngsters mixed into all kinds of street-fights. In consequence the Parlement of Rennes decreed the confiscation of all arms borne by students and ordered the enforcement officials to inflict corporal punishment on any young culprits caught with the weapons on their persons. At night occasionally, noisy gangs of students tramped through dark, quiet streets, waking up the inhabitants with their wild shouts and their roaring songs, unhooking signs, banging on walls, or acting out comedies under the light of smoking torches at the cross streets. When the collegians were out for a night, prudent burghers barricaded their doors.

Julien Maunoir came safely through the dangers, no doubt owing to the reserve as well as the simple piety of his character. And yet he attained a remarkable influence over his companions. He induced some to give up bad associates; others he persuaded to destroy evil books. He won several of the intemperate to sobriety; he prevailed upon many others to moderate their passions for gambling. What moved these youths to accept his counsels? For one thing they respected him for his solid and hard-won successes in the classroom. But much more they gave him their confidence because of his evident goodness. They had observed his deep piety in their common devotions and his pained embarrassment at blasphemous or indecent speech. Once having heard his advice they found that "good Julien Maunoir" was neither a censorious busybody nor a dour fanatic, but a kindly friend whose prudence measured well with his charity. The extent of that charity, however, they would never learn from him. Often he divided his dinner with beggars; sometimes he even deprived himself of a meal that he might have food to give to the hungry. Julien was a true son of Isaac and Gabrielle Maunoir who shared their small profits with the poor.

As his schooling moved along the boy made steady progress in spiritual matters. The services in the churches of Rennes became his preferred pleasure, especially the solemn high Masses and the chanted Vespers in the Cathedral of Saint Pierre with Bishop de Cornulier presiding. The meetings of the Sodality of the Blessed Virgin in the college chapel found him an unfailing participant, intensifying the devotion to the Mother of God which his devout parents had planted in his heart. Preserved in the presbytery of Saint-Georges-de-Reintembault is a simple wooden statue of the Mother and Child, before which Gabrielle Maunoir accustomed her little son to kneel while she taught his lips to form the praises of God's Mother. Now, alone in a strange city and far from the paternal fireside, his love for Mary not only remained but increased, inspiring more intimate thoughts and more fervent prayers to his heavenly Mother. Fifteen years later he wrote: "I recall in memory . . . how she loved me, when I was a scholar, although my malice rendered me unworthy of her goodness."

Even in his college days Julien seems to have practiced mental prayer, under the guidance of one of the fathers. Who was this director? Perhaps he was Père Le Meneust, marked in the college catalogue as Spiritual Father of the students, or Père Porèe, at various times prefect of sodalities, or Père Bouton, director of the Philosophers' Sodality when Julien was in the class of Logic. Boschet affirms that Julien, usually so reserved with people, opened his heart completely to his director.

Noting the boy's attraction for the spiritual, the director proceeded to teach him how to pray interiorly. The priest was not long in perceiving that the lad lived in close union with God, that for his years he was well advanced in virtue, and that the Holy Ghost already was in fact the first teacher of this holy youth.

The director, sensing an apostolic soul when he learned of Julien's salutary activities with his fellow-students, decided to unfold before his vision the heroic apostolate of the missions. He began speaking about the glorious labors of the Jesuit missionaries in Japan, China, Brazil, Peru and, above all, in New France. The lad listened enthralled. One day, as they were conversing, the thought struck Julien that in the vast mission fields numerous souls must be perishing because the laborers were so few. Stirred to a holy ardor he earnestly besought the priest to help him become a Jesuit that he might be sent to save the infidels. It was the generous response that the director had been hoping for. However, he contented himself with an approving word and prudently left to time the testing and strengthening of his youthful penitent's vocation.

There could be no doubt about the young collegian's call to the priesthood. But did God will Him to fulfill that vocation in the Society of Jesus? Possibly Julien had a leaning towards the Jesuits from his early days at the college. In his second year he participated in the splendid festivities by which Rennes celebrated the canonization of St. Ignatius and St. Francis Xavier. The entire city, with the municipality voting to take an active part, joined the Jesuits and their pupils in the enthusiastic observances. Julien marched with his classmates in the grand procession and was present with them at the solemn church ceremonies, in which he may have assisted as an altar boy. Certainly he was profoundly impressed listening to the eloquent panegyrics on the founder and the first missionary of the Society of Jesus. Later, as he progressed through the classes and took a greater part in the sodality's activities, he came to know his Jesuit masters intimately and to admire them devotedly. During his last collegiate years he applied for admission into the Society of Jesus.

His application was acted upon by the Provincial of of the Paris Province, Père Pierre Coton, on his annual visitation of the College of Rennes. Père Coton was one of the foremost figures in the French Counter-Reformation. He had been the confessor and confidant of Henry IV, the confessor and tutor of Louis XIII, a redoubted controversialist against the Calvinists, an ascetical writer of wide influence, and a tireless, intrepid champion of his brethren when storms broke upon the French Jesuits. It was an awed little Breton who entered the room of this great priest. His interview recalls a similar meeting, almost sixty years earlier, at Dillingen, between St. Stanislaus Kostka and St. Peter Canisius. Père Coton, a rare judge of character, was not long in discerning the treasure Providence was offering him. The provincial was one who could recognize sanctity. He had lived as a fellow student with St. Aloysius, he had had St. Robert Bellarmine for a spiritual director, and he had labored by the side of St. Charles Borromeo. When his questioning was terminated there was no doubt in his mind that this boy was of the race of apostles. So Père Coton there and then accepted Julien Maunoir for the novitiate of the Society of Jesus. The humble lad had never envisioned such a prompt fulfillment of his desires. He could only weep as he knelt to receive the venerable provincial's blessing.

There remained his parent's consent, and for this Julien returned to Saint-Georges-de-Reintembault. Perhaps this was his first visit back; there could not have been many, for the college vacations were very brief. The happiness of the Maunoirs on beholding their son again can well be imagined. But their joy quickly turned to dismay when Julien requested their acquiescence in his becoming a Jesuit. Their fondest hopes were shattered. During the last five long years Isaac and Gabrielle consoled their lonesomeness with dreaming of their own dear priest offering his holy mass in their village church, dwelling with them at their fireside, and never far from them in their declining years. But to become a religious, to go away from Brittany, perhaps never again to visit with them, this was asking too great a sacrifice of their love. The prospect became all the more painful if Julien spoke, as he probably did, of going as a missionary to New France. The savage forests of Canada, they surely were a point of no return. What pleas, what persuasions, what prayers the boy poured forth, struggling against the heart-breaking tears and the bitter regrets of strong paternal love! But Isaac and Gabrielle were Bretons; they had the faith, and they consummated their sacrifice. God blessed their generous surrender. Years later the apostolate of their son won from many a grateful penitent in Cornouailles or Lèon a cry that echoed the Gospels: "Blessed is the mother who bore him."

Chapter 3

APPRENTICESHIP

Julien was nineteen when he left his home for the Jesuit novitiate in Paris. The leave-taking must have been overwhelmingly sorrowful for his dear ones and for himself; in all probability they would never meet again in this life. In simple families love reaches deeply, for in their close unity all joys are comprehended. Holiness does not ease the agony of parting. St. Teresa believed that the pain of dying could not be greater than the anguish she suffered on leaving her father's house. Some alleviation eventually came to Julien in the wearisome fatigues of five days' traveling in a jolting coach over the hot summer roads of Northern France. The slow progress also offered many an hour to dream of glorious deeds in God's service, or to long with growing eagerness for the prayerful life he was soon to embrace. The towers and the roofs of Paris, at last coming into view, quickened the holy expectations. Julien made his way through the Faubourg Saint-Germaine straight to a small street, Rue du Pot-de-Fer, where was the Jesuits' novitiate in the old Hotel de Mézières. In his old age Père Maunoir often declared that he had believed himself at the gates of Heaven when he knocked at the novitiate's gates.

His mentioning of Père Coton's name readily opened the door for Julien, but it did not save him from a most painful trial. The novicemaster, Père Jean Brossault, informed the anxious young man seated before him in the guest parlor that there was no Julien Maunoir on his list of postulants. Julien was stunned. What had happened? Had he taken the Father Provincial too literally when he bade him go to Paris as soon as he was ready? Had the admitting letter been misplaced? Was it lost? Père Brossault, a Breton himself, was not very sympathetic with his young countryman; he informed the lad, to the latter's utter dismay, that until word came from Père Coton his entrance was deferred. Without funds or friends, alone in Paris, what was to become of him during this indeterminate wait?

But Julien would not yield to despair. He respectfully asked leave to pray in the chapel. Père Brossault consented. He directed the novice-porter to show the sadly disappointed lad to the chapel. There Julien prostrated himself before the tabernacle and begged God, by the intercession of St. Joseph, to grant him entrance. Julien had made St. Joseph the protector of his vocation, probably on the suggestion of Père Coton at their meeting in Rennes. Père Coton was a constant promoter of devotion to the holy Patriarch, a devotion then but little known. All the while the novice-porter was intently observing

Julien kneeling before the altar, completely absorbed in his supplications. The young brother was deeply impressed, and he marvelled at the postulant's brave faith in his agonizing disappointment. Watching Julien in prayer, he felt convinced of rare merit in this modest, fervent youth. Hastening to the novice master's room, he begged earnestly for the poor candidate, so summarily put off, and yet so evidently holy. Père Brossault deferred to his pleas and agreed to retain Julien until information should arrive from the provincial. Père Coton's authorizing letter came shortly. Accordingly on September 16, 1625 Julien Maunoir was admitted into the ranks of the novices of the Society of Jesus.

From the start the young Breton was at home in the novitiate of Saint-Germaine. The regularity of the house and the practices of obedience were what he had expected. It was not surprising that this youth of such genuine piety shortly became a fervent novice. Père Le Roux, one of his earliest biographers, wrote: "He thought of nothing more than to nourish his inclination for the interior life . . . He devoted himself with intense fervor to all the observances of religious life, without omitting the least." Julien's single aim was, as he later expressed it trenchantly in his motto, "God's will and God's love."[1] This enabled him to meet the difficulties of common life in the novitiate: the clash of personalities, the minute and sometimes irksome regulations, and the training methods, often painful to nature but so necessary for religious formation.

Julien's private journal[2] revealed his advance in prayer and in the awareness of the presence of God. Here

[1] "Le plus grand contentement de Dieu et son plus grand amour."

[2] Much of the journal is available in the many and lengthy quotations of Père Boschet's *Le Parfait Missionnaire, ou Vie du R.P. Julien*

is one of his early resolutions: "I shall try to live in this world as if there were only God, presupposing always His assistance; without that I know that I could achieve nothing . . . Always attentive to that which God desires of me, I shall think of what He could wish of a Jesuit, in order to prepare myself for all things that will be for His service. . . . Ah! how I love Him, this infinitely good God, and how intensely do I desire to be worthy to be loved by Him." These lines are not a mere repeating of the novice-master's conference; for in spirituality, even as a novice, Julien had reached beyond the ordinary. Thus he wrote: "One day at the beginning of my novitiate God entered suddenly into my soul; He spread Himself in the manner of a sweet oil, or a precious balsam, which penetrates and extends all about. In an instant I was flooded with an interior sweetness which aided me very much in elevating myself towards God. Immediately creatures affected me no more, except with disgust; the pleasures of earth from this time were disenchanting and insipid. To these clear blessings succeeded a joy so calm and so profound, that this moment of happiness was for me preferable to all the pleasures which the world could procure here below during an entire lifetime."

Twice during his novitiate the Blessed Virgin favored him in exceptional ways. Retreat notes written at Bourges ten years later testify to this. One favor he described, writing the account in Breton the better to

Maunoir, de la Comp. de Jésus, missionnaire en Bretagne; first edition, Paris, 1697; second edition, Lyons, 1834. Père Boschet declared: "They sent me a copy of the journal which P. Maunoir had written about his novitiate, his years of study and his missionary career." Boschet was scrupulously exact, so his quotations have every chance of being authentic, both as to the letter and as to the spirit.

conceal it: "I remember that one day, during my novitiate, I was steeped in a great sadness at the sight of my past sins, and so I fell asleep. Then this tender Mother with all the charm of her beauty deigned to appear to me during my sleep. She placed on my eyes a precious stone of bright colors. When I awoke I felt in me, together with regret for my sins, an unalterable peace." The second favor he forbore narrating even in Breton, but contented himself by commenting on it: "Before these testimonies of such goodness I vowed to the Queen of heaven an eternal love, and I promised to devote myself to her above all her servants."

The novices of Saint-Germaine numbered about thirty. To all of them Julien bound himself with a profound charity. He esteemed himself as the least among them, only admitted to their ranks by an unmerited favor. He proscribed from his conversation whatever might cause pain to others. The future missionary is discernable in the notes: "I shall study the inclinations of my brothers and the points where one could give them pleasure . . . I shall make every effort to gain them, in order to lead them, in consequence, more efficaciously to God." A high ideal, and it was seasoned with an astonishing maturity: "This compliance, which I shall have with my brothers, will extend to bearing tranquilly their weaknesses and even their faults when I cannot remedy them; but it will not extend to praising them for them. On the contrary, if I judge that they are disposed to profit by the correction, I shall admonish them; but in doing so I shall use such gentleness and circumspection that they will be convinced that I love them and that charity alone has made me speak." To insure that his conduct in the community should be completely charitable, he resolved not to seek the frequent companionship of his fellow Bretons. Such abstaining entailed hard sacrifice for a Breton boy living far from his native province, which was so different from the rest of France in its interests and viewpoints. Yet Brother Maunoir aimed not at becoming an unfeeling ascetic. Great was his joy when he welcomed into the novitiate at Christmas, 1625, a Breton friend and former fellow student at the Collège of Rennes, Vincent Huby. In later years Vincent was to be Julien's superior at Quimper, his helper on the missions, his mentor in the work of the retreat-house of Vannes, and always his very intimate friend.

Two events varied the quiet course of the noviceship. One was the death of Père Coton at the novitiate. The intrigues of the Paris Parlement had darkened the last days of the great Jesuit Provincial; but God afforded him a final consolation, for which he had often prayed, that of dying on the feast-day of his beloved St. Joseph. Both Julien Maunoir and Vincent Huby owed their admission in a very special way to Père Coton. Were they among the privileged novices who witnessed his last hours when he received Viaticum on his knees, supported by two religious? At least they were among the throngs who filed before his mortal remains, laid out in priestly vestments, in the Jesuit church of St. Louis. The other event was the change of novice-masters. Julien saw Père Brossault depart with keen regret. He had long forgotten that first cold reception, having found in his superior a very good and very kind father. The new master of novices was none other than his former prefect of studies at Rennes, Père Le Meneust. His coming recalled many happy memories to Brother Julien and Brother Vincent; and they deemed themselves privileged in the opportunity of finishing their religious apprenticeship under his direction.

On the termination of the novitiate Brother Maunoir was sent to the College of Henry IV at La Flèche in Anjou for a three year course in Philosophy. The change from the quiet recollection of Saint-Germaine to the noisy hustle of an institution counting 1,500 students was about as complete as possible. La Flèche, as the college was popularly known, had been founded a quarter of a century before by Henry IV, as a testimony of his attachment for the Society of Jesus and also of his affection for this corner of Anjou, the scene of his happiest childhood memories. The monarch erected the college on a magnificent scale, planning a mother house from which all the other houses of the Society in France would draw their strength and traditions. When the new philosopher arrived the buildings, only lately completed, still shone in all their bright newness.

The external splendor of La Flèche was more than equalled by its spirit. The standards were high, the scholars eager and the professors excellent. The philosophy faculty maintained the judgment of Descartes, one of the first students of the college: "I must honor our masters by saying that there is no place in the world, as far as I can judge, where philosophy is better taught than at La Flèche."[1] The faculty was headed by Père Claude Tiphaine, of whom Msgr. Coëffeteau, an eloquent Dominican and Bishop of Marseilles, declared, "If Aristotle and St. Thomas were to be lost, one could find all their doctrine in the head of Père Tiphaine."

[1] Letter of Descartes to a friend at Rennes, cited by Père Rochemonteix, S.J., *Un Collège des Jésuites Aux XVII et XVIII Siècles,* 4 vols. Le Mans, 1889.

Julien Maunoir profited greatly by the instruction of these able professors. He may have been of only average intelligence, as Brémond says; in that case he must have applied himself steadfastly, for he achieved a constant success throughout his course. Even in competition with such brilliant minds as Jean Pinette, Isaac Jogues and Vincent Huby, he showed himself one of the ablest in scholastic disputations.

Undoubtedly the secret of his success was his motivation. One finds written in his journal: "God wishes that I become a saint and a scholar. I resolve to use all the means which I have in the Society of acquiring holiness and learning. . . . When I have done all that is in my power, whether I shall succeed or not, I shall be equally content, and l shall receive from the hand of God the measure of sanctity and of science which He shall be pleased to give me. If those with whom I study make greater progress than I in the sciences, I shall not be jealous; I shall praise them highly and with all my heart. . . But if it should come out that I have more success than they, I shall consider it as a present which I have received from Heaven . . . God forbid that I esteem myself more for that, or that I esteem others less. I shall neglect none of the prescriptions touching studies; but I shall put up a guard against a certain overeagerness for knowledge, which is a common temptation for persons having the opportunity and the inclination for the sciences. [1] This overeagerness causes trouble and betokens excess; it dries up the soul and slackens the fervor of devotion . . . I shall not have then an ardor nor an energy except for virtue."

[1] "Sciences" here is used in the older sense which included any branch of higher learning: theology, philosophy, physics, mathematics, etc.

This long quotation cited by Boschet and by Le Roux [1] evidences a steady growth of the young philosopher in the virtues of obedience, humility, self-conquest, charity and courage. Ardent expressions of the love of God and of the desire for God's love occur in the excerpts. Thus one reads: "I felt, with a very pure joy, as if two angels had taken my heart from my breast and that they had pressed it to expel all that it held of natural affections. From that moment there were grounded in me the desire and the resolution of living on earth, in spite of all mundane hindrances as if I lived in Heaven, and of fulfilling here below the ministry of the angels above." One also finds instances of mystical favors from our Lord and His Blessed Mother. But always the practical and the apostolic notes stand out: "My vocation which destines me for the salvation of souls, became more dear to me still. An interior voice repeated to me four or five times with a tone of wonder, 'Ah if you knew! if you knew!' I understood then what a grand thing it was to cooperate with Jesus Christ for the conversion of men. I was marvelously strengthened to follow our Lord completely and everywhere. To conquer souls with Him I must undertake to endure the greatest fatigues, to expose myself to the greatest dangers, to ship-wrecks, gibbets, racks, to all forms of frightful death; for God is my strength."

These thoughts were written in an atmosphere of reality, for in the scholasticate of La Flèche missions and martrydoms were very live topics of conversation. Reports from abroad of Jesuit labors were continually read

[1] Le Roux, Guillaume, S.J., *Recueil de Vertus et des Miracles du R.P. Julien Maunoir, de la Compagnie de Jésus, Missionnaire en Bretagne;* first published in Brittany, 1715; second edition Saint Brieuc, 1848.

at table, eagerly listened to and more eagerly discussed in the recreations. Such reports brought news from Japan of the blood of Jesuits flowing freely in the cruelest of persecutions. They carried accounts of fugitive English and Irish fathers, just across the channel, being tracked down like wild beasts and butchered on the gallows. Other reports told of missionary-scientists at the Imperial Court of Peking, or detailed the vast projects of the civilizing padres in Paraguay. But the narrations of the apostolic adventures among the savages of the trackless Canadian forests, the premier mission-field of France, held the community spellbound. La Flèche knew much about Canada. For ten years it had had for its vice-rector, Père Enemond Massé, the pioneer Jesuit of New France, who never tired of relating his experiences in evangelizing the red men. Though he had gone back to Canada in 1625, accompanied by two former students of La Flèche, Père de Noue and Père Lalemant, the memory of Père Massé and his vivid accounts of the Indians remained a veritable legend in the scholasticate.

One of the philosophers, Isaac Jogues, caught the apostolic flame and carried it even to martyrdom. Though slightly younger he had preceded Julien at the scholasticate by a year. Since Isaac had made his novitiate at Rouen, Julien did not meet him until 1627. They were soon attracted to each other. Ardent young religious, they must have often discussed the missions, especially during the glorious celebrations for the beatification of the Japanese Jesuit martyrs, Paul Miki, John de Goto and James Kisai, which were held in the June of 1628. Isaac hesitated between Ethiopia, Japan or Canada; Julien had thoughts only for Canada. But this was all planning for the distant future; the French Jesuits did not send scholastics [1] to the missions. But soon, on the completion of their philosophical studies, the young religious would find very present opportunities for their zeal. In 1628 Isaac was sent to the college of Rouen, and in 1630 Julien was appointed to the college of Quimper.

Quimper, with which Julien Maunoir's long connection now began, was the chief town of the west of Brittany. Situated amidst steep wooded hills at the confluence of the Steir and the Odet and standing at the head of the Odet estuary, Quimper was a quiet river-port, gray and full of shadows, a jumble of slanting roofs dominated by the purple-gray mass of the Cathedral of St. Corentin. Since 1620 Quimper possessed a Jesuit college, the College of St. Yves. In its first years the institution lacked even a building. The situation was remedied by the zealous Arch-deacon of Cornouailles, M. Jean Briant, Abbé of Landévennec, loaning his prebendal house for the classes. Constructional delays forced the fathers to use the gift of the hospitable abbe for fifteen years. From its start the College of St. Yves was popular; by 1630 its students numbered over a thousand. The Jesuit community, though small, only seventeen all told, included some remarkable priests. Three were especially regarded in Quimper: Père Jean Brossault, the constructive leader of the college; Père Guillaume Thomas, a venerable laborer among the Breton-speaking population; and Père Bernard [2] an indefatigable confessor.

[1] Scholastic, term in the Society of Jesus, for those not ordained who were candidates for the priesthood.

[1] Père Bernard was first a special counsellor of Bl. Julien Maunoir, and later his closest co-operator. He was born at Rennes, March 13, 1585, the youngest son of a sturdily religious family; the father, Pierre Bernard, a lawyer of the Parlement of Brittany, was known

The class assigned to the young regent [1] was the Fifth. Its modern equivalent would be High School Sophomore. The subjects to be taught by him were Latin and Greek. How large would be his class? It would include at least three hundred students! The number is extraordinary according to the present-day pedagogy; but such classes were the usual practice in French Jesuit colleges of the seventeenth century. Discipline was maintained by *monitors*, lay assistants who were employed to hear recitations and to keep order – with a liberal use of the birch-rod as the need arose. At Quimper one of the monitors was an Irishman, John Callaghan (Calganus, they called him). He received a salary of eighteen livres, which enabled him to finance his own studies. Callaghan, a somewhat literary soul, summed up his biography and his functions at the College of St. Yves in a neat epigram:

Versor in Armorica, peregrinis ductus ab oris;
Rex sum, nec regno; dextera sceptra gerit.

which may be turned:

Brittany, scene of my labors, I come from a foreigners strand;

as "the successor of St. Yves" because of his advocacy of the causes of the poor; five of his six sons became religious, two Capuchins, one Carmelite and two Jesuits. Since there was no Jesuit school at the time in Brittany, Pierre Bernard sent all his boys to the Jesuit college of Anchin, near Douai, in Flanders. His youngest son, Pierre, entered the Society of Douai, made his novitiate at Tournai, and then was called back to France. After his ordination he was stationed at Nevers and at Moulins. When the College of St. Yves was opened he was appointed to Quimper. For a decade Père Bernard worked in the town and its environs. He was so tireless in preaching, hearing confessions and visiting the prisons, hospitals and the homes of the poor that he was universally esteemed for his zeal, sagacity and simplicity of heart.

[1] The title of a Jesuit teacher, not yet ordained a priest.

Quimper, in Bl. Julien's day.

(FROM AN OLD PRINT)

The Cathedral of Quimper, in Bl. Julien's day.

(FROM AN OLD PRINT)

King I am (yet without rule); the scepter I swing in my hand.

No doubt he wielded it. Master Maunoir would have had no hesitancy in invoking that secular arm. Years later he noted in his journal the utility of the "white rods" of his catechists not only for explaining the religious charts but also for repressing giddy children. Naturally gentle Julien, when the occasion called for it, could be a stern disciplinarian.

Beyond his task of imparting knowledge, Master Maunoir made special efforts to foster in his pupils piety and industry. He dictated to them an order of the day, and also a method for prayer and a method for study; then he held them to strict observance of the prescriptions. Some of the more vigorous spirits about the college, not at all impressed, inquired sarcastically: "What does the new regent teach his students? To recite pater nosters, to wear the airs of juvenile ascetics?" But before long the example of Julien's students gained considerable emulation. For himself the new master held but one present ambition, to become an efficient teacher. When Père Bernard urged his young confrère to take up the study of Breton [1] so that he might instruct the neglected peasantry of the neighborhood, Julien replied: "You know that my class is my mission and that to conduct it well the languages I must learn are Latin and Greek." Recalling his resolutions at La Flèche he added, "If I study any other, it will be that of Canada, where, I believe, God is calling me." But Père Bernard was not

[1] Julien Maunoir, a native of upper Brittany, the eastern half where French was spoken exclusively, knew no Breton. Only in lower Brittany, the western half, was the ancient Celtic language the common tongue. Even Père Bernard did not speak Breton.

Chapel of the old Jesuit College of Quimper.

dissuaded. He continued his prayers to gain this zealous young religious for his beloved Bretons.

Providence sent another messenger, Dom Michel Le Nobletz. For more than a year the venerable missionary had been all alone in his ministry; the death of Père Quintin, O.P. had deprived him of his only assistant. One thought sustained him in his hopeless prospects, the heavenly promise of a successor. The promise was made again, one night in November 1630, at Douarnenez, when Dom Michel heard an interior voice saying: "He whom you seek is not far distant; you will find him at Quimper, at the college of the Jesuits, of whom he is the youngest." Though it was the middle of the night Dom Le Nobletz set out upon the road, plodding the fifteen miles through the darkness to Quimper. Just before seven o'clock, he was knocking at the door of St. Yves College asking for the teacher of the Fifth Class. Julien, answering the call, was surprised and pleased to find himself in conversation with the renowned and holy missionary. The interview was brief and utterly devoid of the dramatic. Dom Michel said not a single word to the wondering scholastic about Providence's designs in his regard, but contented himself with speaking about the vocations of St. Peter and St. Andrew, of the grace God gave them in calling them to His service, and of their generous loyalty in leaving all to follow him. That was all. The veteran embraced the young Jesuit and straightway departed. On his return to Douarnenez Dom Michel informed his friends that he had met his son in Christ.

Julien Maunoir on his part was intrigued by the strange subject of the vocations of St. Peter and St. Andrew. He sought out Père Bernard for clarification. The latter had no difficulty understanding the inference as a discreet invitation to the regent to offer himself for the Breton Mission. One point he missed: the invitation was for himself also. If Julien was bidden to imitate Peter, Père Bernard was bidden to imitate Andrew, submissive in the hierarchy of the apostolate to his younger brother. Only in the passing years would Père Bernard discover the divine plan completely.

The younger religious, deeply impressed, began to ponder whether or not God had designed him for his native duchy. But what of his complete ignorance of the Breton language? Once more, it seems, the Blessed Mother came to his assistance. About two miles north of Quimper, in a quiet countryside, stood the ancient Breton shrine of Ty-Mamm-Doué, *The House of the Mother of God.*[1] The Quimperois loved to frequent it. Each year the students of St. Yves, led by their teachers, marched in pilgrimage to the shrine. Julien, some days after his meeting with Dom Le Nobletz, decided to visit the holy place, though for no special reason save to honor the Mother of God. As he was walking along, there came suddenly into his thoughts the descriptions that Père Bernard had been giving him of the spiritual dereliction of Lower Brittany. As he pondered on the words of the older Jesuit an interior inspiration presented to him the bishoprics of Quimper, Tréguier, Saint-Brieuc and Léon as fields open to his zeal, and intimated to him the means which he should employ for the salvation of these four dioceses. Forthwith he found himself

[1] Ty-Mamm-Doué can be traced back to the first years of the fourteenth century, just a few years after the Holy House of Loreto. The present chapel, which was built in the middle of the sixteenth century by the de Furics, the seigneurs of the place, either replaced or included the original shrine. Possibly the little oratory, still part of one corner, is the old sanctuary.

forming a resolution to learn the Breton language. He later asserted that during this heavenly visitation his soul did nothing but acquiesce in the will of God. Totally absorbed in thoughts of such an extraordinary vocation, Julien arrived at the threshold of Ty-Mamm-Doué. Entering the chapel he offered himself to God, urgently petitioning that, as He had destined him to instruct these neglected people, He would grant him the ability to speak their language. Then he addressed himself to the Blessed Mother, confidently begging her: "My good Mother, if you deign to teach me Breton yourself, I shall know it in a brief time, and I shall quickly be in a position to gain servants for you." [1]

On his return to the college Julien hastened to inform Père Bernard of all that had happened and of his purpose to learn Breton, if permission were granted to him. Père Bernard heard him with joyful approval. But Julien soon encountered strong opposition from other members of the college staff. Some reminded this young regent that his project was incompatible with the necessary preparation of his classes; others deplored the waste of his fine talents for classical studies. All predicted certain failure. No one, they assured him, could ever speak Breton unless he had been accustomed to it from infancy. Undeterred by the opposition Julien wrote to the Provincial at Paris for authorization to study the Breton language. A favorable reply arrived on the Feast of Pentecost, 1631, a remarkable date in view of what followed. After only eight days of study Julien Maunoir gave his first catechetical instruction in Breton. With the passage of two months he was preaching without note or

[1] Boschet, p. 40; second edition (all quotations from Boschet and from Le Roux are from the second editions.)

TY-MAMM-DOUE.

The venerable shrine of the Blessed Mother where Bl. Julien dedicated himself to the Breton Missions and prayed for the gift of the Breton language.

preparation.[1] Surely this was a singular grace indeed. Julien himself was convinced that he owed the boon to the Blessed Mother; and so he made it a point to begin his Breton teaching in the chapel of Ty-Mamm-Doué, the place where he had begged God and His Blessed Mother to enable him to learn quickly the difficult tongue.

In a short time the new Breton speaker was teaching every Sunday and free-day in Quimper and in the hamlets nearby. Before two years were over he had catechised in twenty parish churches, shrines or hospitals. Sometimes on a single Sunday he would visit three localities. Yet his college work did not suffer; the Jesuit catalogues show that every year he was advanced with his pupils to be their teacher in the next higher class. Douarnenez and its neighbor, Ploaré, were the places he went to most frequently; both were rich in memories of Dom Le Nobletz and both produced good crowds. The first time Julian stood in the pulpit of Douarnenez's parish church, Sainte-Hélène, he looked down upon a congregation of eager faces that reached to the door. Was not this young Jesuit the one whose coming Dom Michel had foretold to them? Was he not to be their patriarch's successor? No doubt most had come out of curiosity. But they returned steadily, to become in time a most faithful congregation. Julien Maunoir, even as a beginner, had a rare talent for teaching Christian doctrine. He presented the matter interestingly and with a liveliness that touched the heart as well as the spirit.

These happy preludes were not without their trials. One occurred on the feast of the Visitation, 1632. On the

[1] Boschet, pp. 41, 42; Le Roux, p. 6; Séjourné, Xavier, S.J., *Histoire de Julien Maunoir, S.J.*, Paris, 1895, T. I. pp. 39, 40.

eve, Julien had stopped at Ploaré to sleep before preaching next morning at Douarnenez. During the night he had a dream in which he beheld the congregation abandoning him in the middle of his sermon and leaving him in the pulpit all alone. On awakening he dismissed the dream as a ridiculous fantasy. At the sermon hour he was in the pulpit of Sainte-Hélène's preaching on the Blessed Mother. Hardly had he launched into his discourse when some unknown miscreant opened the great door of the church and began shouting "The Egpytians! The Egyptians!" Now "Egyptians" was the local name for the thieving gypsy bands who roamed the highways stealing anything they could lay their hands on. The church emptied at once, everyone rushing home to secure his property. The young preacher in the pulpit was left all alone, ruefully beholding his dream come true. But actually there had been no Egyptians, nor was anyone able to discover the identity of the evil-doer who had raised the false alarm. Julien, undaunted by what he believed to be a trick prompted by the Evil One, that very evening had the church bell rung to reconvoke the faithful. Ashamed of their flight they came back in large numbers and crowded right up to the foot of the pulpit. The young preacher spoke very practically to them on the ruses of the Enemy of mankind and on the absolute power of God's mother over the minions of Hell.

The apostolic apprenticeship lasted for three years. It was ended for Julien by a serious illness. The burdens of large classes and the labors of preaching all over the countryside had taken their toll of his strength. He finished the school year completely exhausted and suffering from a weakness of the chest. The Provincial withdrew him from teaching and sent him for rest to the small residence of Tours. The change was a hard sacrifice for

Julien and also for Dom Le Nobletz and Père Bernard. The last two could only hope that the good God in His own time would send back the future missionary of Brittany.

The period of quiet in the pleasant climate of Touraine restored Julien's health. He was given a small class of about forty boys in the new college of Tours. They were easy-going lads rather than industrious scholars, so he paced the lessons to their capacities. With his strength restored Julien began religious instruction in the prison, the hospital and the church of St. Pierre le Pellier. In the Fall of 1634 the Provincial, satisfied with the recovery of his young subject, ordered him to repair to the theologate of Bourges to take up the final studies for the priestly ministry.

Chapter 4

PRIESTLY PREPARATION

When Julien Maunoir came to Bourges in 1634, the old cathedral city was still an important center of French life. For one thing the Prince de Condé, governor of Berry and Bourbonnais, maintained his semi-royal court in the historic town. Its citizens took a special pride in the newly opened Jesuit college of Ste. Marie, where Julien was to make his theological studies. The Prince himself was one of its most generous benefactors; in conjunction with Père Coton he had founded the professorships of Dogma, Scripture and Hebrew. In 1624 he enrolled his son, the Duc d'Enghien, the future victor at Rocroy, as a student of Philosophy. The young duke achieved such success that at the end of his last term he defended in public disputation the theses of the philosophical course. The Prince de Condé presided at the exercises; and among the spectators was the new theologian from Brittany.

The rector of the College de Ste. Marie was Père Louis Lallemant, the renowned authority on prayer and asceticism. Julien had heard much of Père Lallemant from Isaac Jogues, who had had him for a novice-master, and from Jean Rigoleuc, who had been trained by him in the Third Year of Probation. [1] The young religious had only a short time to profit from the conferences and the direction of the master, for Père Lallemant died on Holy Thursday of the next year. Brief as the contacts were Julien cherished them for life. Among his companions in the theologate were three future Canadian missionaries: Paul Ragueneau and René Ménard, in the first two years, and Gabriel Lalemant, the martyr of the Iroquois, in the last two years. Most of his fellow students, however, were not Jesuits but secular clerics and religious of different orders, for Bourges was a general theologate.

Julien, now twenty-eight, brought to the lectures and disputations of Bourges the studious plodding of his days at La Flèche. It paid off well later on. The wealth of scriptural quotations which characterized his missionary preaching had its source in these hard working years; so too, the wide acquaintance with St. Thomas evident in his priestly writings. Dogmatic theology furnished him with what approached mystical knowledge, for he wrote: "If God is the reason for it, God is also the principal object of it." To moral theology, convinced of its vital

[1] Three years of a Jesuit priest's preparation are specifically devoted to spiritual formation: the two years of his noviceship at the start and a third year on the completion of his studies. The last year is called the Third Year of Probation, or the Tertianship.

necessity for the missionary-confessor, he devoted himself energetically and persistently. In the future years Père Maunoir's facility for solving problems of conscience was proverbial with the Breton priests.

The more absorbed he became in his sacerdotal studies, the more his soul was flooded with reverential awe of his coming priesthood. He wrote: "I tremble every time I think upon the sacred mysteries, and I dread the day when it will be given me to accomplish them. Oh the grand and terrible power which God gives in them to men! One thing frightens me still more, it is the thought that priests, ministers of the Lord, clothed with so high a dignity and exercising functions so divine, could have low inclinations, views totally human, even criminal attachments." His considerations did not remain speculative but ended in resolutions of strong detachment: "Far from me all vain and fruitless joys, all useless conversations, all human satisfactions. The man destined for the altar should think only on divine things." If he dreaded the grandeur and the responsibilities of the priesthood, Julien reassured himself by dwelling on its power to work so much good for the salvation of his neighbor. In his second year at Bourges, on the seventh day of his annual retreat, he put down in his notes: "In my Communion I felt an extraordinary ardor for the salvation of souls and a burning desire to obtain it by all sorts of means. Then our Lord spoke to me interiorly: 'I have worked long periods for them, I have wept, I have suffered, and I have died for them.' These words touched me more than I can say; and the ardor which I felt before grew to such a point that, if it had been necessary to die at that moment to save a single soul, I would have died with all my heart." God communicated more spiritual favors to this fervent theologian; years afterwards Père

Maunoir revealed to his disciple, M. de Trémaria, that it was during his theological studies that he had received the gift of continual prayerful union with God.

Bourges had its measure of trials. Half way through the course the desire for Canada began again to perplex Julien. The Jesuit community was all absorbed in the prospects of the Canadian Missions. The reading of the *Relations* [1] was listened to with rapt attention, and the constant topic of conversation was the men and the deeds in the forests of New France. It was common knowledge that the rector, Père Lallemant, had been begging for three years to be sent to Quebec. On the final refusal he turned to training personally Paul Ragueneau and René Ménard for the much desired mission. Then in 1636 Gabriel Lalemant, the future martyr, came to Bourges; he had two uncles, Père Jérôme and Père Charles Lalemant, who actually had written *Relations* from Canada. Julien could not but be affected by the universal enthusiasm. The plight of the Iroquois and the Hurons had, and always would have an appeal for him. [2] And now there was the possibility of martyrdom. Surely here was greater service for God than the relief of the neglected peasantry of Brittany. Yet, had not God chosen him for the Breton Missions? What of the mysterious vision of the four bishoprics? What of the mastery in but a few days of the difficult Breton tongue? On the other hand possibly the good harvests in the environs of Quimper and Douarnenez had satisfied for the favor of

[1] The letters and reports sent by the missionaries in Canada to France.

[2] During all the years of his apostolate in Brittany, Bl. Julien was frequently making comparisons and allusions to the Canadian Indians.

Ty-Mamm-Doué. Maybe elsewhere than in Cornouailles God had prepared a greater apostolate for him. The Good Shepherd, did He not leave his secure fold to seek out the sheep that had wandered into perilous dangers? The lot of the Indians was certainly far more precarious than that of the Bretons.

Meanwhile letters from Père Bernard back in Quimper pleaded with his young confrère to remember Brittany, her sorrows and the field which God had shown to him. They urged him to keep up the practice of the Breton tongue. But most of all they cautioned him not to be enticed by visions of the Canadian Mission, since there could be no possible doubt about his vocation for Brittany. But was Père Bernard, devoted so to the Bretons, capable of an impartial judgment? And further, would not acquiescence in the persuasions of the priest who was his dearest friend be for Julien a yielding to merely human sentiments? Père Bernard not only penned letters but had constant recourse to prayer. So too did Dom Michel Le Nobletz, who seems to have had a divine premonition of Julien's perplexities. At Le Conquet the patriarch, in public and private, kept asking prayers for the vocation of his successor.

A serious illness brought all irresolution to an end. In mid-December, 1636, Julien was laid low with a fever which left him in great weakness. An inflammation appeared in his left arm and quickly swelled to frightening proportions. The doctors tried in vain every remedy they knew. On the ninth day the dreaded gangrene set in. It ascended to his armpit: if it reached his heart, his death was certain. The community in deep sorrow knelt about the sickbed, pitying their well-beloved brother in his excruciating agony.

The sufferer accepted his impending death calmly and joyfully. It was Christmas Eve: what a better day to go to God? He asked for Viaticum and prepared himself fervently for the last communion. While waiting for the Sacramental Lord, he was suddenly inspired to vow the dedication of his life to the salvation of the Bretons if health were restored to him. Then briefly he besought the Blessed Virgin, the Guardian Angels of Brittany, and the patrons of the duchy, St. Corentin, St. Pol-de-Léon and St. Yves to sponsor his vow with God. With a special reverence he received the Holy Host. Almost at once he sensed the affirmative response of Heaven. The infection was arrested and, in a short time, the swelling disappeared entirely. The attending doctors declared the recovery to be truly a miracle.

Dom Le Nobletz had foretold this vocational trial quite some time before it occurred. Marguerite Le Gac, his housekeeper, testified under oath to the bishop of Saint-Pol-de-Léon, Msgr. de Laval de Bois-Dauphin, that Dom Michel had said at Douarnenez two years before the sickness: "But before he returns to these cantons, God will try his virtue by a sickness, which will serve only to affirm his vocation and to make abundantly clear God's providence for the salvation of Lower Brittany." As if in further confirmation of his vocation Julien, shortly after his recovery, experienced a dream similar to Francis Xavier's in which the saint beheld himself bearing on his shoulders a giant Indian. Years later Julien in his manuscript life of Dom Michel Le Nobletz described his dream; "It seemed to me that I carried on my shoulders a peasant of Cornouailles. One easily recognized him by his little bonnet of red wool, his *bragou-braz,* [1]

[1] Great-coat.

even his buttoned gaiters, and all the other details of the Breton costume."

When the invalid's health was sufficiently restored, the superiors allowed him to catechise in the nearby parishes of Berry on his weekly holidays. The good results of Quimper and Douarnenez were repeated. Within the year the superiors granted Julien a far greater permission, something he had earnestly requested, ordination at the end of his third year. Today that is the usual time, but in the seventeenth century the young Jesuit theologians received the priesthood only in the fourth year of their studies. On the Vigil of the feast of the Holy Trinity, 1637, Julien Maunoir, in the thirty-first year of his age, was ordained a priest. Next day, Trinity Sunday, he celebrated his First Mass. According to Père Le Roux, he never forgot the date, celebrating each anniversary with lively gratitude. Unfortunately none of his spiritual notes on his momentous event have survived. Only in his *Journal of the Missions* is there one remnant thought: he noted with satisfaction that henceforth he had the ability to administer the Sacrament of Penance–the thought, at least, of an apostle.

The work of the last year at Bourges was principally a preparation for the grand examination that covered the entire field of theology. Occasionally there was an opportunity for sacerdotal work. One such severely tested the metal of the recently ordained priest. Père Julien tells of it in his *Journal of the Missions.* [1] The domestics of college had complained that their sleeping quarters were haunted. Père Le Mairat, the rector, ordered the young priest to spend a night in the troubled dormitory

[1] *Latin Journal of the Missions,* pp. 15, 16; cited by Séjourné, S.J., *Historie de Vénèrable Julien Maunoir, S.J.,* p. 62.

with the frightened servants and to report next morning any extraordinary happenings. Armed only with a ritual and holy water, Père Julien began his vigil. What he experienced convinced him of the reality of the preternatural occurrences: there were terrible noises, which both he and the servants heard, and there were displacements of furniture and the breaking of a holy waterfont before their eyes. Père Julien courageously kept repeating the Church's prayers for exorcism, and frequently sprinkled the troubled room with holy water. The struggle proved a hard one before the evil spirit was banished. It was the first of several clashes which Bl. Julien Maunoir was to have during his lifetime with the powers of darkness.

On the completion of the theological course, to his surprise and disappointment, Père Maunoir was not sent back to Brittany, as he had expected. He was assigned to the College of Nevers as teacher of the Class of Humanities and as confessor for the sodalities. However, he took up the new tasks resolutely; he always esteemed highly the apostolate of the classroom. By a singular good fortune he had for his Prefect of Studies, Père Jean Rigoleuc, his old professor of Humanities at Rennes. It was more than good fortune; Père Rigoleuc, now a holy and skilled master of the spiritual life, proved a wise and experienced counsellor for the young director of the sodalities of Nevers. There were also frequent opportunities for wider priestly work; during Advent and Lent Père Julien conducted missions in nearby country parishes.

Despite the fruitful prospects at Nevers, one question persisted in his mind: why had he not been sent back to Brittany? The answer was, and Père Julien learned it with sorrow, that he was not wanted at Quimper. The bishop, Msgr. Guillaume Le Prestre, was decidedly opposed to "missions." "There were no Huguenots in his diocese," he protested, as though missions were solely for the conversion of heretics. And he declared, further, that this type of ministry had never been exercised in Cornouailles—ignoring the very recent labors of Dom Le Nobletz and Père Quintin, O.P. He even issued a decree against any proposed missions. Certainly in such circumstances there was no place for Père Maunoir. What he found harder to bear, was the opposition of the Quimper Jesuits. They were flatly against starting any new project; for they felt that they had more than enough problems in their crowded college with its very small faculty and its heavy financial burdens. And if the young missionary were stationed at Quimper, they had no one to spare as his companion. Père Bernard? He would be most willing; but what of depriving the Quimperois of their beloved apostle? Beside, he was fifty-three, and he could not even stammer in Breton. Better postpone the missions and wait for a more opportune time. Such was the opinion of Père Flouet, the Rector, and his judgment was concurred in by the Provincial, Père Dinet.

There was little left for Père Julien but to pray and to wait. Pray he did especially to Notre Dame d'Espérance (Our Lady of Hope). And he waited patiently too, while he pursued his classroom work and his priestly ministry at Nevers. One course still lay open to him, permitted by the Jesuit rule, an appeal to the Father General, Mutius Vitelleschi. In the circumstances Père Julien felt justified in sending a letter of appeal to his major superior. He began the letter with a description of the sad condition of the neglected peasantry of Lower Brittany. Then he recounted the incident of his cure and of his vow. He listed the marks of his special vocation, stressing his remarkable acquisition of the Breton tongue in a few weeks that followed his pilgrimage to Ty-Mamm-Doué. He concluded by earnestly petitioning the Father General to send him back to the poor Breton people, who were in such dire spiritual perils and whom with all his heart he longed to save. Father Vitelleschi was quite impressed by the apostolic spirit revealed in the letter of his young subject. In a short while he communicated to the Father Provincial at Paris his wish that Père Maunoir was to be assigned to the mission of Lower Brittany.

One preparation still remained, the Tertianship, the third year of probation which all Jesuits must make between the completion of their studies and their final vows. Julien Maunoir, with seven other young priests, spent this year of spiritual renewal under the direction of Père René Ayrault at Rouen. Père Ayrault was well prepared for his task for he had witnessed sanctity in heroic reality. At the Roman College he had had as a fellow student, St. Aloysius Gonzaga, and as his spiritual counsellor, St. Robert Bellarmine. He still retained clear memories of both saints; only eighteen years before, in 1621, Aloysius had been beatified, and in that same year Robert Bellarmine had died. When he described to his tertians the modesty, the mortifications and the prayerfulness of the young saint, Père Ayrault spoke with the authority of an eyewitness. When he explained the principles of asceticism he repeated what he had heard in the conferences of his former spiritual counsellor. The Third Year of Probation was rich with spiritual experiences for Julien. Once again he made the long retreat of thirty days; [1] and this time as a matured and experienced reli-

[1] A Jesuit priest makes the long retreat twice in his career; once in his first novitiate and once in his tertianship.

gious he went through the *Spiritual Exercises*. In his study of the Constitutions of the Society of Jesus, one of the duties of this Third Year, he found how the spirituality of St. Ignatius was applied to concrete situations. The time order of each day, threaded with meditation and prayer, kept him continually, almost solely, occupied with God. Probably it was during this year of asceticism that Julien Maunoir fixed that life-long program of bodily mortification which his robust health alone sustained and which recalled the austerities of the ancient Celtic anchorites of Brittany.

A few apostolic expeditions were permitted the young fathers, mainly during Lent. On one such Père Maunoir preached a mission in the Norman town of Bernay, in the diocese of Lisieux. He had some remarkable successes. One was the reconciliation of an unforgiving mother with her son, from whom she had been estranged because of a fancied injury. The woman in her bitter hatred refused even to see her son. Père Julien pleaded and pleaded with the obdurate woman, but all to no avail. As a last resort he knelt down, right in her presence, and invoked her guardian angel. The hardened heart was softened; and the mother, repentant, publicly embraced her son. Another success was the grand procession which Père Maunoir organized to conclude the mission; in the ranks walked all the confraternities of the parish, all the magistrates of the city in their colorful robes, fifty diocesan priests, numerous friars and Benedictine monks, the Benedictine prior carried the Blessed Sacrament. The Bishop of Lisieux was so pleased with the results that he brought the missionaries to another of his towns, Orbec-en-Auge. On the day of arrival Père Maunoir converted a condemned criminal in the shadow of the gallows; up till then the hardened wretch had blasphemously spurned all priestly ministrations. During the first night of the mission a destructive fire, started by a fierce lightning storm, threatened to reduce the entire town to ashes. Père Julien at the head of a quickly organized procession and bearing the Sacred Host led the praying crowd towards the conflagration. The raging flames died down quickly and the catastrophe was averted. Needless to say every succeeding sermon of the mission was thronged.

Brittany was not forgotten at Rouen. Hopes were nourished, plans were formed and continually prayers were said for her people and her priests. Letters from Père Bernard arrived regularly. Unfortunately for the most part they brought only sad reports of a frightful pestilence that was raging in Quimper. No remedy seemed to avail to stop the epidemic; every known one had been tried. The plague was universally considered in Quimper as a visitation for the failure to punish the mutilation of the statue of St. Corentin by a libertine. The Jesuits, who had to close their college, devoted four of their priests to the exclusive care of the victims of the pestilence. Père Bernard, one of the four, seemed almost to multiply himself in his ministrations of the dying. When the disaster was reaching its climax he heard a voice distinctly saying: "Have recourse to St. Corentin." He went straightway to the magistrates and urged them to make a public vow of reparation to their ancient apostle. They agreed to do so and made the vow with the greatest public solemnity. The pestilence ceased almost immediately.

Père Julien followed Quimper's sad trial with deepest sympathy; he hoped that within a few short months he would be in the town laboring for its people. The recourse to St. Corentin appealed strongly to him, who was to be the restorer of the cults of the ancient Breton saints.[1] His third year of probation was completed in August 1640. As quickly as possible Père Maunoir was on the road to Quimper, where he knew Père Bernard would be waiting for him with the heartiest of welcomes.

Père Julien found it good to be back again in the ancient capital of Cornouailles, treading its labyrinth of streets and alleys. He found one great change: the College of St. Yves was now standing on its own premises, close to the northern rampart of the town. True the building was not entirely completed;[2] but at least the Jesuits were dwelling in their own home. Their financial situation, however, was still a heavily burdened one. The harassed rector was quick to inform the new arrival that in his opinion the project of the missions was still impossible. He repeated the old objections: no revenues, no companion, no prospect of the bishop relenting. To the young priest's query about the task for which he had been especially sent to Brittany the rector's reply was: "Your mission will consist of preaching two or three times a year in our Locamant priory." Locamant was a small holding ceded to the Quimper Jesuits for the support of their college. But, two or three sermons only to its sparse congregation! That surely was a dispiriting prospect on the threshold of one's life career. Père Julien accepted it; God alone could measure the grandeur of his obedience.

[1] According to Brémond, Julien Maunoir's restoration of the cults of the ancient Breton saints completely refutes Renan's charge that Jesuit practices destroyed the vènèrable and unique character of religion in Brittany.

[2] The chapel, wherein reposed later on the relic of the heart of Bl. Julien, was not finished until the eighteenth century.

There was still Dom Michel Le Nobletz. On receiving the news of his successor's arrival at Quimper, he dispatched a message begging the young priest to come to him at his retreat in the fishing village of Le Conquet on the tip of Cap Saint-Mathieu. Le Conquet lay in the diocese of Léon; and the old patriarch had been living there ever since his expulsion from Douarnenez, [1] practically a solitary. Almost completely immobilized by infirmities, brought on by excessive austerities, he was unable to move far from his cabin on the lonely beach. Any request of this grand servant of God was a command for the Quimper Jesuits, and so the rector readily granted the permission for the visit. Père Julien made the journey in the beginning of November. On the evening of his first day on the road he received the unexpected news of the death of Msgr. Le Prestre, the bishop of Quimper.

At Le Conquet Dom Michel eagerly awaited the traveller. When he beheld him, tears filled the old man's eyes and he exclaimed, as he embraced his disciple: "O Lord, take me from this world when it shall please Thee. Now I shall die content, since my eyes have seen him whom Thou hast promised to me, because he is prepared to achieve the conversion of these people whom Thou confided to me and whom I place in his hands." Next day the venerable missionary made a general confession of his whole life to his young confrère, an act of touching humility indeed. Then Dom Le Nobletz, ringing his bell, convoked all Le Conquet in the parish church, and there he presented to them Père Julien as his successor in the missions of Lower Brittany. In the view of all he handed over his bell and his catechetical

[1] Cf. p. 18.

charts to the young priest. After that he made him preach a short sermon in Breton; then he had him hear confessions; and finally he led him around in visits to the sick and the poor. It was veritably an investiture.

That evening Dom Michel held a private conference with his youthful successor. Bringing out his old notebooks on moral theology, he indicated a page to Julien and bade him read it. What was the astonishment of the latter when he began to read the solution of a case of conscience that had been perplexing him! His astonishment mounted as the old priest penetrated further into his thoughts. Julien had resolved to do some extensive reading in Baronius' *Annales Ecclesiastici* and also in the history of France, once he was permanently established in Quimper. Now with what amazement he heard the venerable missionary saying to him: "My son, you have work indeed on your hands. Don't waste time reading Baronius and the history of France. What you have to study are the Sacred Scriptures." After that there was no limit to the disciple's trust in his master. That night Dom Michel placed in Père Julien's hands the rule of conduct which he had drawn up for himself; it had received the approval of Père Coton and its model was St. Ignatius Loyola.

Next day the conferences were resumed. Dom Le Nobletz began by movingly describing the spiritual rewards awaiting the Breton missionary, no matter what obstacles or contradictions might block his labors. Then he took a practical turn, explaining his methods of preaching, of hearing confessions and of teaching the catechism by his *enigma* [1] charts and his didactic hymns. He even spoke of ways of travel, advising journeys by

[1] *enigma* chart – Explained in C. VIII and also in Appendix III.

land rather than by sea, since on the highroads and in the inns one found greater opportunities for imparting religious instruction. Finally he counselled his young friend to husband his strength for God's work in Brittany, urging him not to be as careless of health as he had been. "The exhausted horse tumbles into a ditch and leaves his rider there," was his shrewd summary of the years of his own invalidism. When Dom Michel ceased speaking, Père Julien could not find words to express his gratitude. He knelt down and begged the blessing of the old priest, who, after he had imparted it, knelt himself to seek the blessing of his youthful successor. Mutual farewells were said, and Père Maunoir set forth on his return to Quimper, more strongly determined than ever to enter the course God had marked out for him.

But how were the obstacles to be overcome? The vicars of the chapter of Quimper, ruling during the vacancy of the see, were not more favorable than the deceased bishop had been; to them also the missions were a novelty in which they could discern no particular advantages. However they did grant to Père Maunoir the ordinary permissions to preach, catechise and hear confessions throughout the diocese. Père Bernard solved the problem of a companion assistant. An urgent letter from Dom Michel prompted him to offer himself for the task, despite his age and his lack of the Breton speech. Now, he recognized Dom Michel's reference to the two apostles in his conversation at the college in 1630; he was to be the Andrew to Père Julien's Peter. The superiors approved of his offer; and with a zeal nothing short of heroic he set himself to learning the Breton tongue. For the two missionaries the apostolate was still a limited one, surely;

they were allowed only to catechise the inmates of the hospitals and the prison, and the children of the town and its environs. Fortunately the work grew rapidly, and the good results brought generous donations. The Governor of Quimper, M. de Molac, interested Cardinal Richelieu, who responded with a grant of twelve hundred livres. The addition of other gifts finally assured the permanent support of Père Maunoir and Père Bernard. The diocesan authorities too were looking more favorably upon the whole idea of the Breton Missions. It was time to begin.

Chapter 5

FIRST VENTURINGS

In the Lent of 1641 Bl. Julien Maunoir entered upon his apostolate in the Breton Missions. The place he chose for commencing was Douarnenez. He was no stranger in the town; nine years before it had witnessed his first catechising in the Breton tongue. Dom Le Nobletz was highly pleased with the choice. He loved Douarnenez, and he knew that its people still cherished his deeds and his words. With his aged trembling hand he wrote several letters to faithful friends there, begging active support for the mission. Père Bernard accompanied his young friend. As yet he had not sufficient Breton to preach, but he had mastered enough of the language to hear confessions. His zeal and holy example would be invaluable sermons in themselves.

The two priests found an enthusiastic welcome on their arrival. At the town limits they were greeted by a deputation of the citizens, and in the parish church a capacity crowd gathered to hear them. If any were curiosity seekers, they changed before Père Maunoir had finished his first sermon. As he was discoursing on the Last Judgement and describing the ominous signs that would precede it, out of the clear sky there came a great flash of lightning and a terrific clap of thunder. Sudden fright froze the hearts of everyone. Père Julien allowed a moment for his hearers to regain their composure. Then in measured tones he spoke: "Fine indeed, if it suffices for a bolt of lightning and a burst of thunder to throw your souls into such terror! What will it be when the anger of a vengeful God will flash upon you and manifest itself by all the signs which the Gospels describe to us?" No, there were no laggards after that. For six weeks the missionaries preached, catechised, heard confessions and visited the sick in the town and in the seven neighboring hamlets. In his official report Père Maunoir wrote that he and his companion had instructed ten thousand souls during that Lent.

At Le Conquet Dom Le Nobletz eagerly welcomed news from the mission. He redoubled his prayers and consecrated anew his sufferings that God might bestow still greater blessings upon the work. He sent letters of encouragement and advice, recommending strongly his didactic hymns. Père Maunoir used them frequently; he also composed some of his own. He had all the religious songs printed and distributed in all directions. The songs caught on at once; everyone in Douarnenez and its environs, children and adults, took special delight in singing them. Père Julien's didactic hymns, naive and gracious in form, conveyed to the simplest minds instructions that were as solid as they were agreeable. They became the source of innumerable conversions, for many the beginning of truly remarkable piety.

Miraculous cures, deliverances of the possessed and other spiritual favors, all of which Bl. Julien attributed to the intercession of St. Ignatius, manifested God's approval. One instance deserves citation, there is such a ring of Brittany about it. Eléanore Thépot, a poor old widowed fishwife, had obtained from Heaven the favor of bearing the pain of our Savior's Crown of Thorns every Friday. After twelve patient years she now askd Père Maunoir for some alleviation of her excruciating suffering. She said: "I still wish to suffer more, if it pleases God. The only reason of my asking for relief is that old age has come upon me and I cannot earn my bread, except by carrying a heavy basket of fish every Friday from Douarnenez to Quimper. I fear that my poor head, so filled with pain, will be unable to bear such a burden on a journey of eight leagues." Touched by her faith Père Julien applied a holy relic to the old woman's head. She was freed from the pain, but only on the Fridays when she labored for her livelihood; on other Fridays, when for some reason she did not work, the pain returned. A temporary respite, that was all Eléanore Thépot asked; she continued to suffer voluntarily for Christ until her death.

On Easter Monday Père Maunoir terminated the first Breton mission with a great procession. He had frequently promised it during his sermons. The whole countryside came in to participate; over six thousand persons were present. The piety and modesty of the children, marching by in long files, captivated all hearts.

How proud the parents were as they beheld their daughters, robed all in white and crowned with flowers, accompanying the statue of the Blessed Virgin, or as they saw their sons in the guise of angels, bearing the instruments of the Savior's Passion! Enthusiasm mounted high and the immense throng joined in singing lustily the religious songs. Few restrained their tears. The first mission was long recalled at Douarnenez. Père Julien gratefully regarded all its consolations as helps from God to sustain him in present and future trials. The first experiment more than satisfied the Provincial, Père Dinet; on his subsequent visitation he placed in writing an order that Père Maunoir and Père Bernard were to be employed solely in the Breton Missions.

Douarnenez was a terrain well prepared by the earlier labors of Dom Le Nobletz. Next must come a missionary expedition into abandoned places. Such were the isolated islands off the northwest coast. The Ile-de-Sein, five miles from the rocky cliffs of the Pointe du Raz, was chosen for the start. The trip out was almost completed when the fathers learned that the entire male population were away on their seasonal fishing. There was nothing to do but put about, return to the mainland and wait for a more favorable opportunity. On landing the missionaries found a messenger with a pressing invitation from Dom Michel to repeat at Le Conquet the good work of Douarnenez. They re-embarked and made the long sail to Cap-Saint-Mathieu. They were received with an enthusiastic welcome; the old patriarch had seen to that.

Since Le Conquet was in the diocese of Saint-Pol-de-Léon, Père Maunoir and Père Bernard repaired to the episcopal town for the necessary authorization of its bishop, Msgr. Robert Cupif. A matter of routine, so they thought, for this prelate was known to be favorable to their project. But his frigid reception quickly disabused them, and to their dismay they heard the bishop refusing them all approbation. His opinion of the missionaries and their work had been completely changed by an ecclesiastic of his entourage. Coldly Msgr. Cupif informed the two Jesuits that he did not want in his diocese missions given by religious. Let them content themselves with teaching the youth; his own priests were fully capable of administering to the needs of his people. His words certainly closed the door to their best hopes. Modestly and humbly the fathers accepted the hard blow. The bishop was touched by their humility. He bade them not to depart from Saint-Pol without visiting him again.

The two missionaries first sought spiritual help in their disappointment. Dwelling at Saint-Pol was a much revered Breton mystic, Marie-Amice Picard; she was reputed to have shared for years in the sufferings of the canonized martyrs. To her prayers and reparations the fathers recommended themselves and their cause. Then they invoked the aid of an assured friend, M. l'abbé du Louët, the Vicar General of Saint-Pol-de-Léon but soon to be Bishop of Quimper. He was a holy priest, much after the mind of Dom Le Nobletz. M. du Louët gave the two Jesuits a kindly welcome. When he had heard their story he promised them his fullest assistance. Dismissing the fathers, he went immediately to the episcopal palace to plead their cause. With earnest cogency he presented the missionaries' apostolic plans, their excellent qualifications, and the great blessings that they would surely bring to the diocese. Boldly he challenged the bishop. "Prove their zeal! Send them to the islands of Ouessant and Molène! These islands are abandoned in their wild seas. No one knows when a bishop has visited them. These two priests are devoted and brave and eager to go. Why not profit by their good will?" Msgr. Cupif was impressed. When shortly afterwards Père Julien and Père Pierre returned to visit him, they were received most affably. True the bishop asked them to postpone the mission at Le Conquet; but he offered them instead Ouessant and Molène, and there the needs were far more urgent.

The island of Ouessant lay twelve miles off the coast, across a perilous stretch of water, notorious for its swirling cross-tides, cruel reefs and blanketing fogs. The passage in a small fishing smack, threading the maze of rocky islets and rolling on the long sea-swells of the vast Atlantic, called for iron courage in a landsman, such as Père Maunoir. An old Breton proverb ran: "He who sees Ouessant, sees his blood." As his boat drew near Père Julien realized why Ouessant was called "The Island of Terror"; just before it lay a frightening barrier of jagged, foaming reefs that had to be pierced; and beyond loomed up from the water's edge a precipitous escarpment, reaching to heights of 190 feet. For the ascent of this almost perpendicular wall the islanders had fashioned a winding flight of steps. A stranger attempting this dizzy climb alone courted almost certain death.

The fisherfolk of Ouessant, thanks to the isolation of their sea-girt home, were singularly free from the grosser vices. Among them theft was unknown, impurity uncommon and drunkenness rare. But in matters of the faith they were sadly ignorant. Among the three thousand inhabitants, according to the missionaries, scarcely a dozen had more than a cursory knowledge of the Holy Trinity and the Incarnation, or of the Ten Commandments. How could it have been otherwise? Within the memory of man no bishop had set foot upon the island. The few priests who sojourned on the island were themselves woefully ignorant. They were scarcely able to maintain the fruits of the mission preached by Dom Le Nobletz some thirty years before. Poor Dom Ians, they had little save their personal devotion to give to their flock. Once two well educated priests proposed to devote themselves to the islanders; but they never reached Ouessant; for their boat was smashed on the treacherous reefs and they were drowned in the fierce breakers.

On the Vigil of St. Peter and St. Paul, June 28, 1641, Père Maunoir and Père Bernard landed on Ouessant. They announced the opening of the mission on the next day. At daybreak an eager crowd filled the church and over-flowed into the adjoining graveyard. Père Maunoir had the pulpit placed in the portal of the church so that everyone within and without might hear him. The islanders followed his words with the closest attention. "It seemed that the breath of the Holy Spirit passed over the souls of all the people," Père Maunoir wrote. When he finished the crowd still stood around the pulpit, silent and motionless, waiting for the father to start in again. This he did, but only after singing High Mass. Again he was listened to with the same fervent attention. In the afternoon, before Vespers, came the time for the Catechism. But not a single answer could Père Julien elicit. Not from the elders, silenced by shame for their ignorance. Not from the children, bashfully hiding their faces and not daring to look up at the strange priest. The day's exercises were concluded with a stirring sermon on the torments of Hell and the joys of Heaven. The preacher was frequently interrupted by cries of repentance and of faith; his hearers were moved as never before in their lives.

The Reefs of Ouessant.

The Isle of Sein.

The need of the people for religious instruction was so pressing that the missionaries changed their program and gave the first place to catechetical exercises. They wrote to Dom Le Nobletz to send them from Le Conquet a capable catechist who would help them overcome the reluctance and timidity of the islanders. Dom Michel dispatched his best assistant, Jeanne Le Gall, a little orphan girl, who had acquired a special facility in explaining his religious charts. A bit of pious strategy was used in the employment of Jeanne, who came to the island on the pretext of visiting cousins. She was seated among the girls of her own age during the catechism-hour; and when the questions were asked, she volunteered the answers, modestly but with all assurance. Père Julien warmly praised her, both for her responses and for the manner of her replying, and rewarded her with a gift of a rosary. Before long the other girls were essaying at least timid replies. And when they left the church they clustered around Jeanne seeking to learn her answers, which she gave to all with simple devotedness. The stratagem soon bore ample fruit. The young girls, desirous of the praise and the rewards, now eagerly sought to be interrogated; and the young men, moved by rivalry of their sisters, followed their example. In a few days all the islanders were competing for the privilege of answering the questions.

But often what ignorance appeared in their well intentioned replies! Even to the question: "How many Gods are there?", some answered, "Two"; others, "Three"; others still, "Five." How more discouraging could prospects be for the missionaries? But Père Maunoir possessed a potent remedy, his *cantiques spirituels,* with their explanation of the essential truths and of the principal moral duties. One of the island priests learned these didactic hymns and joined Père Julien in singing them in the church. Jeanne Le Gall taught them to the children and young girls in frequent rehearsals. The simple fisherfolk were charmed; and soon all the islanders were chanting the new, pious songs and learning, in an easy, pleasant way, how to honor and serve God. In consequence, so Père Maunoir wrote: "Fire blazed forth in the midst of these waters; the Holy Spirit enkindled such an ardor in the souls of these islanders that, with everyone thronging to the instructions, it was necessary to preach out in the fields. The crowds of penitents were so great that to satisfy them we had to repair to the confessional at three o'clock in the morning and to remain there almost the entire day until eight o'clock at night, and often until nine. Père Bernard, that he might awaken more easily, slept on a table." Père Julien omitted to state that he himself slept on the flagstones.

When everyone had gone to confession—it was the first time in their lives for many—they were prepared and assembled for the general communion, which would be for many the occasion of their first holy communion. The reception of the Blessed Sacrament was followed by an impressive ceremony in which the islanders solemnly promised to abandon superstitious customs and also to guard themselves against the common evil of excessive drinking. The hearts of the two missionaries overflowed with joy: "It seemed to us that there was found again at Ouessant something of the marvels of which the apostles testified at Jerusalem, when they announced the gospel. In the morning, when we went to the confessional, in the evening on our retiring, and during the day, when we visited the sick, everywhere on our way we encountered men penetrated with the most lively sorrow and weeping for their sins. Some asked us what they should do to expiate their faults, or to repair the time lost. All ceased not to praise and exalt His mercy." God sanctioned the work by miraculous favors; one instance was the cure of a blind child. Père Julien and Père Pierre in all their success gave credit only to God: "How good Thou art, my God! How numerous are the graces which Thou dost pour out on these poor fishermen! . . . Never were we more convinced of the words of the apostle: 'Neither he that planteth is anything nor he that watereth; but God that giveth the increase.' (I Cor. 3, v. 7)"

The mission was terminated by a grand Eucharistic procession, with the pastor of the island carrying the Blessed Sacrament. The terminus was a chapel, considerably distant from the parish church. In a nearby field, where more than four thousand people had gathered, Père Maunoir preached his last sermon, exhorting his deeply moved listeners to perseverance. The time for farewells came, and great was the weeping and crying of the good people. The two missionaries proceeded to the shore escorted by the entire population. In the very last moments, right at the top of the escarpment, the sick were brought for the fathers' blessings. Père Manuoir asserts that God cured several. After the dangerous descent had been negotiated and the missionaries were seated in a little shallop, they looked up and beheld the cliffs filled with the islanders, hundreds lining the ridges, hundreds more clinging to every advantageous rock, some even crowding the narrow shore. All kept calling for a final blessing. Père Julien, standing the stern, raised his hand in the sign of the cross and pronounced a final benediction on the good, simple fisherfolk of Ouessant. The boat started on its course; but not a soul left the cliffs until the little craft had passed beyond sight. The mission to the islanders of Ouessant had lasted three weeks. Père Maunoir concluded his report: "May God bless them! I believe that He will be served on this island and that the fervor will endure for a long time."

The boat was put upon a southward course for the isle of Molène. The crossing of the seven and a half miles of shoals and reef-strewn waters took two hours of careful sailing. Molène was much smaller than Ouessant; it stretched no further than a half mile, and it rose, at its highest point, scarcely sixty feet above the sea. A desolate looking place it was; but its five hundred inhabitants made it an attractive spot for Père Maunoir and Père Bernard. To their surprise the missionaries found the islanders prepared for them. Some of the children had crossed over to Ouessant during its mission and had learned the religious songs. On their return they taught them to their companions. The elders acquired the hymns from hearing the children constantly repeating them. Old and young eagerly participated in the catechetical exercises. For the rest it was as at Ouessant: formal sermons, visitations of the sick, confessions of the entire population and a general communion. Because of the small population the mission was completed in eight days. But they were eight days of fervent spiritual renewal, which God blessed with extraordinary graces.

In the midst of the campaign on the islands, a letter arrived from Dom Le Nobletz warning his young successor of an opposition that was being organized against him on the mainland. Two priests, jealous of his successes, were spreading suspicions and false accusations against him. They even presented petitions to Bishop Cupif and to Père de Launay, superior of the Quimper Jesuits, decrying the missions and requesting that Père Maunoir be recalled to the college and that he be banned from apostolic work. In their petition to Père de Launay, while praising the zeal of the youthful missionary, they bemoaned his imprudence—he organized questionable dances, he sanctioned them by his presence, and he even contributed songs to them. The rector, accepting the accusations at face value, dispatched a reprimand to Père Julien and Père Pierre. Anxious not for themselves but for the future of the missions, the two priests sought testimonials from the priests and the leading laymen of the islands. These immediately responded with abundant approbations, citing the wonderful spiritual results and the brief time in which they were obtained. The letters were put into documentary form, notarized and sent to Bishop Cupif and to Père de Launay. The calumnious attack collapsed, completely disproved.

The malcontents, however, were not finished. They turned to an indirect attack, an assault on the character of Dom Michel Le Nobletz. The truth is that they were not worthy priests; and Dom Michel's holy life stood as an open rebuke to their own. They raised a whole mixture of charges: Dom Le Nobletz had collected from Cornouailles a crowd of irresponsible youths who filled Le Conquet with frivolous and dangerous songs: Dom Le Nobletz had joined in singing these unseemly ballads at crossroad gatherings; Dom Le Nobletz had employed a woman, one Jeanne Le Gall, to explain his ridiculous *enigma* charts; Dom Le Nobletz had even allowed this woman to usurp the ministry of preaching. Msgr. Cupif, again too quickly impressed, ordered an official examination of Jeanne Le Gall, proscribed any singing of the religious songs, and commanded the people of Le Conquet under pain of excommunication to send back the youth of Cornouailles (actually these had come for the purpose of making a mission under Dom Le Nobletz). The bishop also severely reprimanded Dom Michel for sponsoring missionaries as indiscreet as Père Maunoir and Père Bernard, though he softened his rebuke by kindly exhorting the venerable patriarch to correct his mistakes.

At her examination Jeanne Le Gall more than satisfied her rigorous interrogators; and Dom Michel, when he presented his *enigma* charts at the inquiry, won emphatic approvals. There remained the religious songs; but on these Msgr. Cupif, realizing his ignorance of the Breton language, would make no pronouncement. The calumniators, notwithstanding, spread a false report through Le Conquet that he had condemned the songs and forbidden with threat of excommunication their singing. Dom Michel on his part issued no defense, though he assured his friends that God would soon vindicate him and his protégé. Nor would he condemn his two adversaries, remarking only that they would not have the power of injuring him for long; indeed they both died very shortly.

The new attack had been going hardly a few days when a flotilla of barques and fishing smacks sailed into Le Conquet. The boats bore several hundred islanders on their way to the nearby Monastery of St. Mathieu for the Sacrament of Confirmation. All the way across they had been singing the religious songs; and now when they landed they made the cliffs of Cap Saint-Mathieu echo with their powerful choruses. Forming a procession the new arrivals proceeded on to the abbey. As they marched along they continued their singing, increasing in enthusiastic volume as they drew near their goal. The crowd that gathered to watch the procession, when they recognized the chants, tried to stop the singers. They shouted that these songs were forbidden and that those who sang them would be excommunicated. The simple-minded islanders scandalized cried to each other: "How can they excommunicate us for singing what we learned from the holy fathers, the Tadou Santel? [1] They took up the chanting again, and in a more vociferous chorus than ever befort. Menacing sticks failed to silence even the children, who were the larger part of the procession.

A riot was imminent; but fortunately it was prevented by arrival on the scene of M. l'abbé Pencrec'h, the theologian and penitentiary of Notre-Dame-du-Folgoët. Speaking in Breton he asked the children to sing the chants for him. They did. M. l'abbé listened intently; and he heard not a single line that was contrary to Catholic doctrine. Then and there M. Pencrec'h bade the islanders keep on singing their religious songs, and with all their hearts too. Some of the bystanders protested, crying out that the bishop had forbidden these very chants. Whereupon the abbé sought out Msgr. Cupif and explained to him the true character of the religious songs, completely justifying Dom Le Nobletz and Père Maunoir. The bishop generously determined on an open vindication. The next day he had the Prior of Recouvrance, M. Le Denmat, declare from the pulpit and in his presence that the Bishop of Saint-Pol-de-Léon, now better informed, blessed the religious songs, their authors and all who would sing them.

When the islanders waited on Msgr. Cupif to thank him for sending them the missionaries, they presented him with the affidavits of the priests and leading laymen of Ouessant and Molène. The bishop assured his visitors that he entertained a high regard for

[1] Already the Bretons were beginning to call Père Julien *an Tad Mad*, "the good father."

Père Maunoir and Père Bernard. A few days later the missionaries themselves brought the prelate the detailed report of their work on the islands. It so pleased Msgr. Cupif that he asked the two priests to preach there again in the following Lent. Further, he requested Père Maunoir to come to him after Easter and teach him the Breton tongue that he might better understand and help his flock.

During all the contention the most active champion of the missionaries was the vicar-general of Léon, Msgr. René du Louët, the bishop-elect of Quimper. In gratitude the fathers offered to conduct a mission in his future diocese. The place chosen was the Ile-de-Sein, five miles due west of that massive headland, the Pointe-du-Raz. Reaching the Ile-de-Sein proved the most perilous journey yet for the missionaries. After embarking at Douarnenez they sailed for many wearisome hours along the cliff-lined southern shore of the Bay of Douranenez. Then they navigated the treacherous waters of the Hell of Plogoff and of the Bay of the Dead, doubled the Pointe-du-Raz, and at length battled through the clashing winds and tides of the Raz-du-Sein. An old Breton prayer petitioned: "Save me, O Lord, from the channel of Raz, for my barque is so small and the sea is so great." The two priests must often have said that prayer as their small boat tossed about in the swirling masses of water.

A length they drew near to what seemed to be a huge raft floating on the vast ocean. Brizeux, Breton poet, thus describes the Ile-de-Sein: "So low on the horizon, that she seems a raft, encompassed by a thousand reefs, on a level with the sea." The island measures a mile and a half in length and a half a mile in width. No part of it is more than a few yards above high water; the danger of its submersion is very real when the terrible Atlantic storms rage. The Ile-de-Sein is just an arid rock, with not a tree and precious little vegetation, save the barley and parsnips which the women raised in little patches of earth, mixed with seaweed. Cultivating these meagre plots was the women's work. Offshore fishing was the men's occupation the whole year around. Life was hard and lonely on this isolated reef, so much so that priests could not be found who would share its harsh loneliness. For years on end the fisherfolk of Sein were without the ordinary consolations of religion. Yet, as the missionaries soon discovered, the people were remarkably good. They had not always been so; in former days the islanders of Sein were known as the "demons of the sea," with a sinister reputation as ship-wreckers. Their wonderful change was effected by Dom Le Nobletz while he was evangelizing the islanders some thirty years before.

When the missionaries' boat at length docked at the little quay of the Ile-de-Sein, it was two exhausted and famished priests who stepped ashore. Held back by contrary winds they had been thirty-six hours on the water, and during that time not a morsel of food passed their lips. Père Julien seldom mentioned personal hardships; but this time he noted how much he had suffered from the unforeseen length of the passage. But if Père Maunoir and Père Bernard had been angels, they could not have received a more enthusiastic welcome. "Now we shall have the Mass," the islanders exulted, and "we shall learn the way to heaven." The welcoming group, to the astonishment of the fathers, chanted the *Veni Creator* and escorted them to the island-church, which to their further surprise they found well kept and filled right to the door. Why think of exhaustion?

Why think of hunger? These poor people, so long without priests, were hungering for the Mass. Right away Pére Bernard began a low Mass. He proceeded in great, painful effort, but he forced himself to finish. Then Père Maunoir prepared to sing a high Mass. Hardly was he vested in his alb, when he felt himself becoming faint. Seriously weakened by hunger and seasickness, he was now nauseated by the odor of a pile of gutted fish outside the sacristy's window. He invoked St. Corentin, the the patron of Cornouailles, and his weakness quickly passed. He sang the high Mass through, and after it he held a catechesis and then preached a sermon.

The familiarity of these isolated fisherfolk with the ceremonies and chants of the Church caused Père Maunoir no end of wonderment. Who could have been responsible? He got the answer in his first conversation with the captain of the island, François Guilcher, called familiarly François le Sû (François of the South) because his house stood on the southern shore. In his youth he had lived for a while on the mainland, where he learned a little French and a little Latin. When Dom Le Nobletz was preaching on the island in 1613, he found in François le Sû such an earnest helper that on leaving he made the good-hearted fisherman a present of de Ponte's *Meditations on the Mysteries of our Holy Faith.* During all the subsequent years Dom Michel kept up a correspondence with the faithful captain, sending him books, hymns, *enigma* charts and spiritual counsel. François Guilcher on his part used his influence with his fellow islanders to maintain the practices of religion. Every Sunday morning he led the whole population in procession to the church, where under his direction they read aloud the Mass prayers and chanted parts of the Divine Office. At the end of the devotions François announced the feasts and fasts of the week. In the afternoon he assembled them once more in the church to sing Vespers and to listen to a reading from one of Dom Michel's books, or even a simple exhortation by himself, if it were a solemn feast-day. On Good Friday the captain brought everyone on the island to the cemetery and, standing at the foot of the calvary, he read to them the Passion of our Lord. During the forthcoming mission François Guilcher was again to prove himself a valuable auxiliary, especially in teaching the religious songs.

The islanders responded whole-heartedly to the missionaries. They stopped all work so that every one could have ample time for considering his eternal salvation. They made each exercise with great faithfulness; even the children, clustering around their elders or held in their parents' arms, seldom turned their gaze from Père Julien. Nor were the islanders content with sermons and catechetical lessons. On the conclusion of the day's exercises they followed the fathers to their lodgings and interrogated them, often far into the night.

How the priests survived the demands upon them was a wonder. Père Bernard, held all day in the confessional, with but a quarter of an hour for his humble meal of barley bread and dried fish, and then occupied all evening with consultations, could find scarcely more than three hours for repose. Père Maunoir had to preach all the sermons and conduct all the catechetical exercises, since his companion had not sufficient knowledge of the Breton tongue for the pulpit. Of course he had a large share of the confessions too. Yet he sought no more rest than did Père Bernard. Both missionaries felt amply repaid for their sacrifices; as Bl. Julien evidenced in his *Journal*: "How wonderful it was to see these men, before approaching the holy tribunal, asking pardon of one another; to observe the tears of the penitents, as they confessed their sins; to witness their ardor for instruction in the service of God." By the third day the islanders' veneration for the missionaries reached the point where they were bringing them their sick to be cured. They were not disappointed. Six persons recovered from very serious throat ailments and two were cured of deafness when Bl. Julien prayed over them and anointed them with holy oil.

For the present moment the mission was succeeding beyond the best expectations. But what of the future, after the fathers had departed? Would the people of Ile-de-Sein be once again enveloped in spiritual isolation, a flock without a priest, a Christian community without the Eucharist? Père Maunoir pondered earnestly and prayerfully. At length a solution occurred to him: why not have the captain of the island ordained a priest? [1] François Guilcher had many qualifications: he was free, since he was a widower; he was virtuous, sagacious and zealous; he had the maturity of his sixty years; and he enjoyed the full confidence of his fellow islanders. True, the little Latin of his youth must have faded by this time. But a sojourn at the Abbey of Landévennec, of which the Ile-de-Sein was a dependency, would equip him with a knowledge sufficient for reading the Missal and the Breviary, and for hearing confessions. Discreetly Père Julien sounded out François. The captain replied that he had often dreamed of the priesthood, but that he never dared to speak about it, stopped by the thought of his lack of education and by the consciousness of his un-

[1] The practice was not uncommon in the early church and in medieval times, especially in the shortage of priests after the Black Death.

worthiness. If, however, the father was of the opinion that he should become a priest, he would do whatever the father prescribed. Père Maunoir was satisfied. He bade François go to the Abbey of Landévennec and spend a year there. He assured the humble fisherman that he personally would request the Benedictines to prepare him for the priesthood. The islanders joyfully learned of François le Sû's vocation; and they offered to raise a fund from their paltry earnings to defray the expenses of their captain during his stay at Landévennec. But, as will be seen later, the priesthood of François le Sû was not to be easily achieved.

The mission on the Ile-de-Sein lasted for eight days. At its conclusion the fathers, instead of going directly homeward, set sail for the distant Le Conquet to consult with Dom Le Nobletz. They were fortunate in having as their pilot François le Sû, for the voyage was a rough one with a storm threatening all the way. It was near midnight when they made shore. But hardly had they landed when the storm broke with furious violence. Drenched in the fierce downpour and unable to pierce the inky blackness, the little party was stranded on the rocks. After a time a stranger joined them and conducted them through a difficult pass in the cliffs to a path that led to Le Conquet. The sailors were convinced that their deliverer was an angel. More extraordinary still, they were not long on the path when they encountered Dom Michel, lantern in hand, leading a search party for them. The old patriarch had received at least no human message of their coming.

Dom Le Nobletz would hear no reports until the rain-soaked travellers had been warmed and fed. Then, his heart overflowing with holy joy, he listened to the detailed recital of the missionary triumphs on the Ile-de-Sein. Dom Michel doubly welcomed his old friend, François le Sû; and, when he learned of the captain's priestly desires, gave them his most emphatic approval. In the conference Père Maunoir and Dom Le Nobletz agreed that the abundant harvests of Ouessant, Molène and Ile-de-Sein warranted the extension of the missions to the whole of Lower Brittany.

Chapter 6

WIDER FIELDS

On their return journey to Quimper the missionaries decided on a detour to the Abbey of Landévennec. They had a double purpose: a pilgrimage to the shrine of its founder, St. Guénolé, one of the great Celtic saints of Brittany, and an arrangement with the Benedictines for the training of François le Sû. They arrived in due time at the shore of the Rade de Brest. To cross the fifteen miles of that wide roadstead to Landévennec they could find only one small boat, and that was piloted by a boy of twelve. Père Maunoir and Père Bernard loath to relinquish their project embarked on the dubious craft. They were far out on the great bay when a hurricane struck, threatening every minute to capsize the little shallop. The storm raged for twelve hours. Near its end the helpless craft was run down by a heavier boat, and only with difficulty were the fathers rescued from drowning. After their landing they had still far to go to reach the abbey. For long hours the two priests, weighed down with heavy packs, had to trudge through the rainy blackness. At length they arrived at the monastery gate, drenched to the bone, famished and exhausted. A warm-hearted Benedictine welcome soon restored them, and next morning they were able to say Mass at St. Guénolé's tomb. When they presented the story of François le Sû to the abbot, Dom Pierre Tanguy, he readily promised that his monks would afford every help to the good fisherman.

The two priests resumed their homeward journey to Quimper. There Père Maunoir took a month's respite from the missions, a practice which he followed each year of the forty-three of his apostolic career. He loved those periods of quiet calmness in the College of St. Yves; there was regular observance, common life, and above all renewal of spiritual strength. In the beginning, perhaps, there was danger that with his predilection for prayer Père Julien would prolong those days of retirement. Dom Le Nobletz feared as much; for in a set of instructions [1] for his young successor he made the following observations: "It is necessary for him to make retreats from time to time, but he ought not to delay too long in them . . . It is a temptation for him to love religious solitude more than the exercises of the mission . . .

[1] Dom Le Nobletz made out two sets of instructions for the guidance of Père Maunoir and included them in a letter to Père Bernard, who was to transmit them to Père Maunoir; hence the instructions were written in the third person, not in the second. Both sets of instructions are given in full in Séjourné's *Histoire de Julien Maunoir, S.J.* Vol. I, pp. 415-417.

He will pray better in the midst of the world and in the midst of labors than in religious solitude." The saintly old priest, himself a mystic, promised that he would receive more heavenly illuminations while preaching than while studying in his room. God had plainly called Père Maunoir to a most active apostolate, and Dom Michel dreaded lest he might be turned from it. Actually there was little to fear.

Outside of the eight days of his annual retreat, Père Julien's rest was filled with pastoral activities. Each day found him at the Hospital of St. Anthony, instructing the sick poor, hearing their confessions and preparing them for death. He frequently visited the prison, bringing the Lord's forgiveness to despairing criminals, and, on occasions, reconciling the condemned at the hour of execution. The figure of Père Julien, wandering about in search of the poor and afflicted, became a familiar sight in the streets and alleys of Quimper. Nowhere was he venerated more as the Tad Mad. It would be impossible to count the number of sermons he preached in the parishes of Quimper and its environs; the local pastors never called on him in vain. When he came to help the flock, he also strove in a friendly way to intensify the shepherds' zeal. He frequently gave conferences and exhortations in the convents of the nuns. Whatever free moments of his "Leisure" he had left, he devoted, especially in his early years, to his religious songs, revising old ones, composing new ones and preparing both for publication. Père Maunoir's rest periods in actuality constituted annual missions for Quimper.

One day when he happened to be at the college, Père Maunoir was called to the parlor. On entering he found standing there none other than François le Sû dressed in his fisherman's garb, seaman's jacket and blue bonnet. The good man's story was soon told. He had been with the Benedictines at Landévennec for a few months and the monks had assured him that he knew enough to receive Holy Orders. Would the father present him to the Chapter of Quimper [1] for the authorization needed for ordination? Père Julien was not surprised at all, either at the presence of this extraordinary aspirant for the priesthood, or at his request. He took good care, however, to furnish the fisherman with a black coat and a black hat for his appearance before the chapter. He sped the simple captain on his way with the assurance that God would assist him if He desired him to work for His glory.

The canons were in session when François walked in on them. His examination by them was over in a few minutes. Astonished at his appearance they asked him who he was and what had brought him there. The old fisherman replied naively that he was from the Ile-de-Sein where there were no priests, no Mass, no sacraments, and that he wanted to be a priest that he might come to the aid of his neighbors. What studies had he made, he was asked. He answered again with the same simplicity that when he was about sixteen he had studied in two little books, the *Rudiments de Codret* and the *Sentences de Caton* [2], but that after four years at Léon, where he had also studied French, he had returned to his island and there had followed the occupation of a fisherman for forty years. The canons at first listened with mild surprise to this elderly, white-haired aspirant for the priesthood. But, as they heard him out, and

[1] A diocesan chapter is an ecclesiastical body that assists the bishop in the governing of his diocese. The members bear the title of canon and their place of meeting in the cathedral is called the chapter house.

[2] Two elementary Latin books, then in wide usage.

learned the paucity of his attainments, their wonderment turned to amused forebearance at his preposterous request. Some scarcely suppressed their laughter. Dispensing with further questioning, the gentlemen of the chapter dismissed the old fisherman as unqualified for the priesthood. They bade him go back to his boats and his nets.

Poor François le Sû! Utterly disconsolate he shuffled along the pavements of Quimper: at his age to have reached to such high hopes, and then to have been dashed into complete disappointment! What a heart-breaking disillusionment! Providentially Père Yves Pinsart, O.P., the prior of the Dominicans of Quimper and Theologian of the Cathedral of Quimper, encountered the poor fellow. Noticing the very evident discouragement of the old fisherman, the kindhearted prior inquired of him why he was so cast down. When François sadly confessed the reason, Père Yves, as wise and as learned as he was kindhearted, made him turn around and come right back with him to the chapter. There, Père Pinsart, relying on his office as Cathedral Theologian, spoke very plainly to the canons: "You have a duty to give a pastor to the Ile-de-Sein where none of your priests will consent to go. It is true that this man's attainments are meagre, but in pressing necessity the Church can always ease her prescriptions. Finally, in my opinion, you will be rash indeed to dismiss so lightly a candidate seemingly sent to you by God Himself."

The Dominican's strong words impressed the canons and they agreed to resume their interrogation of François le Sû. They placed a missal in his hands and told him to read any passage. François by chance opened to the Gospel of St. Matthew, to the lines where Peter confesses the divinity of Christ and is promised the primacy. He read the passage to the end firmly and intelligently, to the surprised and growing interest of his examiners. One of them asked him if he understood what he had read. The white-haired fisherman responded by translating the entire section into French, and with such ease and clarity that the astonished gentlemen of the chapter remarked to each other that there were many pastors in the diocese who could not do so well. Finally they proposed some cases of conscience such as he was likely to hear in the confessional. François solved the problems so much to the approving satisfaction of the canons that, recognizing the finger of God, the chapter without further delay issued the documents requisite for ordination.

After expressing his deep gratitude to his advocate, Père Pinsart, François hastened to Père Maunoir and gave him a full account of his adventure and of his success. Père Julien bade him depart at once for Saint-Pol-de-Léon, where some days later Msgr. Cupif conferred upon the erstwhile fisherman the sacrament of Holy Orders, making him a fisherman of men. Now Dom Guilcher, François le Sû returned to his native Ile-de-Sein to say his first Mass in the presence of its entire population. What heights of happiness for these good people: at last, a pastor for their island, and he, their neighbor and their kinsman, their own François le Sû! Msgr. du Louët, who visited the island many times later, always declared that he had never met a more faithful pastor than this good priest. Dom Guilcher shepherded his island flock for seven years, and then died in the odor of sanctity. To this day his memory is blessed in the Ile-de-Sein.

The Breton Apostolate widened considerably in the second year, 1642; missions were given in thirteen different localities in the four dioceses of Cornouailles, Léon, Saint-Brieuc and Dol. To the perils of coastal voyaging this extension added the hazards and fatigues of overland journeys over wretched roads; sometimes there were not even roads. Dom Le Nobletz recommended a preference for land-travel, for it offered far more opportunities of meeting the peasants and giving them the word of Life. Times innumerable Père Maunoir joined parties of peasants on their way to market and chatted with them about produce and prices so that he might turn their thoughts to the purchasing of Heaven. "Faith, hope and charity, contrition and confession," he was wont to say to them, "there are the coins that will buy Heaven for you."

Hardships were never absent in the moors, forests and mountains. In bad seasons the missionary had to trudge along often up to his ankles in mud and water. Père Julien never traveled by carriage; he went on foot, and only in his old age did he proceed on horseback. When he reached the destination, usually he had to begin his labors right away, no matter what the cost. Père Le Roux, himself a veteran of the Breton Missions, describes the painful experiences of Père Maunoir thus: "When he had to get up early to preach, despite his need for rest after a long fatiguing journey, he went long before daybreak through the mud to the church; and after giving his instruction he remained in the confessional until late at night, soaking wet and penetrated with the cold. . . Only those who have gone through it can comprehend how much it cost human nature. It is not enough that in these circumstances one should repress the fear of rheumatism or other sicknesses; rather one is obliged to scorn life itself and its every comfort."

Shrine of the Heart of Bl. Julien.
Roz-Avel, Quimper.

But it was by the price of such painful sufferings that Père Julien and Père Bernard purchased their marvelous harvest of souls. The reports of Père Maunoir to his superiors in Paris and in Rome note for the year 1642 fifteen thousand Bretons solidly instructed and carefully prepared for the sacraments; for the year 1643, twenty thousand; for the year 1644, fifty thousand. The peak was reached in 1648 with sixty thousand, a figure equalled in 1649. In less than ten years Père Maunoir and his lone companion, Père Bernard, preached to, catechised and heard the confessions of more than a quarter of a million souls.

Such successes aroused bitter enmities among the malicious. There was even an attempt to assassinate Père Maunoir. The incident occurred in the town of Plozévet, on the Bay of Audierne, while Père Julien was preaching out-of-doors to a large crowd that filled the town's square. He was speaking from the top step of the calvary, and was extolling the virtues of Saint Corentin. A crazed desperado shouted from a window that he would end the sermon and fired a blunderbuss at the preacher. One shot grazed the head of a peasant, two pierced the coifs of country-women, others dug into the wood of the cross, and one struck the biretta of the missionary. The furious crowd rushed on the house of the miscreant. They would have killed him, had not Père Julien, hurriedly placing himself in the doorway, pleaded with them not to harm the unfortunate wretch. After some anxious moments he succeeded in calming the angry peasants. Strangely enough, on that very day Père Maunoir had implored of God the grace of dying for love of Him. [1]

[1] Boschet, p. 138.

The bishopric of Dol, for reasons going far back in history, included certain parishes deep within the limits of the bishopric of Tréguier. Because of their remoteness from their episcopal city they had been neglected, and in consequence ignorance and its attendant evils reigned in them. Père Maunoir sought and obtained authorization to conduct missions in these parishes. His choice for a beginning was the island of Brehat, in the English Channel, just off the northern tip of Brittany, between the bishoprics of Saint-Brieuc and Tréguier. When he and his companion came to the coast to seek passage out, they received all sorts of fearsome warnings against adventuring among people notorious as poisoners, sorcerers and murderers. The two priests paid scant attention; the islanders of Brehat, no matter how evil, had souls to be saved.

The charity of Père Maunoir and Père Bernard was to be amply vindicated. The people of the island had never heard missionaries before, but they had good hearts, and they gave the fathers a warm welcome. Nowhere did Père Julien meet with more docility and repentance, more fervor and humility, more eagerness in learning the religious songs and more ardor in singing them. The marvels of the Ile-de-Sein seemed surpassed. On their departure the fathers received a most touching tribute of gratitude from the islanders. Père Maunoir thus describes it: "If they had lost their own father, they could not have shown a more lively sorrow. Nearly all escorted us to the port, keeping a mournful silence, which was broken only by their sighs and sobs. The children in troops climbed to the summit of the cliff at the foot of which the missionaries were to embark on their departure. At the moment when the ship unfurled its sails and started to glide over the waters, the children began to sing a Breton hymn. They prayed to the Holy Family to preserve from all perils those who had employed themselves in saving their souls. Even when the fathers were at a considerable distance the childish voices in the chant of farewell still pursued them."

The boat made the mainland at Lannevez, where the two fathers had planned to open a mission. They were on shore but a brief time when they became aware that the natives universally suspected them of being English spies. An English raid on this part of the French coast was always a possibility. The several days which the strangers had spent on the island of Bréhat seemed sure proof that the two had been lulling its inhabitants into a false security. The appearance of two British warships offshore, at this very time, confirmed the worst suspicions. Not a single soul attended the opening service of the mission. And then, after nightfall, the English vessels made a descent upon the Ile-de-Saint-Maudet, only a short distance from Bréhat. At once the islanders of Bréhat and the neighboring Ile Verte lit beacons to alert the mainlanders. Rumors flew all along the coast that the English were ravaging and burning in the islands. Great land-beacons began to flare out into the night, and in every belfry the tocsin was ringing to rally the coastal defenders. Crowds of armed peasants quickly gathered. About the two strangers, arrived from Bréhat just this very day, there was doubt no longer: they were not priests, but disguised British spies. Angry shouts for vengeance arose in the crowd assembled at Lannevez. The situation grew ominous, for the mob in their terrified panic might murder the fathers.

What was to be done? Père Maunoir proposed immediate flight; he was very frightened, and he was very young. But Père Bernard, the veteran, would hear no mention of flight; it would be taken as an admission of guilt. No, far better to place themselves in the hands of God and stay. The brave counsel of the old priest invigorated his young comrade's spirit. Courage restored Père Julien walked towards the approaching mob, crying out to them: "No, no, my brothers, we have not come to betray you to any enemies; we have only come to defend you against the enemies of Heaven. Before you commit any rash act in your terror, I beg you send to the Ile-de-Bréhat and find out what those fires mean, and what you have to fear. In the meantime observe us closely; and if we do anything else than teach you how to gain Paradise, then treat us as you please." His wise words calmed the agitated crowd. A deputation was sent off to Bréhat. They came back with the information that the enemy had retired, though not before ravaging the Ile-de-Saint Maudet. As for these two priests, the deputies reported that everyone on Bréhat, to a man, venerated them as saints. That washed out the spy-charges.

But the suspicious in Lannevez were not yet satisfied. They kept asserting that never had they seen priests garbed as these two strangers, without starched linen rabats, but with enormous hats and three-winged birettas. The three wings, to the superstitious worriers, presaged plague, war and famine. About the only encouragement the fathers received was when boatloads of youngsters rowed over from Bréhat to take part in the mission. Up from the beach they came in parade formation, loudly chorusing the religious songs as they marched along. But the only effect the marching chanters had upon the suspicious was to deepen their misgivings that these strange priests must be wizards. How could they draw an island's entire population after them, except by magical charms? How could they make children learn in eight days as much of the catechism as ordinarily would take three months, except by some sort of occult practices? When the fathers changed their lodgings to a poor peasant's cottage near the church, the worriers held only one explanation: they did so to seek hidden facilities for diabolical enchantments. The affair was really getting far beyond an old wives' tale.

The village children brought matters to a head. So fascinated were they by the questionings and the singing that they could not be kept from the mission even by the most menacing prohibitions. They would steal out of their homes in the early morning and spend the whole day following the prayers, venturing answers at the catechesis, learning and practicing the religious songs. It was too much for the elders of Lannevez; so when their neighbors of Paimpol proposed jailing the missionaries as sorcerers, they readily concurred.

Fortunately there were some level-headed persons in the village, and they succeeded in having a committee sent to seek the counsel of the prior of the Premonstratensian abbey of Beauport, Père Martin, whom the whole country-side held in reverence. When the prior heard the description of the missionaries' garb, he informed the delegates that the costume, for which they were reproving the two priests, proved to him that they were fathers of the Society of Jesus. He warned them that it would be a grave mistake to accuse these priests of magic and enchantments, and a tragic one, if thereby they were deprived of liberty and life. He assured the deputation that these priests had come among them only to rescue their souls from Hell and to open to them the gates of Paradise. As proof of his confidence in the fathers Prior Martin dispatched forthwith two of his religious to Lannevez to salute the two Jesuits in his name. He sent along refreshments and the assurances that he would bear the expenses of the mission and that the fathers would lack for nothing during their sojourn in those parts.

The words and acts of the charitable Prior of Beauport effected a complete change of heart in the peoples of Lannevez and Paimpol. They could not hurry to the church fast enough to seek the fathers' forgiveness for their rash judgments and their harsh treatment. The priests accepted the poor folk's amends with such humble kindness that they won the complete confidence of everyone. Profiting by the good dispositions of the people Père Maunoir ascended the pulpit and preached a powerful sermon on the torments of Hell. He spoke so effectively that he was repeatedly interrupted by the cries of the congregation for God's mercy. After the sermon the preacher with Père Bernard went directly to the confessionals. The first biographer of Bl. Julien adds that the penitents' tears flowed abundantly.

Word of the good to be obtained spread abroad, and though it was August, the harvest time, such a concourse gathered from the dioceses of Tréguier, Saint-Brieuc and Dol that a dozen missionaries could not have heard all the confessions. The two priests had to forego all preparation in their preaching, trusting in God solely to inspire their words. The spiritual songs again proved most valuable; many acknowledged that in singing them they learned more about the truths of religion in eight days than they had known in all their lives.

The mission that had begun so hopelessly ended in a singular triumph. Heavy rains, during the last days of the missions, had beaten the wheat flat; a ruined crop seemed certain. The congregations prayed unceasingly for better weather, but the rains continued without letup. Père Maunoir alone retained hope; he announced that the closing procession would be organized as a great petition for the saving of the harvest. He redoubled his prayers and continued every one of his preparations. His faith was rewarded; just as the files of the children began to march, the rains ceased. A month of splendid weather ensued and brought an abundant harvest.

The procession itself was a glorious success. The marching ranks were augmented by the islanders of Bréhat, who came for the occasion in several enthusiastic boatloads. To satisfy the people of Paimpol, now anxious to offset their initial opposition, the route of the march was extended to their village. A hundred of their men, bearing arms and forming a guard of honor, escorted the procession to the center of Paimpol where it was welcomed by the ringing of the church bells and the discharge of muskets. The Premonstratensian canons came from Beauport to participate, wishing to honor both the missionaries and the marchers. Père Maunoir echoed the gratitude of all; "Honor and praise to God alone, to God who disperses the darkness with the most resplendent light and teaches us never to lose confidence, even in the midst of the most violent persecutions." At the conclusion of the procession, Pére Julien prepared to address a final sermon to the large crowd. He had hardly announced his text, when the realization that these were his farewell words dawned upon the assembly; they broke into such crying and lamenting that he was obliged to descend from the pulpit. The crowd followed him to his lodgings, many kneeling to beg his blessing, and others, despite his objections, kissing his hands or the hem of his cassock. Their homage continued into the night and ended only when Père Maunoir promised to return soon for another mission.

Early in the next year, February 22, 1643, Père Maunoir assisted the bishop-elect of Quimper, Msgr. René du Louët, in his solemn entry into his episcopal city. The newest shepherd of the ancient diocese of Cornouailles was a prelate of rare merit who would dedicate himself unswervingly to the reforming of his diocese. Wasting no time in lamenting unfortunate conditions, Msgr. du Louët set for his first task the visitation of his entire diocese. Quimper had not had a canonical visitation in two hundred years. The zealous prelate proceeded in this task not only as a bishop but as a missionary. He traversed the length and breadth of Cornouailles, penetrating to the most remote hamlets, not drawing back even from the tides and reefs of the coastal islands. He commissioned Père Maunoir and Père Bernard to go before him to prepare for his coming; and frequently he brought them along as assistants. This was a new phase for the Breton Missions.

The visitation was begun in the cathedral of Quimper. At the wish of Msgr. du Louët the two missionaries preached preparatory sermons and conducted daily catechetical instructions. They repeated the sermons and instructions in all the nearby villages. God sanctioned their labors with remarkable cures and conversions. One of the first practical results was the organization by Pére Maunoir of a group of noble ladies for the visiting and nursing of the sick poor in the hospital and the prison. As a rallying point for the newly awakened zeal the bishop and the fathers chose the devotion to St. Corentin, the apostle of Cornouailles. His cult had been in the process of revival since the plague of 1639; [1] and a shrine to contain the relic of the patron of Cornouailles had just been completed in the cathedral. Amidst a splendid celebration manifesting the universal joy of the people of Quimper, Msgr. du Louët placed the relic in its repository. St. Corentin's shrine soon became renowned for its extraordinary favors. One such was the cure of a young girl, Françoise Gubaer, a paralytic who had been horribly burned as she sat by a fireplace when a flaming brand rolled out upon her helpless feet. The two missionaries prayed over the afflicted child and recommended her cause to St. Corentin, and Père Julien anointed her with oil from the shrine's vigil-lamp. A few minutes later the girl's mother was amazed to behold her daughter walking to her and crying out that she had been cured by St. Corentin. Both burns and paralysis had totally disappeared. [2]

During the preliminaries in the visitation of the rural districts the fathers had to spend large portions of their time in preparing the country-folk for the sacrament of Confirmation. Very large numbers had to be instructed, for years had passed since anyone had been confirmed. Père Maunoir estimated that in three country-parishes, Brasparts, Pleyban and Saint-Ségal, hardly less than 13,000 persons, of all ages, received Confirmation during this visitation.

Msgr. du Louët came to realize that lasting remedies for the evils he encountered could be achieved only by arousing his pastors to zealous vigilance. He decided on convoking a synod; he fixed the date and appointed Père Maunoir for the opening sermon. While awaiting the gathering of the clergy the two missionaries, at the behest

[1] The account of the revival during the plague has been described in Chapter IV, pp. 80-81.

[2] *Latin Journal,* ad ann. 1643; cited by Séjourné, Vol. I, p. 184.

of the bishop, journeyed to Saint-Pol-de-Léon to enlist the prayers of a holy mystic, Marie-Amice Picard. On the road back Père Julien thought out his opening sermon. He preached the discourse with such unction that he won the wholehearted approval of the assembled pastors. Msgr. du Louët, profiting by such good dispositions, announced to his clergy that he was sending Père Maunoir and Père Bernard into their parishes to be their auxiliaries in the care of souls. He bade the pastors receive the two Jesuits as they would receive himself and give to them the most zealous co-operation.

At the conclusion of the synod the bishop sent the missionaries to the remote parishes of the west coast. The first was Audierne. A generation before its inhabitants had resisted the efforts of Dom Le Nobletz; but now chastened by a terrible disaster, the loss of over half their ships in a storm, they proved themselves most amenable to religious exhortation. Their mission turned out well-nigh a complete success. In the environs of the Pointe-du-Raz the fathers encountered extremes of ignorance and superstition. At Cléden the penitents knew so little about Confession that they complained of the interrogations of the missionaries: "You new priests are very curious, you wish to know too much. Why don't you act like our priests? They ask us if we know our religion; and when we answer yes, they tell us to say five paters and five aves for our penance and give us absolution. Is anything more necessary?" At Plogoff the fishermen, except for attending Mass, made no distinction between Sunday and working days; "Do we not have to eat on Sunday, as on other days? We must then go to our fishing." Dances held at night, sometimes even in country churches, were a source of grave disorders. Many local customs were grossly superstitious: beating the statues of the saints to obtain the return of menfolk out on the ocean, throwing the sweepings of the chapel into the sea for the same purpose, praying in honor of the new moon, offering buttered bread to propitiate the malign spirits of the fountains, leaving seats for dead ancestors around the St. John fires. Sadder to relate, occasionally avaricious priests traded on the superstitions of the poor people, particularly in connection with novenas of masses for the dead. A few such unworthy clerics even attempted cures by magical practices. Père Maunior wrote that an entire book would not suffice to describe the pacts and sorceries inspired by hell in these isolated folk: an exaggeration, certainly, but indicative of the evils with which he had to contend. But Père Julien's determination and his understanding sympathy triumphed eventually; culpable priests made open reparation for their scandalous practices, and their example induced the people to abandon the remnants of a long-dead paganism. The general confessions were almost uncountable; and the intense and solid fervor of the penitents augured well for the permanence of their reform.

Missions were given in other parts of Brittany during that year, at Penmarc'h, Rostrenon and Ty-Mamm-Doué. In late August Père Julien was back in Quimper to prepare himself for his final vows. The letter of the Jesuit General, Father Vitelleschi, authorizing Père Maunoir, Père Huby and others to make these vows, ends with the words: "I ask our Lord for the most abundant treasures of His grace for each one of them. May they be able to find the efficacious means to respond fully to their vocation." This letter is preserved in the Jesuit archives in Rome; in the margin, next to Père Julien's name, is an annotation in the hand of a later superior, "Respondet cumulate" (He is responding abundantly). On September 8, 1643 Père Julien Maunoir pronounced the solemn vows which made him a professed father in the Society of Jesus.

Chapter 7

IN FULL SWING

In the years 1640-1650, Bl. Julien Maunoir established the *Breton Missions* as a permanent feature of life in Brittany. In the next thirty years he was to devote himself without stint or respite to this apostolate. It would be wearisome and of little purpose to trace his long course from mission to mission. More profitable would it be to give a general consideration of the work and a detailed description of its outstanding practices.

From 1640 to 1683 Père Maunoir conducted 400 missions in seven dioceses of Brittany: the four Breton-speaking, Quimper (Cornouailles) [1], Saint-Pol-de-Léon,

[1] The diocese of Quimper was occasionally called by its ancient name of Cornouailles.

Tréguier and Saint-Brieuc; and three of the four French-speaking, Dol, Rennes and Vannes. He averaged ten missions a year, each of four to five weeks duration.[1] Trudging along the highways and the byways—only in old age did he go by horseback—he crossed and recrossed the peninsula countless times. Père Julien became the most familiar figure in the old duchy, in its towns and hamlets, in its fields and forests, on its rocky headlands and coastal islands. What this tireless road-traveller of God was achieving was in fact the re-evangelization of the Breton people.

From the very beginning immense crowds attended Père Maunoir's missions. Even in the early years, when there were only himself and Pére Bernard, the count showed annually over 30,000 participants. After the association of priest cooperators had been founded the numbers increased threefold, reaching 100,000 attendants in 1664, and again in 1665. In a single mission at Irvillac, in 1644, one of the earlier years, 10,000 people made the exercises; at Landivisiau, in 1668, at the height of the movement, 30,000 people received Holy Eucharist at the general communion. These figures of Père Maunoir would appear astronomical, were they not supported by numerous testimonies: the official reports of the Fathers Provincial of the Province of France to the Father General, several letters of Quimper Jesuits, preserved in the general archives of the Society of Jesus, and statements of many diocesan priests who had assisted

[1] A listing of all the missions preached by Bl. Julien Maunoir is to be found in Appendix I. The list was made by Boschet in 1697, published again by Le Roux in 1715, checked and amended by Séjourné in 1895. A cursory examination will enable the reader to appreciate Bl. Julien Maunoir's "immense labors", a term used in the prayer sanctioned by the Bishop of Quimper.

him. Notable among the last testimonies was that of M. Vincent de Meur, Superior of the Seminary of the Mission Etrangères of Paris; he noted that he had seen in a small village 20,000 persons making a mission. His observation revealed what had become a common occurrence, the participation in a particular mission by all parishes within a considerable radius.

The mission was usually given at the request of the pastor of a parish. Such requests multiplied considerably once the diocesan clergy began to assist Père Maunoir. Witnessing the wonderful benefits of a mission in which they were helping, these priests became most desirous that their own flocks should be recipients of such blessings. Occasionally fervent seigneurs, or devout châtelaines, solicitous for the eternal welfare of their tenants, sought missions for their estates; the noblesse of Brittany were always close to their peasantry. Sometimes a bishop ordered a mission for a parish that he deemed needful of reform, or better, as a preparation for a canonical visitation. The provision for lodging and boarding the missionaries devolved upon the pastor or the seigneur; it became a considerable problem when the number of priest co-operators reached thirty or forty. Not always were the necessary expenses assured. Père Maunoir by preaching and by soliciting alms was wont to accumulate funds whereby certain poorer and more abandoned parishes might have missions. But more than once Bl. Julien began a mission with no other resource than a simple, unquestioning trust in God's providence.

Many preparatory letters had to be sent out. First of all was the notice to the pastor; this had to be dispatched some weeks in advance, so that he might announce the great event each Sunday at Mass, and also have the news spread through all the parishes round about. Then followed the invitations to the priest collaborators; these often amounted to three dozen messages or more. Finally there were the lists of recommendations to the charitable hosts who were to lodge and board the missionaries. Though Père Maunoir left much to the good will of the hosts, he always insisted that no necessities be lacking for his assistants on their arrival. If the missions were to be in the diocese of Cornouailles, he always paid a visit to the episcopal palace, soliciting the bishop's blessing and official approbation. If the work carried him elsewhere, on entering the particular diocese he went directly to its bishop to present his courteous respects and to beg the necessary authorizations.

The final preparation was prayer. Having constituted the Blessed Mother of God supreme patroness of the Breton Missions, Bl. Julien never embarked on any apostolic venture without first fervently begging Mary's assistance. Next he appealed to St. Michael, especially if he apprehended a possible conflict with gross superstition or diabolism. Celtic to the core, Père Julien continually sought the aid of the ancient saints of Brittany, St. Corentin, St. Pol de Léon, St. Elouan and the patrons of the parishes which he was evangelizing. It was his invariable custom on leaving Quimper for a mission to say Mass on the day of his departure in the Cathedral of St. Corentin. Another custom which he faithfully observed when crossing into a new canton was to invoke the guardian angels of the territory.

Père Maunoir usually arrived at the place of a mission on Saturday evenings. This afforded him the opportunity of announcing and explaining the entire programme of the exercises at the Sunday Masses, thus assuring good order all through the weeks to come. He always went directly to the parish church to reverence the Blessed

Sacrament; as he used to say, "It is but just that the Master par excellence should receive our first visit." Next, prompted by his sincere respect for the diocesan clergy, Père Julien paid a courtesy call at the presbytery.

During this preparatory day groups from the more distant parts, not infrequently with their pastors at their head, were converging on the village. They came from all directions appearing in every road and bypath. Every class and every age walked along in these groups: gentry and peasants, rich and poor, great and simple. The lodging and feeding of so many strangers must have posed most serious problems in a small village. Of course the people from the immediate neighborhood would bring their own food and would go back to their homes at night. But the visitors from remote parishes must have had to depend on relatives, friends, or on the charity of the villagers. In the milder seasons many slept in the fields. After the inception of the priest-assistant system the apostolic clerics could be frequently seen in the marching crowds. The priest would trudge along with a pack on his back, a breviary in one hand and a staff in the other. Only a few, well advanced in years, ever rode on horseback. As has been noted Père Julien made the lodging and the boarding of these zealous priests his personal responsibility.

Directly after the Sunday Vespers the mission was opened with a solemn procession of the Blessed Sacrament. At its termination Père Maunoir entered the pulpit and read the bull of indulgences; then he announced once again the time order for the morrow and for all the subsequent days of the mission. These preliminaries over, he preached the first sermon, enumerating the saving advantages of the holy exercises, warning against the neglect of them, and appealing in moving accents to the piety and the courage of his crowded congregation. Even the merely curious found it hard to resist the compelling unction of his words. The great majority, of course, were but waiting for such an appeal.

When the first service was over, Père Maunoir sought out the parish bell-ringer to give him his instructions for the days to come. The most important was the ringing of the great bell of the church for a quarter of an hour every morning at four. "If you are a little before four, it will do no harm; but if you ring later than four, I shall not forgive you," Père Maunoir admonished the bell-ringer. Lest he should sleep beyond four, on the first morning the priest himself got up at three to awaken the bell-ringer. Folks started earlier in those hardier days. A few other arrangements remained, the assigning of rooms and beds to the assisting missionaries, the posting of the schedule of Masses, with the altars and the hours, and the allotting of the different tasks for the morrow (preaching, catechising, hearing confessions, teaching religious songs and explaining the charts). In a final common act the missionaries knelt down together for the recital of night prayers. Then they retired for the all too brief hours of repose.

The rising hour was four, whatever the season. Père Julien, always up a little before hand, went from chamber to chamber, ringing a hand-bell and pronouncing salutations such as, "Signum magni Regis est, alleluia (It is the standard of the great king, alleluia)." The priests replied, "Eamus et sequamur illud, alleluia (Let us go and follow it, alleluia)." The last one to arise incurred a small penance; he had to serve his brethren at table or read during the meals. The penance was given and received in an amiable spirit.

All this while the great bell in the church steeple was booming out its grave and solemn sounds to the four quarters. Indoors and out everything was in motion as a sort of pleasant apprehension ruled in the town. Unforewarned travellers, awakened by the continual tolling of the bell, at first imagined that a great fire had broken out in the neighborhood. The slamming of doors and the rushing of footsteps in the streets only confirmed their fears. Throwing open the windows they called to the passersby to find out where they were hurrying so early in the morning. "The mission, the mission," was the universal answer. Curiosity brought the strangers down into the streets, and soon they were moving along with the hastening groups.

At the last sounding of the bell the one or two missionaries who had been assigned to stand at the church portal entered the edifice to lead the morning prayers of the congregation. The rest of the priests gathered at the lodgings of Père Maunoir for the recitation of the Holy Office. They followed that by meditation in common, a practice never omitted, save when the press of penitents called every one to the confessional. At the completion of the meditation Bl. Julien led his priest-assistants through the streets in solemn procession. Two by two they marched, attired in surplices and chanting alternately the *Veni Creator*. So they entered the church and advanced up into the sanctuary, where they knelt in a common act of adoration of the Blessed Sacrament. One group began vesting for their Masses, while the rest betook themselves to the confessionals. When the first celebrants finished they exchanged places with some of the confessors, and so it went until all had offered up the Holy Sacrifice.

The first Mass at the high altar was usually said by Père Maunoir. As the missionaries were filing into the church, the morning prayers of the people were reaching an end in an act of offering to God the Mass which they were about to hear. The priest, leading the prayers, had just previously explained the purpose of the Holy Sacrifice and the need of offering it with the priest. During the vesting the congregation sang a cantique [1] that embodied all this doctrine. During the Mass quietness reigned, for it was considered a time for silent, personal prayer. When the Mass was over one of the missionaries explained to the people the proper manner of thanking God; and then they in turn chanted a cantique that embodied their sentiments of gratitude.

Now Père Maunoir mounted the pulpit for his first discourse on matters of eternal salvation. He began by a series of questions to which he most earnestly sought responses from the congregation. Indeed he encouraged his hearers to interrogate him on their problems of faith and morals. Their questions, proposed even so simply, afforded him a good estimate of the knowledge or of the ignorance of his auditors. His own clear responses gained him the deepest confidence of the congregation. The answers and the questions of the people furnished abundant material for the formal sermon which he now swung into. A fervent teacher was preaching a practical

[1] The cantiques were didactic poems, with the principal purpose of teaching dogmatic truths and moral duties. So far, to give an idea of their nature and use, the somewhat cumbersome term *religious song* has been employed. The Breton term is *Canticou Spirituel,* the French term is *Cantique Spirituel.* From now on, for practical reasons, *Cantique* will be used. The English *Chant* can have secular implications; and *Hymn,* usually means a short composition of two or three stanzas in which emotional devotion is emphasized.

sermon to a doubly-interested audience. Often this catechesis-sermon started a stream of penitents toward the confessionals. When the sermon was concluded Père Julien went straight to his place among the confessors.

Now it was time for the missionary in charge of the singing to teach the cantiques. He led the people from the church to a nearby chapel; or, if the weather were good, he gathered them in the cemetery, always a part of the churchyard. First he chanted the verses himself, pausing occasionally to comment on their meanings. Then he induced his audience to sing the cantique several times until, familiar with the air and the words, the delighted crowd raised a mighty chorus in the fields. This common singing served both as a relief period and as a means of keeping up devotion; it rested the spirits of the people and at the same time it made them keener to profit by the next exercise of the mission. The singing was prolonged until the second sermon, which took place at ten o'clock. The priest most renowned for his oratorical abilities was chosen to preach this sermon.

At the end of the discourse Holy Communion was distributed to those of the faithful who were disposed to gain the indulgence. Père Julien, standing on the steps of the altar, himself prepared the communicants. First he spoke to them of the sentiments of faith, repentance, respect and love, with which they ought to approach the Sacred Table. Then he helped them to make acts of these virtues, interrogating them in the following manner, as Boschet reports:

> "All of you who are prepared to communicate, do you believe that it is really and truly the body of our Lord Jesus Christ, which you are going to receive?"

They responded all together, "We do believe it."

"And is it truly to render glory to your God, to pray that He will pardon your sins, and to preserve yourselves from relapses that you desire to communicate? Is it truly to find the strength to practice virtue, in a word to obtain the grace to live well and to die well?"

All responded again, "Yes, it is for that."

"But do you not tremble in the presence of a God so great, so powerful and so holy, you who are nothing but the dust of the earth, nought but miserable sinners? Why the angels of heaven, all holy as they are, tremble before His infinite majesty, and you, unfortunate culprits who have so many times merited hell, are you not frightened by the thought of receiving Him!"

The face of Père Julien was inflamed, as he pronounced these words in tones so terrible, that truly the communicants all cried out, "We are all filled with fear."

"And this God so good, could it be that you have hearts so hard as not to love Him for the future? It was to gain your love that He made Himself a small baby; that after you were created He redeemed you; that He died for you on the cross; and this same God, who right now is coming to give you His Body and His Blood, is it possible that you would not love Him?"

It would be difficult to express the tenderness of heart with which Père Julien spoke in that moment. His words reached into the depths of his hearers' souls, and all responded, "Indeed, we do love Him!"

"How often have you offended this God so good and so lovable, this God who is going to feed you with His Body and Blood! Ah! Is not your sadness the deepest sorrow, and will you not beg His pardon with all your hearts?"
Only tears and sighs and groaning responded to the query.

"If you desire God to pardon you, then it is necessary that you pardon with all your heart those who have offended you. Do you pardon them?"
All responded. "We do pardon them!"

"If truly with a good heart you pardon your enemies, then I assure you that God will also pardon you. But in the future offend no more a God, who shows you so much mercy. Are you strongly resolved to obey His commandments and those of His Church, not to violate any one of them? Are you resolved to repress your criminal desires, and to fly the occasions of sin?"
"We are so resolved."

"These resolutions, who will give you the strength to accomplish them? The very One whom you are about to receive, if you do so fervently. But are you truly desirous, are you impatient to assist at this heavenly banquet, to eat this Lamb without stain, who would make all of you Christians gentle and patient, sober and chaste and holy like Himself?"
"We are!"

"Do you beg the Eternal Father to give you His well-beloved Son that He may be all to you, and that you will never more act with Him except with a single heart and a single soul?"
"We do supplicate that."

"Do you beg the Blessed Virgin, Saint Michael, Saint Corentin, the holy patron of this parish, and all the saints of Paradise to render the dispositions of your souls more perfect still? Do you ask them, themselves, to adorn this palace of your soul, where God is going to descend with all His angels?"
"We do beg them all for that."

"Since it is so, let us all chant together the cantique that contains the Acts before Holy Communion. As you chant it, make your hearts echo to the words which fall from your lips." [1]

Then Bl. Julien intoned the first stanza. The communicants repeated it after him. When in this manner they had chanted the whole cantique, they approached the altar rail. Their devotion at the moment of reception moved even the most casual bystanders. After Communion, Père Maunoir chanted the cantique of thanksgiving, and the communicants repeated it after him, stanza by stanza. Then the communicants were left to themselves, so that in complete silence and recollection they might converse with God as their fervor inspired them. The busy Père Julien was never in a hurry when things sacramental were concerned.

A quarter of an hour before midday Père Maunoir rang his hand-bell; it was the signal for the missionaries to alert themselves for an interruption of their labors. At midday the bell was rung a second time. The priests, quitting the confessionals or the catechetical groups, gathered in the sanctuary for the recitation of the *Angelus*. Then they filed out of the church and proceeded to their dwellings, in the fashion of the early

[1] Boschet: pp. 268-271.

morning, two by two, reciting alternately the *Te Deum.* The crowds in the streets parted respectfully for the procession of chanting priests, greatly edified by their gravity and prayerfulness. Bl. Julien conducted the group to the lodgings where the common refectory had been established. Before dining the priests on their knees made an examination of conscience, terminating it with the *De Profundis.* The meal was taken in silence, though there was always reading from the scriptures or spiritual books by a priest appointed for the task. Recreation followed. Usually it took the form of a conference on missionary problems and was presided over by one of the more experienced priests. The discussions sometimes lasted for two hours.

All during the time of the common recreation Père Maunoir would hold a large scale catechesis in the church. He set a high value on this exercise; and Heaven had blessed him with a unique facility for teaching Christian Doctrine by question and answer. If the particular mission was the first ever held in the parish, he started as if the people had never had any instructions in the mysteries of the Faith. He made the progress of his teaching always depend upon the knowledge of his auditors. The people loved these sessions: everybody, grown-ups as well as children, men and women, rich and poor, took the keenest delight in responding to his adroit questioning. He was always kindly; but no one escaped as his white wand pointed out respondents indiscriminately. These catechetical exercises, supplemented by the cantiques, were what enabled Père Maunoir to instruct a whole district in a month's time. After a mission it would be hard to find a parishioner who did not know what to believe, what to practice and what to avoid for his eternal salvation.

Bl. Julien Maunoir, S.J. preaching the great mission of Kerlaz, 1658.

MEMORIAL WINDOW IN VILLAGE CHURCH.

At two o'clock, with their conference completed, the missionaries walked again in solemn procession to the church, where a crowded congregation was awaiting Confession. Most of the priests, joined by Père Maunoir, began to hear the penitents. A few, designated for the task, occupied the congregation with teaching them the examination of conscience and the method of confession, or by training them in the saying of the beads, or by explaining the religious charts. At the end of the instructions the people were dismissed for a period of relaxation. After a sufficient interval they reconvened in separate groups in the churchyard, the cemetery, or a neighboring chapel to learn more of the cantiques. As previously, the missionaries interrupted the chanting to emphasize or explain a point. The lay catechists, men and women, led in the singing and took a special part in the discussions. It was in these out-of-doors exercises that they rendered their great service to the Breton Missions.

At length there came the evening sermon. During the winter it was given at four o'clock, and in the summer at five. The subjects, especially during first week were: the end and purpose of man's existence, and the four last things, Death, Judgment, Hell and Heaven. These sermons often brought the most hardened sinners to repentance. When the desire for conversion seemed attained, the topics became more practical: the sins of each state or calling, the obligation of doing penance, and the sure routes to salvation to be found in the sacraments, especially in Confession and in Holy Communion. Then followed explanations of the dangerous occasions of sin, of temptations and the ways of conquering them and of the sovereign, powerful remedy of prayer for all times, places and occasions. Finally and never omitted was a glowing description of the tremendous rewards of ultimate perseverance.

When the evening sermon had been concluded, the pastor, accompanied by his curates, proceeded to the altar for the Exposition and Benediction of the Blessed Sacrament. Night prayers were then recited by the congregation, led by one of the missionaries from the pulpit, a cantique was sung, and, as the final act, the examination of conscience on the day's work was made. Though the bulk of the congregation now left, confessions continued to be heard until seven o'clock. Then the missionaries returned to their lodgings, walking in the two files and praying aloud all the way. Before partaking of the evening meal the priests, directed by Père Maunoir, recited Matins and Lauds for the next day. At supper, as at dinner, there was reading. Immediately afterwards a conference on apostolic methods was held. It served as a recreation; though the matters considered were serious enough, they were discussed in an atmosphere of relaxation. Père Julien, who always presided at the night conference, contributed by his gentle gaiety to the amiable sallies and witty remarks that were bandied back and forth. At the end the priests knelt for common night prayers. Before their retiring Père Maunoir assigned to each missionary his task for the morrow.

Such was the day-to-day programme of the Breton Missions. There were variations, especially on the day preceding a General Communion, when absolving the throngs of penitents became the first concern. Sermons and instructions were abbreviated, or even omitted, for the priests were held in the confessionals through the whole day with but brief respites for their two meals. Sometimes when the throngs were very great, the missionaries began hearing at four in the morning and stopped only at eight at night. Changes were made for special services; thus on the final day all attention was given to the procession, the grand climax of the mission.

From the start of these weeks of spiritual regeneration to their finish, great crowds were always in attendance, and they were enthusiastically fervent crowds too. Early in the morning, often before it was yet light, good numbers foregathered at the portal of the church. As they stood there in the darkness they chanted cantiques to shorten the time of waiting, or to nerve themselves against the rigors of the cold. Throughout the day they kept moving in and out of the sacred edifice, ceasing only when the missionaries departed for their night's rest. The sermons frequently had to be given out-of-doors. Where were the churches that could hold five thousand, or six thousand, or more? In a country parish the pulpit was erected in an open field, which the people rapidly filled to its boundaries and beyond, the more venturesome climbing into the trees the better to see and to hear. In a town the preaching platform was set up in the market place, often against the base of the calvary. The faithful packed the entire square; and they crowded the balconies, the windows, and even the roofs of the adjacent buildings. Never were speakers listened to by more receptive audiences. Emotionally the Bretons were a reserved people; but the burning words of Père Maunoir and his assistants quickly brought tears and cries of sorrow from those thronged congregations. Nor was it an effervescent emotionalism; the large groups daily besieging the confessionals evidenced the enduring solidity of their convictions. Many of the penitents stayed patiently near the confessionals all day long; some sought the missionaries in their dwelling places even at night. Many waited a whole week for their chance to be heard; there were instances of strong souls fasting for three days until they had made their confessions. Père Maunoir declared: "There is not a single one of our days which has not been consecrated to hearing confessions, and very often from morning until evening." The figures, which he duly reported for each mission, indicated that a very large number were general confessions.

Of all the exercises, perhaps the most affecting was the General Communion for the Dead. By receiving the Blessed Sacrament in the church where the mission was being given and by reciting the prescribed prayers, a plenary indulgence could be gained for the souls in Purgatory. To deliver their dear ones from out of the cleansing fires into the joys indescribable of heaven appealed strongly to every Breton. No other people, not even their Celtic brethren of Ireland, lived in such real unity with their departed kinfolk. Brittany was a land peopled by the presence of the dead. Prayers for the dead were part and parcel of the Breton's daily life; requiem Masses were said as often as the Church allowed, and All Soul's Day was one of the outstanding days in the year. All this is still so today in Brittany. Père Maunoir, the Breton, preached the indulgence with urgent eloquence.

To assure the greatest possible response, he set aside a special day for the General Communion of the Dead, and invited every parish for a dozen miles around to participate. He made the most detailed preparation for the event: in letters to the neighboring pastors he recommended that they have their people confess in their own churches, lest anyone be prevented from confessing by the crowds at the mission; he also requested that the pastors bring with them their own ciboria, completely filled with unconsecrated hosts, accurately counted. He left nothing to chance; always he held one of the assistant priests in reserve to celebrate Mass at the latest hour in case the supply of hosts should give out.

All through the evening before the day of remembrance the bells in the churches of the countryside tolled the funeral knell, slowly and solemnly sending their sad, sweet message over the fields, through the woodlands, on the highroads and in the narrow streets of the towns. At the first sounds of the tolling bells everyone, in the great mansions and in the thatched cottages, knelt down to offer a common prayer for all the dead of the district; it was their first act in the great commemoration of their dear departed. Very early next morning devout groups trod every road and lane converging on the church of the mission. As they walked along they kept reciting the rosary, alternating it with chanting the poignant cantique of the Holy Souls:

"Brothers, parents, friends,
In God's name hearken to us,
In God's name, pray! pray!
We are in fire and anguish,
Fire over our heads, fire under our feet,
Fire on high, fire below.
Pray for our souls!"

Already, as early as four in the morning, the mission church was thronged to its very door. The Masses were begun; and as they succeeded one after another, the priests in many relays distributed Holy Communion to the seemingly never dwindling throngs. At Landivisiau, where on September 21, 1668, 30,000 communicants received the Blessed Sacrament for their dead, groups of seven missionaries at a time were occupied from six in the morning until three in the afternoon distributing the Sacrament. In the next year in the small hamlet of Lesneven, 18,000 communions were received in the service for the Holy Souls. All the while, as the faithful were filing up to the altar-rail, choirs of children, one choir relieving another, chanted continually the Breton cantiques, first that for the preparation for Holy Communion, and then that for thanksgiving after Communion. The sweet young voices of the children, the murmuring undertones of the priests saying the Masses or administering the Holy Eucharist, and the rhythmic beat of countless steps moving always forward to Communion, these were the only sounds that day. All the rest was silence, but a silence filled with cherished memories of the loved ones who were gone. Emotions deeper than human expression filled men's hearts on the day of the General Communion for the Dead.

The last exercise of the mission was the Grand Procession. It was the crowning event for it epitomized all the preaching and teaching of the weeks past. Père Maunoir attached the highest value to the Grand Procession and prepared it with the greatest care. Endowed with a keen sense of the dramatic, a deep understanding of human psychology and an exceptional ability for handling large crowds, Père Julien was a master of the spectacle. Today he would be famous as a director of immense pageants. Always he worked in the Ignatian tradition, using all good means, simple or magnificent, to lead souls to their ultimate good, God Himself. Thus he planned grandeur in the spectacle to arouse the piety of the people to enthusiastic fervor, and he worked for vivid portrayals of the incidents of the Savior's life to fix the love of Jesus deep in the recesses of their souls. Before the scenes of the Passion, who would not be inspired with a hatred of sin, a penitential sorrow and an inviolable attachment to the service of Jesus crucified? Père Julien also aimed the procession at the conversion of those still resisting the graces of the mission. How many times he saw his hopes realized! Sometimes it was at the beginning that the hardened souls surrendered, sometimes during the marching, and sometimes at the very end of the procession.

On the very first day the Grand Procession was announced; and throughout the whole mission it was constantly referred to. Thus when speaking of some event of our Lord's life, Père Julien would promise his hearers that they would see it depicted in the procession. The distribution of rôles was guided by the fervor of participation in the mission's exercises. By the time that the last week had come around the actors were all chosen and their training begun so that they might stir up in the bystanders the holy sentiments which each was charged to portray. The simple peasants caught the fire of Bl. Julien, and following the missionary's admonition, each one labored his hardest to realize in his own heart the meaning of his particular rôle.

The crowds at the mission doubled and trebled for the Grand Procession. The faithful gathered from miles around, some making sure to arrive on the day before. At Fougères in 1662 forty parishes, each led by its pastor, came for the Great Procession. Local dwellings would be unable to accommodate such numbers, so the visitors set up tents in the fields; some slept out under the open sky. These throngs were not mere thrill-seekers; they had come to share in a tremendous manifestation of faith. The visitors crowded both sides of the route of march, and as the different groups filed by, they joined in sing-

The Grand Procession of the Mission.

(FROM AN OLD PRINT)

ing the cantiques and in swelling the volume of the prayers. When the last marching section had passed, they hastened to the field of the final Benediction to secure a vantage point for hearing the great sermon and for sharing in the supreme adoration of the Sacred Host.

The procession [1] was always headed by a company of men-at-arms, dressed in colorful military apparel and shouldering muskets and harquebuses. They halted from time to time to discharge a volley in the air, thus solemnly announcing the approach of the marchers. A cross-bearer appeared, leading the first division: the Apostles, the Evangelists and the Seventy-Two Disciples, marching two by two, barefooted or shod according to the season. All were garbed in priestly albs and wore crowns of laurel; each one carried the symbol of his dignity or the instrument of his martyrdom. They were followed by the Three Deacons and the Four Latin Doctors: Ambrose, Augustine, Jerome and Gregory. If the costumes and the numbers permitted, the group was preceded by the principal personages of the Old Law, the Patriarchs, the Prophets, St. John the Baptist, and the Sibyls.

Another cross-bearer appeared with the beginning of the second division–the sign of the Redemption was carried at the head of each division. Now came the living tableaux portraying the joyful mysteries of our Lord's life. The first was the *Presentation of the Child Mary in the Temple;* just in front of the High Priest

[1] The description of the procession is based on that given in Séjourné, Vol. I, pp. 217-230. In Appendix II will be found an order of characters in the procession, taken from a manuscript work of 1754, printed in Séjourné. The numerous details are given in the text to enable the reader to appreciate what a tremendous thing the Grand Procession was. It has been described as a Passion Play moving through the streets.

walked the little Virgin between St. Joachim and St. Anne. A brief interval, and then came the groups depicting the *Incarnation.* Four young girls, all robed in white, bore a canopy sheltering the Blessed Virgin. In front of it advanced the Archangel Gabriel, holding a dove in his hand; from time to time he stopped, approached Mary, bowed before her and reverently repeated the immortal salutation. Shepherds in white vests, their broad hats circled with flowers, followed; every so often they turned about to offer their modest presents to the Infant Jesus in His crib, which was carried on the shoulders of four disciples. An angel, holding a tall baton tipped with a star, led the Three Magi, resplendent in their royal mantles and their kingly crowns, each carrying the vessel of his precious gift: gold, frankincense or myrrh. A crowd of little innocents in scarlet robes, accompanied by their mothers in black garments of mourning, recalled the victims of cruel Herod, himself represented, sword in hand, with his escort of fierce executioners. At a little distance behind them, mounted on an ass, rode a young woman closely pressing a baby to her heart, *Mary and the Child in the Flight into Egypt;* Joseph walked at their side guiding their journey. So ended the section on the *Incarnation.* Naive, no doubt, and rude in costume and action; but oh, so real and vital to these peasants and fishermen, living again with Jesus, Mary and Joseph.

The next division dealt with the episodes of the Passion. The theme was evidenced at once when St. Michael appeared leading a file of children, each little one bearing some instrument of the Savior's sufferings. The great archangel held a cross in one hand and a pair of scales in the other, signifying that the Passion brought mercy and justice for all mankind. The first group presented the *Agony in the Garden.* A priest, dressed in a long purple robe, took the part of Christ; he was preceded by an angel bearing the Chalice of Bitterness, and by Peter, James and John. At the pauses in the march the angel knelt in profound reverence and presented the chalice to the agonizing Savior; He tasted it and offered it to His Eternal Father with words of loving resignation. The *Arrest of Christ* followed; a priest, burdened with chains, was dragged along by a band of ruffians armed with swords and clubs. In the third group another priest, crowned with thorns, with a purple cloak draped over his shoulders and a reed in his hands, portrayed *Jesus, the Agonizing King,* as shown by Pilate to the mob. An escort of soldiers and executioners formed His court.

The fourth division, more striking than all the others, offered the spectacle of *Christ Carrying His Cross.* The role of the Savior was considered so sacred that it was always reserved to priests alone. The priest-actor advanced barefooted, bent beneath a heavy cross and covered with sweat and blood. At his side paced Simon of Cyrene, attentive to raise the burden of the cross at the numerous falls; Veronica was also there, hastening to wipe with her veil the bruised and bleeding face. A few steps behind slowly followed, between the two Marys, the Sorrowful Mother, garbed in deepest mourning, with a sword fixed in her breast, the very picture of unflinching courage in overwhelming grief. What this scene must have meant to the many Breton mothers who had lost their sons at sea! After the Sorrowful Mother walked a whole host of saints, who in life had had a notable sharing of the Cross, St. Louis, St. Helena, St. Catherina of Siena and, of course, the Saints of Brittany. They were followed by a double file of virgins, in robes and veils of shining white, holding green boughs in their hands, and these were succeeded by a double file of martyrs, in robes of scarlet, thorn-crowned and carrying the instruments of their sufferings. The section of the Passion was terminated by the women-members of the Third Order of St. Francis. The grey dresses and the black veils of these lay-women, who lived so piously and austerely in the world, added a note of contemporary reality.

Now approached the most solemn division of the procession, the section of the Blessed Sacrament. In it were gathered all the priests; and they were numerous for they had come to this grand ceremony from many parishes. They wore beautiful chasubles and copes; each priest had brought along his best vestment. This priestly body made an impressive sight, chanting the Eucharistic hymns and pacing with slow reverent steps in front of the movable platform on which was the Sacred Host. The great privilege of actually carrying the Sacramental Savior was reserved for the pastor of the mission-parish, or for the bishop of the diocese, if he were present.

The last division was formed from the assembled crowd. They joined in to march in double ranks, singing earnestly the spiritual cantiques. All along the route the spectators joined the marchers in these hymns; so that thousands of voices filled the heavens and earth with the continual praise of God. This final division was the most colorful of all. Over the heads of the marchers waved numerous brightly hued, richly ornamented banners and oriflammes of various confraternities and guilds. In the ranks would be seen many statues of Jesus, of Mary, or of the patron-saints of the parishes, borne aloft on elaborately decorated stands. From the beginning to the end of the Grand Procession everything conspired to make it a deeply moving spectacle, pleasing Breton eyes and rejoicing Breton hearts because it manifested so truly their stalwart Breton faith.

Halts were made along the route at stations previously designated. At these stops the different groups acted out their episodes of the Savior's life, and the missionaries furthered their efforts by brief stirring exhortations. Finally the terminus of the procession was reached, and the marchers found themselves entering a vast open field in which an altar had been erected for the Solemn Benediction and a pulpit had been set up for the last sermon of the Mission. Père Julien, the first to arrive, directed each division as it appeared to a definite place; with the result that when the Blessed Host was brought in and placed upon the altar-throne, everyone was ready for the great adoration. The priests, who had arranged themselves in two choirs and were kneeling on either side of the altar, now began the *Pange Lingua.* While the priests chanted, the Prophets, the Apostles, the Martyrs and the various tableau groups advanced in succession to the foot of the altar and prostrated themselves before the Eucharistic God. The whole scene was permeated with intense fervor and piety. Even the impious were impressed, as on more than one occasion they avowed.

The adoration completed, the ostensorium was veiled and Père Maunoir mounted the pulpit to preach upon the Passion. To touch the hearts of his vast congregation he joined spectacle to words. Thus towards the middle of his discourse, he caused the priest, who in the procession had portrayed Christ on the way to Calvary, to ascend the preaching-platform, staggering under the burden of the Cross. It required little acting for the exhausted priest to carry out his part; he sank under the heavy burden to the floor. Père Julien paused for a brief moment to let the crowd contemplate the sorrowful sight. Then in vibrant tones, that pierced into the depths of their souls, he addressed his huge audience:

> "O sinners, do you see the God whom you have crucified? His sacred head, wherein resides all the wisdom of a God, is crowned with thorns; and it is you, yourselves, who have pressed them there. A cross crushes His shoulders, and it is you, yourselves, who have loaded on this cruel burden. The fruit of your crimes, behold it! Look, look on His adorable face. The angels of Heaven longed to contemplate it; and you, you have bruised and disfigured it!"

Here Père Maunoir ordinarily had to stop because of the great waves of weeping and sobbing which would sweep over the vast crowds. He would wait to allow full course to the people's grief. When he did resume, with a new vigor he cried to his profoundly stirred audience:

> "Engrave forever in your hearts what I am going to say to you: the priest whom you behold here is only a figure of the suffering Jesus; and yet the simple sight of him suffices to provoke your tears. What would they be if you saw Jesus Christ in person, carrying that cross which your sins have rendered so heavy? What would be your sorrow, if He Himself spoke to you to reproach you both for His love and for your ingratitude? If He said to you: 'My people, what have I done to you? What reason have you for outraging Me thus? I came into this world only to give you life; and you, ungrateful ones, you have given Me death.' "

The cries of sorrow that answered that appeal mounted to such a volume that Père Julien had to end his sermon. He descended from the pulpit, resumed his place at the head of the procession and led it back to the church of the mission. The marchers made the return in great quietness. Each one was preoccupied with his own salvation, the good planning more virtuous lives, the converted sinners hastening for confession and penitential satisfaction.

The General Procession, climaxing the entire mission, produced rich and durable blessings. Since the primary consideration in the assignment of parts was the knowledge of the cantiques, the keen competition resulting implanted their lessons of faith and morality deeply and widely, especially among the youth. The participants, earnestly trying to relive the scenes of the Savior's life, could not but be influenced in their own daily lives by the virtues of the holy persons whom they strove to portray. The visiting crowds, observing the true and modest piety of the people making the mission, charmed with the singing of the cantiques, and marvelling at the answers of the children to the catechism questions, sought for the benefits of a mission in their own parishes. But perhaps the greatest fruits were the numerous conversions which the Grand Procession and the discourses brought about. M. de l'Estour, pastor of Caudan, in the diocese of Vannes, affirmed on oath: "The most rebellious, those very persons who heaped mockeries on the missions and the missionaries, became at the end of the procession gentle followers of the Lamb, as malleable as wax exposed to fire. Some, even guilty of the most odious crimes, which they never dared to reveal to any priest, made sincere acknowledgement of them, after they had been witnesses of this last ceremony of the mission."

The General Procession was not without its opponents. Narrow-minded Jansenists and other trouble makers, clerical and lay, labelled the procession and its unique features as "novelties" lacking all episcopal approval. They protested that until then no one had ever heard of children singing before the Blessed Sacrament hymns in the vulgar tongue. Evidently they had little knowledge of tradition. They had never heard of St. Francis Xavier and the children of Goa. Nor did they know of the common practices of Italy and Spain, or of their own Lyons and Toulouse. Another feature which they condemned as utterly degrading was the spectacle of a priest carrying a cross on his shoulder in public. What would they have said of St. Charles Borromeo, Archbishop and Cardinal, proceeding through the streets of Milan, barefooted, a cord around his neck, bending under the weight of a heavy cross? Bl. Julien ignored such captious critics, just as his predecessor, St. Vincent Ferrer, did in his day when he was assailed for similar practices. The entire Breton hierarchy took up Père Maunoir's cause. Not only did they defend him solidly, but several of the bishops shared in his labors, placing themselves under his command. The strikingly abundant fruits of salvation, as well as the numerous prodigies often connected with them, before, during and after the missions, completely silenced the opposition.

The mission was often concluded by the erection of a cross, especially if the exercises had been given for the first time in the parish. It was known as the "Mission Cross," and was set up either within the church or on an open space nearby. Usually the ceremony was held on the day after the Great Procession, with only the local parishioners present. As the years passed on this simple cross became more and more an object of traditional devotion. The people loved to pray before it for their mission cross recalled to them the moving scenes and the salutary graces of the glorious visitation of the Holy Spirit upon their parish. Moving through their grateful memories always was the figure of their own apostle, their beloved Tad Mad, Père Julien Maunoir.

Chapter 8

CHARTS, CHANTS, AND CHAPTERS

One thing Bl. Julien Maunoir made doubly certain: the Breton Missions must rest upon the solid foundations of well-learned religious truths. He was conducting no "Revivals". Emotionalism abounded, of course; but for Père Julien emotionalism was a minor concern. At the best he used it as an aid for instilling in simple folk clear knowledge and strong conviction about their faith and their moral obligations. He kept continually expounding in his sermons the essential verities; the purpose of life, the four last things, the seven sacraments and the ten commandments. Certainly these truths were no forcing-beds of sentimentalism. He never abandoned his primary purpose of making the faith of his Bretons a pre-eminently practical one. To achieve that purpose Père

Maunoir placed great reliance on allegorical charts, spiritual cantiques and devotional books. His constant use of the charts and of the cantiques made both characteristic features of the Breton Missions. His production of books strengthened immensely the permanent good of the missions.

The charts first received prominence in Brittany in the religious instructions of Dom Michel Le Nobletz. They did not originate with him; long before and in far distant places painted tableaux had been employed to illustrate the truths of faith. His particular contribution to this field of religious instruction was twofold: he used the charts on every occasion possible, and he developed to a high degree the process of presenting religious and moral truths in a vivid, highly colored, allegorical or symbolical form. Nothing did he recommend more insistently to his young successor than his allegorical charts, his *taolennou,* as the Bretons called them. Père Julien followed faithfully Dom Michel's directives.

The charts were printed on sheets of parchment, measuring about three and a half feet in height by a half a foot in breadth. Because of their size they could be used only by small groups gathered about them in a house, or in the porch of the church, or at a monument in the cemetery. They were explained to group after group over and over again in the course of a mission. There may have been bigger charts, worked on wood, for pulpit use with larger crowds; but there is no mention of them. Dom Michel's collection counted at least forty charts, to which Père Julien added a few of his own design. Some were simple and easily comprehensible, dealing with such subjects as the Seven Deadly Sins, Hell, the Prodigal Son, the Life of our Lord, especially His Sacred Passion, and the Life of Our Lady. Others, the more characteristic ones, were quite symbolical, often complex and crammed with enigmatic figures that called for considerable explaining, or offered numerous opportunities for moral lessons. Their bizarre titles, *The Wandering Knight, The Chart of the Heart, The Six Cities of Refuge, The Chart of the Three Trees*, challenged attention.

What these allegorical *taolennou* were can best be learned from considering some of the surviving charts. One, very typical, was *The Chart of Desiring*, which traces the journey of a good Christian youth, named *Desiring*, in his search for the *Knight, Love-of-God*. Ten scenes depict the episodes in his quest; and, paralleling each, is another scene depicting a contrasting happening in an evil and worldly life. Numerous figures crowd the chart; all are small, since each scene is only about four inches square. A commentary of Dom Michel Le Nobletz explained the many significances. [1] The episodes begin at the bottom of the chart, the good incident placed on the right side, the contrasting evil one on the left:

> "(1) The first episode presents the point of departure, depicting the break between *Desiring* and his family. To the right stands *Desiring*, his hand in his guardian angel's who affords him companionship throughout the various scenes. Meeting the pilgrim is a shepherd with his flock. He is Jesus, the Savior, dressed in a garment bedecked with red and white lace, carrying at His cincture a horn of oil to

[1] This paraphrase of Dom Michel's commentary was prepared for a film lecture on the occasion of the celebrations for the beatification of Bl. Julien Maunoir. The lecture was published at Quimper, October 2, 1951. No author's name was attached.

cure His sheep, and bearing in His hand a staff to defend them against the wolves. The Shepherd gives *Desiring* His dog to guide him across the desert. To the left are four figures: the father and mother of the gentleman, heart-broken at the departure, his sister, or fiancée, displeased, or disappointed (the devil in the form of a serpent incites her anger), his younger brother, with collared cape and plumed hat to indicate his worldly propensities (a devil-serpent too incites his disdain also). Every detail is intended for future commentary.

(2) In the section to the right *Desiring* is arriving at an abbey, called Humility. Its abbess, the *Lady Humility,* welcomes him. With her are the keeper of the gate, *Fear-of-God,* armed with a halberd, and the faithful maid-servant, *She-Is-Not Anxious-About-Anything,* so named for her prompt obedience. Humility is put in the first stage, since it is basic to all virtues. In the opposite left panel a monstrous devil, father of all pride and vanity, blows a great trumpet calling poor souls to embrace the road of perdition, the beginning of which is pride. *Desiring's* younger brother, already caught in the coil of the devil's tail, is facing towards another youth who allows himself to be turned from the good schooling which he had received in the Abbey of Humility.

(3) At the right, *Desiring,* supplied with the necessary attestations after his probation at the Abbey of Humility, is directed to another abbey, the College of Christian Doctrine. He is accompanied by two maidens, *Simplicity* and *Poverty,* the daughters of *Humility.* Here he imbibes a greater knowledge of virtues and of Christian Doctrine. The place is

Detail of the Chart of DESIRING.

also called the Abbey of Justice. In the opposite panel one sees libertines who scoff at *Desiring* because he goes to the College of Christian Doctrine, preferring themselves to play in the skittle-alley.

(4) *Desiring* is entering the Abbey of Strength, symbolized by its tower. Opposite is a man with a rapier and a frivolous girl in beautiful attire; the first tries to turn him away by menaces, the second, by seduction. *Desiring* remains steadfast and by his holy detestation overcomes both.

(5) Here is depicted the Abbey of Temperance, with its frugal table. On the contrary part are persons addicted to gluttony. They are for pushing the young man from his path; but they struggle vainly because he is guided by *Desire-for-God*, who could not endure such selfish existence.

(6) Next is the Abbey of Prudence. In it *Desiring* labors to implant the cardinal virtues in his heart. By the abbey stands a tree abounding in fruit; it is to symbolize the prudent man who makes all his time productive and who has carefully fortified himself with provisions for his continuing journey. On the other side are shown, in some detail, those who live foolishly, despising all prudence. They employ their youth, the best period of their lives, in dancing and vain diversions; they sing in summer and starve in winter. Their sole preoccupation is in amusing themselves, when they should be doing penance and piling up good works.

(7) In this section stands the Abbey of Faith, first of the theological virtues, with a scroll containing the articles of belief. Its opposite panel is difficult

to comprehend; Dom Michel's commentary offers no explanation. Three persons are arranged upon a red carpet; one is dead, murdered by the other two. The significances are puzzling.

(8) *Desiring* now sojourns at the Abbey of Hope. On the left side are found victims of despair; one has hung himself, the others are rending their garments and tearing their hair.

(9) The Abbey of Charity, loaded with detailed symbols, welcomes *Desiring*. Across in the contrasting section are evil wretches, breathing vengeance, filled with designs of harming their neighbors.

(10) In the last scene *Desiring* enters the Citadel of Prayer, Prayer which perfects all virtues and is their queen. He gains a realization of Christ's words, "Ask and you shall receive." It is in this castle that *Desiring*, by insistent petitioning, finds his *Knight, Love-of-God*, with whom he is united in eternal glory. Opposite to the Citadel of Prayer two persons are depicted; one sleeps and the other gorges himself, all the while that *Desiring* is praying to God. The final issue of their worldly lives is represented beneath them by a fiercely flaming ball of fire; it is Hell."

To the left of the two columns of contrasting panels, and stretching almost the entire length of the chart, looms a large stringed instrument, a psaltery, which is being played by two small female figures, one above the other. Over them flies an angel bearing a crown. The symbolism is quite extensive:

"The upper half of the instrument is colored grey, the lower half, red; the grey signifies the fear of God and the red recalls the Savior's Passion. The two colors also stand for the active and the contemplative life. The colors are joined to show that all prayer, if it be pleasing to God, must proceed from a union of these two lives. The active life includes contempt of self, reflection on one's sins, on death, judgment and hell, on love of the neighbor; the contemplative life embraces meditation on the glory of Paradise, on God, on the love of God, and on the life of His Son. The strings of the instrument signalize the exercise of piety which assures the salvation of the soul. Finally each figure has its special meaning: the lower female is a servant, *Slave-of-All;* the upper female is *Madame-Pious-Considerations;* the angel, above both, bears the rewarding crown, worthy for even a queen to wear."

More on the line of the Prodigal Son is the *Chart of the Knight-Errant*:

"*The Wandering Knight* . . . followed the highroads of vice where *Dame Folly* cut off his hair, as formerly Delilah did to Samson, and despoiled him of his arms. He arrived at Babylon, the seven towers of which are the seven deadly sins, and he sojourned there in the castle of *King Carnality* and *Queen Sensuality*, who have nine daughters: *Libertinage*, *Idleness*, etc. He also dwelt in the castle of Worldly Prosperity, where reigns *King Worldly Love* and *Queen Worldy Prosperity*, in company with their daughters: *Greediness*, *Avarice* and *Pride*. Their nurse is *Negligence*. There is a little dog there called *Pass-Time*. The *Wandering Knight* is sunk in the mire of sin; but *Divine Grace* touches him with a golden rod, and he invokes *God's Help*. *Trial* and *Expiation* come for him. He falls sick of numerous fevers, which are vicious customs. An angel cures him, discovers to him his weakness and conducts him to the castle of *Penance* which is on a very rugged mountain. *Divine Grace* helps him to mount it, presenting to him a crown. There is a woman before the door, very sorrowful and weeping, called *Contrition*. She shows him a serpent trying to rub off his own skin between two stones. The gate is called *Truth* and the key *Mercy*. Finally the *Wandering Knight* becomes *Desiring the Love of God*."[1]

As one may recognize, these charts were aimed not merely at converting hardened sinners but also at leading generous souls up the path of perfection to the mystical heights. This fact is especially evident in the *Chart of the Hearts*, which presents the aids and the obstacles in a Christian's struggle for salvation. [2]

Not all charts treated of the reconcilation of the repentent sinner with his forgiving God. Some were composed for one purpose only, salutary fear. Thus the *Chart of the Sick Man*, after tracing the criminal career of an unscrupulous parvenu in his accumulation of riches by injustice and extortion, ends with the fearsome spectacle of his despairing and unlamented death. Many rejoice at his terrible departure; none mourn him, not even his wife, now freed at last from his oppression. In almost every chart one thing was recognizable, the influence of the *Spiritual Exercises* of St. Ignatius. It was especially evident in the chart, *Imago Mundi*, which was practical-

[1] This summarization was made by Brémond in his *Histoire Littéraire du Sentiment Religieux en France*, Vol. V. *Le Conquête Mystique*, p. 97; Paris 1926.

[2] This chart is so complicated and contains such a multitude of significant details that its description is given in Appendix III.

ly a pictograph of the great Ignatian meditation, "The Two Standards". One sees there maps of Europe and Asia, of Jerusalem, the city of the saints, and of Jericho, [1] the city of sinners. There are swarming crowds of people from kings wearing their crowns to peasants carrying their spades; there are the two leaders who contend for the mastery of the world, Satan and Christ; and finally there are the regions of the Hereafter: Purgatory with its flames, Hell with its dark abyss, and Heaven, where sits enthroned the Holy Trinity.

Some of the charts held a direct appeal for the fisherfolk, often so large a part of Breton congregations. Such was the *Chart of the Harboulin,* based on a nautical manuever of Breton sailors in tacking a vessel, which involved the use of the bowline (Fr. "bouline"), a rope attached to each side of a square sail. To go on the bowline was to hold the sail close to the wind, when direct forward sailing was impossible. Dom Michel directed that in the beginning of the explanation a lesson in navigation be given to the apprentice-seamen, from which some instruction for the good of their souls should then be drawn. The most intriguing of all these "marine" charts, at least for those sea-faring Bretons who had sailed the broad Atlantic to the New World, was the one called *The Counsels,* or *Perfection.* It merits complete description:

> "You see before you a map, depicting a part of North America, all of Central America, with its famous Isthmus of Panama, and the whole of South America. You notice at once, and not without sur-

[1] Jericho is the town given in the explanation of the chart; in St. Ignatius' "The Two Standards" Babylon is the town named to symbolize the capital of Satan's kingdom.

prise, two groups of tiny laborers in knee-breeches, who are toiling stoutly with big shovels to dig canals between the two oceans, in two different places. One group is excavating in the southern part of Mexico, across the Isthmus of Tehuantepec; the other group is digging on the Isthmus of Panamà. So, the problem of Panama was already under discussion along the coasts of Lower Brittany, even in the days of Michel Le Nobletz! Ships of every size, of every shape and of every color are plowing the Atlantic Ocean and the Pacific Ocean; some are speeding along with all sails set, others are proceeding with sails furled, others still are being propelled with oars. They are being steered towards mysterious isles, unknown to geography, or in the direction of an immense continent where the Eternal Father, robed in purple, crowned with a tiara of gold, and holding in His hands the earthly globe, sits enthroned in glory. In one spot a vessel founders on a reef; in another shipwrecked unfortunates are escaping by swimming and holding themselves up by pieces of the wreckage. Ladders and other enigma-signs are sketched on sea and on land.

Everything is symbolical. The Isthmus of Panama represents the great obstacle which hinders us from reaching the eternal shores more surely and more quickly. Far better is it to embrace the toil of cutting through the land than to follow another route, very much longer and more dangerous, of going around South America through the Straits of Magellan, where shipwrecks are of frequent occurrence.

Don Michel supposed that the isthmus had a width of three leagues 'which signifies three kinds of vice: *concupiscentia carnis, concupiscentia oculorum, superbia vitae,* that is to say concupiscence of worldly pleasures, concupiscence of the flesh, concupiscence of transitory riches.' But you have three staves to beat them down: *amor paupertatis et humilitatis, amor mortificationis, amor obedientiae,* that is love of humility and abasement of self, in a word contempt of self, love of poverty and love of mortification.

'One of the two vessels which you see in the Bay of Mexico, is a pirate craft; the other belongs to avaricious merchants. The city drawn on the land, marked Mexico, signifies for us Jericho, or earthly confusion. Those who are trying to cut through a great stretch of land near Mexico, represent the unfortunate worldlings who take greater pains in practicing certain devotions of their own fancying than is required of those who cut through the other stretch in Panama, that is to do the works which our Savior counsels.'

Look now at the three islands, among which many ships are sailing. Each has its own town and its own steeple. The first stop is called *Altum Consilium,* or counsel of perfection; a vessel lies here at anchor, but our guide makes the observation that many are lost here 'because they have undertaken what is beyond their capabilities and they have exceeded the limits of discretion.' The works of the counsels and the religious life were not for them. Another navigator, less ambitious points towards the second island, called *Minus Consilium,* which represents a state of life less elevated though superior

> to ordinary conduct; 'but because the tide and the wind are contrary to him, he has to go with the current on another and a lower course, called *Obligatio,* or obligation, and so he does not arrive at the point he wants, but reaches very well the point where he ought to, and could, save himself. A third craft turns the helm towards *Obligatio;* but alas! the violence of the wind forces it to drift among the rocks of despair and on the sand-bars of temptation and diabolical illusions,' where it is lost with its crew. 'Let us learn then to strive for virtue according to our capabilities,' concludes Michel Le Nobletz, 'following the Apostle's advice, *Aemulamini charissima meliora.*'
>
> A great continent extends its contours in the Pacific Ocean without limits to the bottom of the chart; this is the *Terre Nouvelle, Nova Terra,* where the elect dwell forever; an image of the Eternal Father indicates this significantly.
>
> This mystical geography, is it not ingenious and instructive?"[1]

The explanation of these *taolennou* embraced the whole range of doctrine and morals; there was not a teaching of Christianity but was reached in these tangible catecheses. The sensible imagery of the charts rendered religious truths palpable to the least intelligent, speaking as they did to the eye and the heart as to the mind. The most careless souls, beholding in these mirrors of life the uselessness, if not the ugliness, of their own conduct were brought to sobering thoughts. The influence of the charts endured. Thus fishermen, manuever-

[1] Le Gouello, Le Vicomte Hippolyte, *Le Vénérable Michel Le Nobletz;* Paris (1898), pp. 190-193.

ing their crafts around the rugged Breton coast, remembered the lessons that had been drawn from the turns of navigation, or from the perils of reefs and gales. So too the peasants, following their plows in the fields of Cornouailles, or tending their flocks in the uplands of La Montagne D'Arrée, recollected the applications that had been attached to their toilings.

The unravelling of the enigmas on the charts fascinated the Breton crowds completely. Solving riddles and charades, or probing the meaning of symbols are always keen joys for childlike people. And so the missionaries left much that challenged natural curiosity to the peasants' own divining. Of course the skilled interpreter took over when the matter comprehended deeper significances and stronger applications. Père Maunoir, with his singular mixture of pious simplicity, poetic subtlety and intense zeal, was easily the best expositor. Several of the priest-assistants, and even some lay persons, developed considerable skill in explaining the charts. Poor, simple Jeanne Le Gall as has been noted, possessed an extraordinary power for interpreting the allegories to her docile and highly pleased listeners. Although their discussions of sin and its earthly and eternal punishments might have been severe and often terrifying, yet neither Père Julien nor his associates taught as harsh ascetics, with no eye for the blue expanse of the sea, or the smiling green of the valleys. Frequently they injected a lively humor and gained many a hearty laugh from their appreciative audiences, with their depiction of foppish worldlings or sentimental pietists.

Père Maunoir and his associates made constant use of long, white, wooden pointers in their explanations of the charts. They would rest the pointer on the symbol under discussion, or they would designate by it the per-

Bl. Julien teaching the ENIGMA *Charts.*

From Le Berre's UN GRAND MISSIONAIRE BRETON.

sons who were to answer the interrogations. Occasionally they would bring it down with a good thwack on the backs of the giddy or the heedless, securing strict attention at once. Indeed the long, white pointer became a sort of symbol of the Breton Missionaries. It was also used to marshal the crowds in the Grand Procession and at the Solemn Benediction. On these occasions the priests affixed their rosary-beads to the tips and carried the pointers as pious guidons.

More than once from the enigma charts and the white pointers the people recognized the missionaries whom Dom Michel had promised them years before. So during a mission at Dirinon in 1644, while Père Maunoir was explaining one of the patriarch's charts, a good old soul, one Marie Kéraudy, unable to restrain her joy, cried out: "It is the very same chart which M. Le Nobletz explained to us at the mission of Landernau in 1613. I interrupted his talk to ask him what would become of his pictures when he had gone on. He answered me, thirty-one years ago, that soon the Jesuits would be established at Quimper and that they would give missions throughout Brittany and would explain these very same charts. Look! the prophecy of my holy director is being fulfilled."

Again in 1650, during the first mission at Mûr, a particularly obstinate community, Père Julien was more than impressed by the lively attention of his auditors, especially while he was using his white pointer to indicate the lessons of the enigma charts; when he had finished they broke out into an enthusiastic clapping. Astonished by this unexpected approval he inquired and found out the reason for their applause. Some fifty years before the arrival of the Jesuits at Quimper, Dom Guillaume Briant, a zealous pastor, a holy priest and possibly a martyr (he died, poisoned by evil persons), was pastor of

Mûr. Frustrated by the indifference and hostility of his flock, he finished a sermon with these prophetic words: "People of Mûr, will you never change your lives? Will you always be rebellious to the promptings and graces of the Holy Spirit? No! No! It will not always be so. Today your hearts are harder than stone; but there will come a day when they will be as soft and pliable as wax. Yes, one day, but long after I am gone, you will see in this parish, preachers with white wands teaching the catechism. Then you will recall the truths I am teaching you, and you will reproach yourselves for the disorders into which you daily fall. These teachers will offer to your gaze the spectacle of Heaven, of God and His angels, and the joys of the Blessed. They will carry Rome to your doors, and it will be the hour of your conversion." The old people, who were being questioned, continued to Père Maunoir and Père Bernard: "That is the cause of our rejoicing, the prediction of our old pastor is now being fulfilled to the letter. Do we not behold the preacher with the white wand teaching the catechism? Are we not being taught the truths of the Faith? Did not the procession from Saint-Mayeux to Sainte-Suzanne portray to us the angels and the glories of Paradise? And Rome is at our door too, for you have proclaimed Pope Urban's Bull that accords the plenary indulgences to those who make the mission. After all this, what can prevent our conversion?"

Of much greater popularity and of much wider usage, were the *Cantiques Spirituels,* the didactic hymns that inculcated faith and morality in easily sung stanzas set to well-known tunes. The Bretons everywhere welcomed them. Soon the cantiques became a vigorous feature of all mission exercises, the Masses, the sermons, the catechetical instructions and, above all, the grand processions. And when the mission had become but a memory, its good lessons were kept living memories by the continual and loving singing of the cantiques by the simple folk, as they walked along the roads, or tilled the fields, or sailed the fishing craft.

Long before Père Maunoir there were didactic hymns in Breton as there were in French and in other languages. Dom Le Nobletz himself was the author of a few. However Bl. Julien Maunoir wrote and published so many, and he promoted so successfully their universal usage that he deserves to be considered the Father of the Breton Cantiques. In the very beginning of his apostolate Père Maunoir produced his first chants, as his *Latin Journal* reveals: "In this year (1641) while teaching children and grown-ups, I composed some pious cantiques in Armorican verse, which were compendiums of what I taught." In the following year there appeared in the window of Michel Machuel's bookshop in Quimper a modest volume with this long Breton title: *Canticou Spirituel hag Instructionu profitabl, evit diski an hent da vont dar Barados; composet gant an Tat Julian Manu, religius eus ar Gompagnunez Jesus* (Spiritual Cantiques and Profitable Instructions to teach the road which leads to Paradise, composed by the Father Julien Maunoir, religious of the Company of Jesus). Much corrected and augmented, this little book was to go through many editions, the last as late as 1821. [1] On the first page the author revealed its purpose: "Contraries are cured by their contraries, according to the aphorism of the doctors. We have believed, my dear Readers, that worldly and lascivious songs, which contribute so much corruption

[1] The first edition is not extant, but a second edition is in the Bibliothèque Nationale.

to the manners of Christians, would be rooted out and extirpated by spiritual songs and devotional cantiques, filled with the Christian instructions which are diametrically opposed to them."

Père Julien composed many more cantiques. In the subsequent editions of the *Canticou Spirituel*, he added several new songs, one of which, on the life of St. Corentin, 766 verses long, he also published separately. He produced a collection of cantiques on the Passion, and one in honor of St. Elouan. Many of his cantiques are to be found dispersed through his prose works; thus there are sixty of them in the *Templ Consecrat dar Bassion.* One of the last is a long lament [1] on the Passion of our Lord, which offers a daily exercise on the sufferings of the Savior in dialogue form. A faithful soul asks the Blessed Virgin the causes of her Son's sufferings, she answers, and the faithful soul sympathizes with her. Père Maunoir's manuscript life of Catherine Daniélou contains some cantiques; one especially noteworthy deals with the Maternity of Mary.

How did Père Julien come to write the cantiques? It was because Dom Michel pressed him to do so during the meeting at Le Conquet. The young disciple was not long in finding that the task he had taken upon himself would cost him days and days, and nights too, of nerve-racking toil. He had to compress into the small space of simple-worded verses the most profound religious truths. He had to count syllables and scan lines, he had to search

[1] The lament rhythm, the *gwerz*, was a mode used by the Breton bards to transmit the accounts, historical and legendary, which they composed. Like the ancient bards, Père Julien employed the form of oral tradition and began with apostrophes, such as, "Listen, people of Cornouailles."

endlessly for rhymes, in a Celtic language with all its fondness for rhymes, simple and complex rhymes, internal and end rhymes. When the cantique was completed, he had to find an air for it, one well known and easily sung; and then he had to fit his verses to this tune. Various sources were drawn upon for these musical settings. He did not furnish a musical score with the words; but he indicated by a subtitle the familiar air to which the cantique was to be sung, for example, "Sur l'air, *Bataille, compagnons, bataille, allons camper.*" In a few cases the borrowing was from the music of other hymns: the airs of the liturgical sequences, such as *O Filii et Filiae, Vexilla Regis and Stabat Mater*, or the airs of well-known Breton and French cantiques. But for the most part the tunes employed were those of the popular songs and authentic folk-ballads of Cornouailles, or melodies imported from France, war-songs, pastoral lays and even love songs. The French airs were the most utilized; in the preface of his *Canticou* Père Maunoir acknowledges his debt to the "airs mesurés de Claude Le Jeune, excellent musicien du Roi Henri III." Was Père Julien himself a musician? There is no mention of the fact in any of his biographies, certainly he never composed any melodies for his cantiques. He did possess a good voice, and it was noted that the people loved to hear him sing.

The sources of the cantiques were the Gospels, first of all, then the lives of the saints, the local legends and any other wellsprings of instruction or edification. The cantiques might be classified in two categories, the explanatory and the devotional. The first group explained or paraphrased the whole field of faith and morals: the common prayers, the *Pater*, the *Ave*, the *Creed* and the invocations of the saints and the angels; the virtues, especially charity and mercy, with their corporal and spiritual works; the commandments of God and of the Church; the examination of conscience; the capital sins and their opposite virtues, the sacraments, treated dogmatically and morally; the last things of life: death, good or bad, the general judgment, the sufferings of the Holy Souls in Purgatory, the torments of the lost souls in Hell, the happiness of the blessed souls in Heaven. The second group sought to stimulate the popular devotions: meditation on the Passion, recital of the rosary, the histories of the saints, particularly St. Michael, St. John, St. Corentin, St. Eutropius and Ten Thousand Virgin Martyrs, and finally the pious legends of Brittany, such as the story of Three Drops of Blood.

How did Père Maunoir develop the themes of his cantiques? Consider the excerpts that follow. [1] For a start there is this charming extract from a six page *gwerz*, or lament, on the Maternity of Mary:

"You have carried Him nine months
    Within your two blessed ribs.
You have suffered all kinds of poverty
    While He was within your two ribs.

It was not in a tapestried salon
    That the Savior of the world was born,
It was only in a stable.
    And Mary had every privation there,
She had neither fire nor candle.

[1] These passages are to be found in the excellent work, *Les Missions Bretonnes*, Brest, 1935, by M. le Chanoine Louis Kerbiriou. Some of the quotations are in verse form and some in prose. It would be next to impossible to produce in English the Breton poetic forms and rhymes; the thought context must suffice.

Afterwards her spouse, St. Joseph
Laid Him in a crib.
A gentle ox and an ass at His side,
And under Him an armful of hay."

Since one of the very first purposes of the missions was the uprooting of evils, it is not surprising that some of Père Julien's best cantiques were vigorous attacks on the current vices. With incisive realism they assailed luxurious living, drunkenness, the dancing craze, night revels and the fundamental sin of pride. For warning they cited the terrible punishments of the Old Testament, the fearsome fates of Pharaoh, Dathan and Abiron, Jezabel, Nabuchodonosor, Aman, and Holophernes. Here is a vivid attack on drunkenness:

"This damned wine
'Tis a fierce schoolmaster
Who teaches far more than one sin.

Alas! night and day
He instructs from his chair
In the taverns,
His ink, it is wine,
His books, they are the cups."

Against the dance craze Père Julien cried out to the Bretons of the four western bishoprics, "Listen all, Cornouaillais, Léonards, Trégorois, and Vannetais," and he bade them imagine themselves forced to dance with the devil in the cinders and flames of Hell. As for the night revels he branded them with the burning denunciation, "scol an diaoul," (school of the devil)!

Fear, terrifying yet salutary, was the object of the cantiques on Hell. One such took the form of a dialogue in which the living interrogated the damned:

> "Tell us, wretched souls
> Who suffer so many pains,
> Merited in your lives
> By so many sins,
> Tell us, tell us your irremediable torments."
>
> "No tongue knows how to tell
> How frightful are our pains.
> All of us are doomed
> To dwell among demons.
> Alas! Alas! No one can conceive our pains!"
>
> "Where are your dances,
> Where are your nocturnal gatherings,
> Where is the ball, where are the cards,
> Where are the amours?"
>
> "Alas! in a narrow prison
> Of endless nights we stay
> No more shall we see the day,
> We abide in the midst of fire."
>
> "Where are your revels,
> Where is your delicious wine,
> Where are your savory dishes,
> Where are your costly viands?"
>
> "The gall of the dragons
> Is our drink, for us the damned
> The lizards, the toads,
> The serpents are our food."

The dialogue continues on for considerable length through all the capital sins, assigning to each its appropriate chastisement and emphasizing the despair that arises from the eternity of each chastisement.

The cantique on Death stressed its grim inevitableness. Here is a sample of it:

"Death with his keen scythe
Spared neither Solomon in spite of his wisdom,
Nor Samson in spite of his strength
Nor the parents of Rebecca in spite of their wealth.

What has become of those men
Who would not be satisfied with the possession
Even of the whole world?
Where is the opulent Croesus?
Or Alexander with his victories?
O, pitiless Usurers,
How will the profits of thievery and avarice
Serve you now?

And you, Gentlemen of the Nobility,
Which of your chattels will you carry with you?
Tell us, rich Merchants,
Where now are your silver crowns?
Where are your tradings?
And you, Drunkards,
With your intestines corroded with wine?
Icy death has locked your lips.

And you, proud and senseless Girls?
Today you adore your golden hair,
You idolize your faces in the mirror,
Your hands of ivory whiteness;
But tomorrow?

Rapid is the human journey.
Death in its tragic horror will change

This ephemeral beauty into an unsightly hide,
Devoured by worms and reptiles
In the deepness of the grave."

How different is the cantique on the death of a good soul! It calls upon the Mother of God and the Saints to help the poor mortal who is about to depart from this life. In response the saints file by: Mary, the Blessed Virgin, and St. Joseph, Monsieur Saint Jean and Saint Michel, Monsieur Saint Corentin and Monseiur Saint Pol, Madame Saint Anne and Sainte Barbe, Saint Julien, Saint Vincent Ferrer and Saint Yves. How they energize the soul! They obtain for him graces to confess his sins, to receive Holy Communion and to chant with them the eternal Alleluia. Then the cantique describes the radiant vision of Paradise, the ocean of splendor of the heavenly Jerusalem, the everlasting city with its brilliant mansions, whose locks of pearl are brighter than the stars; mansions beside which the grandest palaces of earth are but miserable thatched hovels.

Those who die in justice straightway become the holy sufferers in Purgatory's cleansing fires. They will never be far from their Breton kinfolk. They are especially loved now, cherished perhaps more than they had ever been in this life. One of the most renowned of Père Julien's cantiques was *The Lamentation of the Departed Souls;* changed only slightly, it is still chanted in Brittany:

"If there still be pity on earth,
In God's name succor us.
My son, my daughter, you are lying down
Upon the soft feathered couch;

And I, your father, your mother,
In Purgatory in the midst of flames.

You are in joy, we are in agony;
You made good cheer, we do penance;
You have satiety of everything,
And we are abandoned in pain."

The life of the Savior furnished the theme of numerous cantiques. On the whole the treatment was restrained; Père Maunoir felt that the gospel scenes spoke well enough for themselves, so he gave them without variations. Still one detail held an echo of Brittany; he represented Christ suspended on the cross in the rain and wind instead of in the darkness mentioned in the text. The cantique, *The Five Wounds,* had lines that heralded the approaching revelations of the Sacred Heart at Paray-le-Monial:

My drink, your vinegar,
My chamber, your side,
Where I shall contemplate your love.
Engrave in my heart
Your cross, your crown, your nails."

The Breton folk welcomed heartily the cantiques on their ancient Celtic saints–very living personages in their daily world. St. Corentin, hermit and first bishop of Cornouailles, under whose patronage Père Julien had placed the missions, naturally received the greatest attention. Four long poems of the *gwerz* genre were written about him. One, *The Arm of Saint Corentin,* prayed that the powerful arm of the venerable apostle, which once saved a city, would now protect his living compatriots and also the Bishop, the King and the Pope. Another celebrated St. Corentin's charity towards a poor exile whom he encountered on a lonely island, the unfortunate victim of a mysterious malady; it stressed the obvious lesson, of course.

Local pious legends furnished subjects for cantiques. Such a one was *The Three Drops of Blood.* A devout townsman of Quimper, on his return from a pilgrimage to the Holy Land, found his wife and children in dire poverty and hunger, because a false friend had stolen the pilgrim's fortune which had been placed in his keeping. The thief denied his guilt, even on oath before the crucifix in the Cathedral of Quimper. Thereupon the image of the Savior came to life and three drops of blood from His sacred foot fell upon the perjured villain. The cantique developed the story at great length and concluded with these touching lines:

> "Venerate, all ye people of Quimper,
> The crucifix in your cathedral.
> Venerate with a good heart
> Each day the three drops of blood.
>
> I hail you, three drops of blood
> That Jesus, my Father, has shed;
> Because of them, O Jesus, lave my heart
> That I be enabled to gain my pardon."

Père Maunoir would not let the Bretons forget Dom Le Nobletz, who had brought so many of them back to the paths of virtue. He composed a cantique for the pilgrims who came to venerate the tomb of the old missionary in the chapel of St. Michel at Douarnenez. Here is the opening apostrophe:

"O Michel Le Nobletz, true friend of the world's
Queen,
During life you lived, a hidden treasure;
But the Bretons knew how to discover you,
You carried your cross, while leading back to
God
Blind sinners. You have left your brethren,
Your parents, too, that you might catechise the
world.
O Father, so compassionate, what do you say to us?
'I pray for you in Paradise.'"

In the long cantique that follows Dom Michel recounts the story of his apostolate. He describes the beginnings at Douarnenez, when he was railed against as a fool, a bigot and even as Antichrist, and when he was in danger of being cast into the sea, because he had cleansed the town morally. Then he tells of his refusal to be discouraged, how he persevered in his task and how God consoled him abundantly. The future promised so well, he asserts, that he planned to live and die at Douarnenez, even choosing the place of his tomb at the nearby village of Ploaré. But the demon Jealousy drove him from the country; and so he came to end his days at Le Conquet in the land of Léon. Now, in Paradise, he prays for those who enter his house to worship in the chapel built there in honor of Saint Michel, his patron.

The cantiques were far more than emotional effusions. Pére Maunoir directed the moral and ascetical ones to a practical piety beyond the ordinary devotions of his day.

"Once, each month, with care sincere
Choose of your faults three or four,

The sources, most likely, of your sins.
Correct them yourself. Be vigilant,
And death will have no terror for you."

In a similiar manner he explained and proposed the eight beatitudes, the daily examination of conscience and the monthly communion.

The appreciation of a Celtic expert, M. l'abbé Kerdaffrec, once curé of Pontivy, summarizes well the value of Bl. Julien's cantiques: [1]

> "The cantiques of Père Maunoir embrace a complete treatment of the truths of the Faith. They lead a man in the accomplishment of the most elementary duties of religion, and they conduct him step by step to his final end, all the while instructing him in the dangers which he must fear and in the resources of salvation which Providence offers him. Thanks to the marvelous facility which the Breton language offers for rhyme, Père Maunoir could put into verse and adapt to the ancient melodies the usual prayers of Christians, such as the Pater, the Ave Maria, the Credo, the commandments of God and of the Church, without adding a word to the text. One finds in these cantiques all the exactitude of a literal translation. The doctrine of the sacraments is presented with the precision of a lesson in the catechism. This luminous simplicity, which Père Maunoir made his rule each time he proposed only to instruct, constitutes, in our opinion, the distinctive merit of his cantiques. What indeed is the cantique in religious instruction, if it is not a substantial abridgement

[1] *Revue de Bretagne et de Vendée,* (1859) t. V. Livraison d'avril, p. 283; "La rénovation religieuse de la Basse-Bretagne au XVII siècle."

of doctrine, presented under the attractive form of a simple melody and a popular air to those whose ruder intelligence would not permit their following the reasoned development of a book or a sermon? . . .

Always simple and precise, Père Maunoir nevertheless knew how to avoid the reef of monotony. When he depicted the capital sins, and above all the vices most common in his time, he traced the strokes with a sure hand, and with a vividness which attests at once to the richness of his imagination and to the profound knowledge which he had of the human heart. His cantiques on Death, Judgment and Hell are full of those strong images, of that sombre harmony, so comformable to the genius of the Breton language. In his beautiful strophes on the Holy Eucharist, the Blessed Virgin, Paradise, the mysteries of the Passion, there breathe through them all that tender piety, that penetrating unction, of which the saints alone possess the secret."

The cantiques of Bl. Julien Maunoir gained not only widespread but also lasting popularity. Today in one section of Finistère the commandments, the morning and evening prayers are often chanted according to formulas long ago received from the Tad Mad. In missions and retreats the modern Bretons still sing cantiques such as: *Var ar finveziou diveza* (On our last moments), *Ar varn jeneral* (The General Judgment), *Var ar maro* (On Death), *Pager berr eo ar vuez* (How short Life is), *Ann ifern* (Hell), *Var ar Purkator* (On Purgatory). [1] These all go back, at least for substance and inspiration, to Père Maunoir.

[1] The author's special thanks is due to Soeur Marguerite Félicie, F.S.E. for this information about the modern use of the cantiques and

By the *Taolennou* and the *Canticou* Bl. Julien taught his Bretons to love and fear God, to obey the Church, to venerate the Blessed Mother and the Saints, especially the ancient holy ones of Brittany, and to remember always their dear departed kinfolk. Through more than three hundred years these two devices have produced rich harvests of virtue. They still do today, as the Bretons sing the cantique *Before the Taolennou*:

"Look carefully at the *Taolennou*
Which are the mirrors of the soul
And which say to everyone
The truth without fear.

Two roads there are, two roads only
Which stay open for every man:
The road to Hell and the road to Heaven,
The road to Death, and the road to Life.

The road to Hell, open and wide,
Through sin sends into fire;
Crowded it has always been
By many people, too bad for them!

Pride, anger, lust, envy,
Avarice and laziness,
With hateful gluttony,
Cause many people to be damned.

Now you should pay attention,
Let good behavior be in your lives;

also for the translation of the cantique which concludes this subject. In this connection he would also recall the cherished memory of an occasion when a charming old Breton nun, Mère Ste. Armelle, F.S.E. so sweetly and so simply sang for him one of these cantiques of her people.

To lose your soul is to lose everything. . .
Too late will it be to lament.

The cantiques constituted only a part of Pére Maunoir's literary apostolate for the Breton Missions. He produced eight books and six unpublished manuscripts, writings of such depth of thought as to make him "one of the richest and most serious writers of the very fecund seventeenth century." [1] The printed works [2] include: the *Canticou Spirituel,* already discussed; *Ar Vuhez Gristen,* a work on the life of Christian virtue; *Ar Vuhez Sant Caurintin,* a life of St. Corentin; Breton cantiques in honor of St. Elouan, noticed above; *An Templ consacrat dar Bassion Jesus Christ,* a devotional work; *Le Sacré Collège de Jésus,* a combination of catechism and Breton grammar and dictionary for the use of priests instructing in Breton; *Chemin assuré de Pénitence,* a manual for confessors; *Abrégé de la science du salut,* an epitome of Christian Doctrine. The unpublished works are *The Latin Journal of the Missions,* and five biographies in manuscript: lives of Dom Le Nobletz, Père Bernard, Catherine Daniélou, Marie-Amice Picard and M. de Trémaria. In view of his toil-filled life, forty-three years of sermons, confessions and conferences, almost without respite, and of endless journeyings all over Brittany, the question arises: when and where did Père Julien find the time to write anything? The fact is, and it seems almost incredible, he did practically all his writing during the brief periods of rest at the college of Quimper. These periods totaled in a single year hardly more than a month.

[1] de la Chevasnerie, *Le Tad Mad,* Dinard (1951), p. 185.

[2] Appendix IV contains a list of all Père Maunoir's writings and their various editions.

Père Maunoir plied his pen with no other design than the glory of God and the salvation of men. For him the book was merely the continuation of the pulpit. Thus the *Canticou Spirituel*, the *An Templ consacrat dar Bassion*, the *Abrégé de la science du salut* and the *Chemin assuré de pénitence*, were but extensions of his oral teachings. *Le Sacré Collège de Jésus* was something more; with its Breton grammar and vocabulary it was an aid for French-speaking curés and vicaires to acquire the indispensable knowledge of the language of their Breton-speaking flocks. The vocabulary contained, besides specifically religious words, expressions current in the crafts, in agriculture and in grazing. Père Maunoir constantly used such terms to render spiritual realities accessible to less speculative minds; he won over many a peasant by discussing with him his daily occupation. In writing the manuscript biographies Père Maunoir's purpose was to preserve the memories of the holy lives of Dom Le Nobletz, Père Bernard and M. de Trémaria, or to describe the prayers and sufferings offered for the missions by the mystics, Catherine Daniélou and Marie-Amice Picard. These works were hardly more than collections of incidents and documents. Later writers would find them most useful for more formal treatment, as Père Antoine Verjus did in his book on Dom Le Nobletz.

The most precious of Père Maunoir's manuscipts is his *Journal Latin des missions*. Drawn up in 1671 and 1672, on the order of Father General John Paul Oliva, it related year by year the more remarkable events of the Tad Mad's ministries, recounting with abundant details the difficulties and combats, the joys and constant progress of the Breton Missions. Every page revealed the true apostle, triumphing in the victories of his Divine Master. The charm of its narration, the grace of its diction, the depth of its sincerity and the veil of modesty covering all successes, made the *Journal* a work of first merit. Unfortunately the account of the first ten years is the only part that has survived; the rest must be sought in the résumés by Fabri or Boschet. If these lost sections are ever recovered, the *Journal latin des missions* will be placed among the best missionary histories. [1]

The rôle of Père Maunoir was not that of a man of letters. He never sought literary renown, and in his missionary wanderings he had no time to spare for the writer's craft. Yet, unwittingly, Père Julien did become an important writer owing to the breadth of his views and the profundity of his thoughts. True, his writings are diffuse and they lack the sobriety that marked the French literature of the mid-seventeenth century. But his pages are alive with vivid pictures of the life of the Breton fishermen and peasants, narrated goodnaturedly, even gaily, in simple, familiar language, well sprinkled with the proverbial sayings that adorn popular conversation. His works abound with scriptural and historical allusions; and by the manner of their citation it is evident that they had been deeply realized in the author's own imagination. His style is always direct, concrete and singularly adapted to his Breton readers.

Père Maunoir did not seek poetic expression, but neither did he avoid it. Often there appears in his writings a fresh and sincere feeling for nature, an attention to the majesty of the sea and the loveliness of the countryside, something scarcely to be found in the literary classics of his day. Like St. Francis of Assisi and St. Francis de Sales, Bl. Julien listened with joy to the song of the nightingale and the murmur of the brook and noted the

[1] Cf. notice of the *Journal* in Appendix IV.

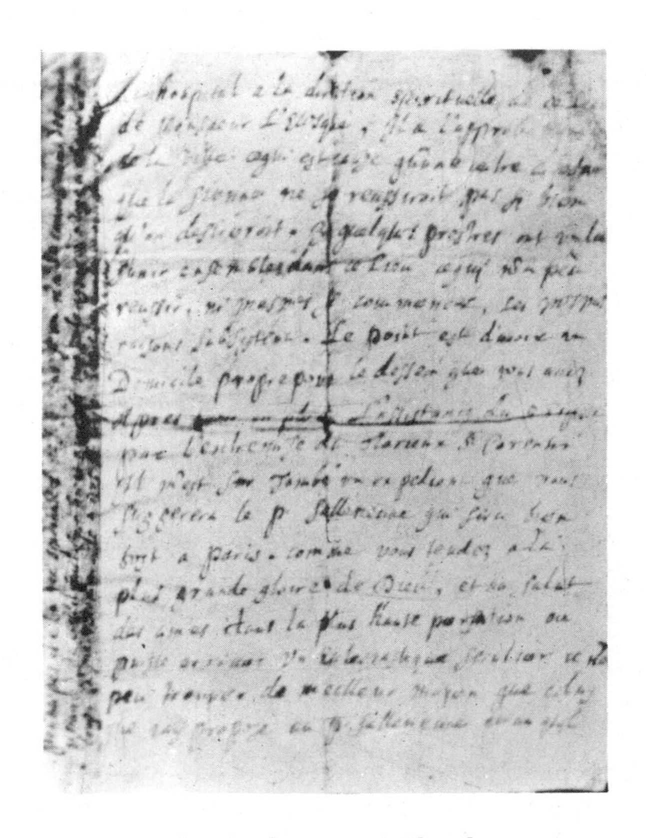

The Handwriting of Bl. Julien.

melodies of their songs. How pleasing it is to encounter in the last cantique of his collection:

> "Come and browse as you will in this grassy meadow. Have no fear in eating your fill because what you consume will grow again overnight. As for me, I shall be praising God for you in the shade of a blackthorn tree, while my watchful dog prowls the shadows in search of a hungry wolf. How glorious this spot is! Here are a thousand weeping-willow trees bordering a swift stream. Stretched out over me, they arch a cradle for my head. At my feet, the swiftly running water in muffled anger seems to scold the rocks in its path. Hearing this, the nightingale breaks out into song, joyful and happy. It seems to defy the anger of the brook. O merry nightingale and you, pure source, since God has given you voices, let us all three carol a song to His Majesty." [1]

Abbé Kerdaffrec, a noted Celticist of the last century, has affirmed that "in simplicity, clarity and unction no other Breton poet has surpassed Père Maunoir." [2]

For the renewal of the Breton language Père Julien's writings were of prime importance. This was especially true of his cantiques, which, so widely sung, furnished the common people with their native literature through three centuries. The Tad Mad valued Breton as a language noble by its antiquity and most worthy of study; so he wrote in his *Sacré Collège de Jésus*. However he has been criticised by modern purists for simplifying

[1] From a French translation in Père D'Hérouville's article, "Julien Maunoir, Ecrivain, Grammarien et Poête," *Annales de Bretagne*, Vol. XI., p. 280.

[2] *Revue de Bretagne et de Vendée*, 1859, pp. 282-283.

the Breton spelling by writing the words as they were pronounced. There is some justice in the complaints. But in his time the orthography of any language was quite arbitrary, and in modern times there has been considerable advocacy of simplified spelling in Celtic languages. As regards the *Sacré Collège,* it should be remembered that Père Maunoir was composing a handbook for middle-aged parish priests struggling for a practical grasp of what was for them a very difficult tongue. There have also been complaints of his bringing in too many foreign words and expressions, especially from the French. In those days that was a common enough practice in all languages. Certainly the seventeenth century was not a golden age for the Breton tongue. Outside of Père Maunoir and his missionaries, few labored to revive the old speech of Brittany; a hundred years elapsed between the dictionary of Guillaume Quiquier in 1632 and the French-Breton dictionary and grammar of the Capuchin, Père Grégoire de Rostrenen, in 1732-1735. Père de Rostrenen thought enough of Père Maunoir's work to utilize the *Sacré Collège* in the preparation of his great dictionary. A Welsh clergyman, the Reverend Edward Llwyd, 1660-1707, included the *Sacré Collège* in his *Archaeologia Brittanica,* a tribute indeed, coming from a broad-minded, seventeenth century Protestant scholar to a Jesuit missionary.

Chapter 9

COMPANIONS IN ARMS

The Breton Missions, would never have been the widespread success that they were without the priest-assistants whom Père Julien Maunoir recruited from the diocesan clergy. Brémond, no indulgent critic, declares emphatically: "This holy alliance is, without contradiction, the capital event, the grandest and essential miracle of this marvelous history. In 1640 when Père Maunoir began, there were two missionaries; in 1683 at the death of Père Maunoir, there will be a thousand; and really one does not know whom to admire the more, the Jesuit who knew how to bring together this multitude and direct it according to his plans, or those very many priests who joyfully submitted to the discipline the Jesuit imposed on them." [1] Pere Julien did more than rally numerous bands of helpers; he also trained them in pastoral work, and so solidly that Brittany had priests, the peers of any in Europe, well equipped intellectually and spiritually for their exacting duties.

With the exception of Père Bernard, his loyal assistant for fourteen years, Père Maunoir was not greatly aided by his fellow Jesuits. At the start some dismissed the Breton Missions as an impractical dream. Others were more encouraging, though they felt that only on rare occasions could they lend a helping hand. The larger student bodies and the heavy financial burdens of the two Breton colleges, Quimper and Rennes, absorbed almost completely the handfuls of Jesuits who manned both institutions; the thousand students of Quimper were directed by only ten priests and four scholastics, the three thousand students of Rennes by seventeen priests and five scholastics. Now and then some did manage to help in the work; thus in 1644 the Rector of Quimper, Père Alain de Launay, originally unfavorable, assisted in the mission of Daoulas-Plougastel, together with other fathers, including old Père Thomas, a strong supporter always. More effective help came during the years 1646 and 1651, when, in addition to Père Thomas, two outstanding figures of seventeenth century French spirituality, Père Jean Rigoleuc and Père Vincent Huby, [2] labored in the missions. Though hampered by an inability to speak Breton the two priests rendered invaluable service in dealing with the clergy and the noblesse in French, and by introducing new devotions.

[1] Brémond, Henri, *Histoire Littéraire du Sentiment Religieux en France,* t. V. p. 112.

[2] Brémond, ibid, cc. II. III.

Bl. Julien never ceased begging his superiors for assistants, even writing to the Father General of the Jesuits, Goswin Nickel. The General was sympathetic and several times requested the local superiors to appoint men for the work, more than once expressing his surprise that hardly one of the numerous Bretons was desirous of the missions. But a large increase of assistants was out of the question; even if the number of the Breton Jesuits had doubled, they would still have been too few for their colleges.

The situation worsened with the death of Père Bernard in 1654. He had been stricken during a mission at Merléac, on the confines of Cornouailles and Saint-Brieuc, and had been brought home quite helpless to Quimper. After a brief convalescence, long before he was fully recovered, the veteran missionary proposed going back to the help of Père Maunoir. Just as he had finished packing his bag, on the eve of his departure, the fatal stroke came. He died on the next day, November 28.

Père Bernard was in his seventy-first year and had been in the Society of Jesus fifty-one years. A simple-hearted priest he had solicited six graces for his dying, as Père Maunoir, his confidant, revealed. They were: (1) to expiate all his faults in this life, so that nothing would retard his happiness in Heaven; (2) to persevere on the missions until death, in order to die in the exercise of charity; (3) to suffer the final agony on a Friday, so as to participate in the Passion of the Savior; (4) to be a short time sick, so that he would not be a burden to anyone; (5) to die on a Saturday, so as to obtain more surely the help of the Blessed Mother; (6) to be interred on a Sunday, since on that day our Lord rose from the dead.

Good, holy old Père Bernard obtained every one of the graces. His funeral at Quimper was a triumph; the entire city participated in his obsequies. Père Salleneufve, the Rector of Quimper, in writing to the Provincial of the Flandro-Belgian Province, in which Père Bernard had started his religious life, paid him this tribute: "If this good father was esteemed and loved by the people outside, he was equally so by our brethren. His attachment to obedience and to the observance of the rules made him beloved always by the superiors; while the goodness of his character, joined with a profound humility and a gentle charity, caused him to be cherished by all. For the completion of these virtues, he had remarkable gifts of prayer and piety, and a great desire to suffer in the missions." For Père Maunoir the loss of the companion of his apostolate was a most painful trial: they had shared the same views, the same ardor for God's glory and the same zeal for their neighbor's salvation. During more than two decades they had been one heart and one in mind; now their intimate union was broken.

His old friend's passing raised a new embarrassment for Père Julien. The Jesuit rule insisted on a companion. Where would he find one? No one could be taken from the Quimper staff. Nor at the time was there anybody in the Province of France available. Finally Father General Nickel directed the Provincial to assign Père Robert Jacquesson as the companion. However, this young priest had yet to complete his third year of probation; so Père Maunoir had to be content with different fathers, as they could be spared. Père Thomas, despite his great age, must often have been chosen, for he knew Breton so well. But this venerable priest died in 1657.

At one time Père Julien's reiterated pleas seemed finally answered, when two priests, Père Triguier and Père Taillard, were assigned to him. But both proved disappointments. Whether because of lack of courage, or of prudence, or because of some character defect, they did not respond to the wishes of Père Julien. Both tried to evade the assignment, alleging, among other reasons, ignorance of their mother tongue. Père Triguier later became a good missionary; but Père Taillard, in 1671, left the Society of Jesus. A more likely associate next appeared in Père Pierre Champion, a young professor at Quimper from 1657 to 1660. A close friendship developed between Père Julien and Père Pierre. Maunoir saw in the young priest his eventual successor and began teaching him his methods of the mission apostolate. But Breton proved too difficult for Père Champion. He was transferred to French-speaking Brittany, where he labored arduously and successfully for souls. Ten years later Père Maunoir tried again to train him as his successor, but once more Père Champion failed to master the Breton.

That decade witnessed a succession of assistants. The first was Père Antoine Poncet, back from eighteen years in Canada, where he had been tortured and almost killed by the savages. A Parisian, he had to begin the study of Breton. Possibly the task proved too difficult for him too; at any rate after a year Père Poncet was sent out to the French Caribbean. Père Jacquesson, who had come in 1660 to study Breton and to minister to the poor of Quimper, succumbed to the heavy fatigues of his labors and died in 1663. Occasionally the Jesuit communities of Rennes and Vannes would send helpers for missions in the French-speaking part of Brittany; but but there was no permanency in such aid.

At long last in 1668 Bl. Julien's prayers were answered when he received for his companion a priest who was to measure up to his ideals. He was Père Vincent Martin, a Breton by heart no less than by birth, who loved his native land dearly and spoke its language perfectly. This young recruit, he was only in his fortieth year, gave promise of becoming a first-class missionary; he was endowed with a vigorous constitution, he was courageous and virtuous. He brought to the work a well developed gift of eloquence, which was to find the fullest exercise in the pulpits of Lower Brittany. Père Vincent was truly a child of the Breton Missions; as a little lad and as a youth he had often mingled with the crowds of country folk listening to Père Maunoir. He conceived such a veneration for the Tad Mad, that on the completion of his theological studies he volunteered to be his helper. Bl. Julien, discerning the fine qualities of his new assistant, at once felt a deep affection for him. The more the older priest observed the younger one's eagerness in sharing his burdens, the more he thanked God for this companion of his later years. So he wrote to the Father General, John Paul Oliva. The General, to help the Breton missions, exempted Père Martin from the Third Year of Probation, writing to the Provincial: "I exempt Père Martin from the Tertianship and I readily substitute for it the mission of Lower Brittany. It is but to change the trials of a single year for those of a whole lifetime, the first are not the most difficult." Assured of a permanent Jesuit companion, Père Julien could now plan for a new feature in the Breton Missions, retreats for special groups. But of that more in a later chapter.

The diocesan priest assistants, who contributed so effectively to the success of the Breton Missions, were organized by Bl. Julien Maunoir near the close of the first decade of his apostolate. As he was completing those ten years, 1640-1650, two problems kept pressing upon his thoughts: first, how to guarantee the permanence of the good achieved; and second, how to extend and exploit future possibilities. Every solution seemed to go back ultimately to a large increase in assistants. Père Bernard, old and infirm, could not labor much longer. Nor would the one or two priests whom the Jesuits might eventually spare bring the answer. Manifestly the need was for many, many workers. But where could they be found? And how could they be trained and organized?

Père Maunoir had given some thought to the diocesan clergy. In a mission at Dirinon in 1644 he had received help from nine secular priests; he was highly edified by their zeal and ability. Two years later, while he was giving a mission with Père Rigoleuc and Père Huby at Vannes in Upper Brittany, he was aided by twelve local priests. He observed the secular assistants carefully, and he was again very favorably impressed. Still he did not formulate any definite plans. At length in 1650 he came to a decision. That year had been a painfully laborious one for Père Julien, weakened by a grave illness and yet deluged with work. The whole task of preaching had devolved upon him alone, since Père Bernard had not sufficient fluency in Breton; besides the hours in the confessional were almost endless. He must have often wondered how much longer he could continue. One day a holy widow, possibly his loyal helper, Catherine Daniélou, asked him in great simplicity: "Why do you do alone the work of twenty priests? Why don't you invite the curés and the vicaires to join in your labors? You would have help, God would have glory, and the neighbor his salvation."[1] It was just along such lines that Père Julien had been recently thinking. But for the moment he could give only intellectual acceptance. In the next year he brought the idea to its realization.

At Mûr, in the heart of Lower Brittany, the pastor, M. Guillaume Galerne, was reviving the ancient devotion to its patron, St. Elouan, and was rebuilding the ruined shrine of this old Breton anchorite. When he was ready for the laying of the cornerstone, he asked Père Maunoir and Père Bernard to prepare the people for the solemnity by preaching a great mission. The exercises were attended by a concourse of thousands of pilgrims from all the dioceses of Lower Brittany. The most extended efforts of the two Jesuits proved hopelessly inadequate, so the pastor and six other priests joined in the preaching and in the hearing of confessions. So impressed were the volunteers with the fruits of their labors that they petitioned their bishop, Msgr. du Louët, for permission to work steadily with Père Maunoir. The bishop readily gave his consent. Then M. Galerne and his friends begged Père Maunoir to receive them as assistants and to dispose of them in all things that regarded the ministry of the missions just as he did with Père Bernard.

What must have been Père Julien's joy! Here at last was the answer to his reiterated prayers. Deeply moved he replied to M. Galerne and the six priests: "You are giving an example which will go far to sanctify all the priests and to save the whole of Brittany. We all have the same goal, the glory of God and the salvation of souls. We have a single Master; consequently we shall be united in a single mind and in a single heart. And

[1] Boschet, p. 189.

since you wish it, I shall deal with you as I do with Père Bernard. I love him as my brother, and I honor him as my superior." And thus began the association of priest assistants. Bl. Julien was to develop it into one of the most vital factors of the Breton Missions. Within a dozen years he would be directing three hundred missionaries; before his death he would be leading more than a thousand preaching and teaching assistants.

Quite providentially for the success of the new venture Père Rigoleuc and Père Huby were stationed in Quimper. Both contributed much to the intellectual and spiritual formation of the new priest assistants. Père Rigoleuc, restricted to hearing French confessions, employed his extra time in training the younger priests. He held spiritual conferences, gave doctrinal lectures and taught the theory and practice of preaching. It was Père Rigoleuc who gave the initiative that made the association a sort of pastoral novitiate. Père Huby worked in much the same way. In addition he established the devotion of the Perpetual Adoration of the Blessed Sacrament, which was to become a unifying bond and a source of countless graces for the priests. He first began the devotion at Quimper, in the cathedral of St. Corentin, and shortly afterwards inaugurated it in Vannes, whence it spread to all parts of France and to the rest of the world. Brémond rightly makes much of the influence of these two Jesuits on the character of the missionary priests' association. But it should be noted that the contacts of both these priests with the association were brief and only in the first years. The organizer, director and promoter for thirty years was Père Maunoir. It is well to add that in his work with the priest assistants he always enjoyed the hearty support of the Breton bishops. Or course, from the very beginning of the organization he had the emphatic approval of Dom Michel Le Nobletz.

Père Maunoir's procedure with the missionary assistants usually followed pretty much of a set pattern. Some time in advance of the mission Père Maunoir would make his selection of the co-workers. He would choose thirty, forty, or even fifty, if the expected numbers of the faithful warranted it. He had hundreds of priests on his lists. Some few worked very often, most helped occasionally. Père Julien always gave consideration for parish duties, preoccupations, health and aptitudes. On his completion of a particular list, Père Julien would send to each priest the following invitation:

> "MONSIEUR,
>
> The Master of the harvest says to you, as to other evangelical workers: 'Lift up your eyes and see the fields covered with grain ready for the reaper!' The mission at . . . will commence on the . . . day of the month of . . . Come and help us. The Master of the harvest calls you; see what He promises you: 'He who harvests, receives the recompense of his labor, and amasses the fruits of eternal life.' You will be well repaid. I await a favorable response, and I am in union with your holy Sacrifices,
>
> Monsieur,
>
> Your most humble and obedient servant in Our Lord,
>
> JULIEN MAUNOIR
> priest of the Company of Jesus." [1]

[1] Boschet, p. 259.

The assembling of a group of the missionary associates and a typical day of their activities, have already been described. [1] The following Order of the Day will recall their routine:

4:00 A.M. Rising.
Recitation of the Office in common.
Meditation in common.
Procession to the church, (chanting the *Veni Creator*).
Masses or Confessions.
Breakfast.
Various occupations (preaching, catechising, hearing confessions or teaching cantiques).

11:45 A.M. Bell for the common visit and the *Angelus*.

12:00 P.M. Procession from the church (chanting the *Te Deum*).
Examination of conscience, *De Profundis*.
Dinner, with reading.
Recreation, conference on mission problems, one hour.

2:00 P.M. Procession from the church, (chanting hymn).
Various occupations, as above.

7:00 P.M. Procession from the church, chanting the *Te Deum*.
Recitation of *Matins* and *Lauds* in common.
Supper with reading.
Recreation, free discussion of mission problems, presided over by P. Maunoir.
Night prayers, in common.
Assignments for next day.

9:30 P.M. Retirement.

[1] Chapter VII, pp. 113-120.

The priest assistants rallied to Père Maunoir from all parts of Brittany. Every diocese without exception contributed its representatives. Most spoke Breton, for the bulk of the missions were in Lower Brittany; yet French-speakers joined in goodly numbers, especially when the mission was given in Upper Brittany. Once in a while priests from other parts of France came, not only to observe but to take an active share in the labors; even in the Breton-speaking districts there would always be some French confessions, particularly among the noblesse. In the ranks of the missionary associates one encountered all classes of the clergy: hundreds of young priests and old pastors; religious of the various orders, Dominicans, Franciscans, Carmelites, and Jesuits; ecclesiastics of noble lineage, such as M. de Trémaria, the Count de Saisey, and the Marquis de Pontcallec; doctors of the Sorbonne, like M. Vincent de Meur, the first superior of Les Missions Etrangères de Paris, and M. Esnault, well known as a missionary in France; at least one founder of a religious congregation, Dom Jean Leuduger, the first director of the Daughters of the Holy Ghost; vicars-general, as M. de Kerlivio of Vannes; several bishops, notably, Msgr. René du Louët, of Cornouailles, Msgr. Charles de Rosmadec of Vannes, Msgr. Balthasar Grangier of Tréguier, Msgr. Denis de la Barde of Saint-Brieuc and Msgr. Pierre de la Brousse of Saint-Pol-de-Léon.

To all these ecclesiastics, of high or of low degree, Bl. Julien Maunoir was the Tad Mad just as much as he was to the simple folk. They were content with whatever employment he assigned them, executing his commands with as much promptitude as if they were bound by the vow of obedience. To them his rule guiding their conduct was no restraining chain but a precious aid for their own holiness. They served under Père Maunoir joyfully. Seldom were there grumblers among them. How could there have been, when their admiring eyes beheld Père Julien continually bearing the heaviest burdens, the first up and the last to retire, and always all to all, to the missionaries as to the peasants? Aged veteran missionaries assured Père Boschet that it was hardly possible to find more than a few complainers. Those who did not entirely approve of Père Maunoir's methods, and among them were some of his Jesuit brethren, were yet filled with veneration for his person. All, after his death, were unanimous in rendering homage to his virtues. Père Le Roux, at the beginning of the eighteenth century, received so many and such enthusiastic testimonies from the surviving priest assistants that he declared their depositions to be the greatest collective tribute ever given to a spiritual father.

Père Julien returned the affection of his co-laborers; truly he loved them as his brothers. To serve them was his continual thought. Thus on every mission he made the provision for their lodging and their meals his special personal concern. When he assigned them to their tasks, he did it with a gentle command, and in his casual dealings with them he was always genial and humble. Bl. Julien Maunoir deeply sensed the importance of the parish priesthood. Brémond notes it: "One of the rare merits of this missionary is that he does not have an undue reliance on the *missionary*: I mean, the priest of passage who for a few days fixes the curiosity and stirs the sensibility of the crowd. The crowd quickly forgets the eloquence of the stranger, they forget even his miracles. With clearer vision, Maunoir desired to make parish priests perpetual missionaries and the parish life an uninterrupted mission."[1] His brothers of the secular priesthood, in Père Julien's opinion, were courageous souls upon whom he could call for the noblest heroism. This expectation was evidenced in his reply to complaints that he did not moderate the zeal of his missionaries, many of whom had fallen into grave illnesses, a few had died under the burden of the work. The charges came less from the missionaries than from their friends. To the complaints Père Maunoir answered that for the soldier of Christ sometimes there arise circumstances so pressing that it is his duty to expose his life for the glory of God and the interests of His kingdom. And he added the observation: "How happy are the faithful ministers of the Gospel who find death in the service of the King of Kings; immortal glory will crown their valor!"

The union which flourished between Père Maunoir and his brethren of the diocesan clergy caused Père Champion to remark: "The Holy Spirit united them and showed both the members of religious orders and the members of the diocesan clergy a model of the union which should inspire them, and the blessings which flow from such union and cooperation. It is rare to find such cooperation among the workers in the Vineyard; yet Brittany was edified to see how beautifully M. Le Nobletz cooperated with Père Quintin, O.P., how Père Maunoir worked shoulder to shoulder with M. de Trémaria, M. de Kérisac and the thousand or more of the missionary assistants, and how Père Rigoleuc, S.J. and the priests whom he had trained labored together for the good of souls."[2]

[1] Brémond, *Histoire Littéraire du Sentiment Religieux en France* Vol. V, p. 117.

[2] Champion, S.J., *Vie du Père Huby, ed. Paris,* 1886, V. I, p. 5.

The rejuvenation of the Breton clergy was the second achievement of Bl. Julien Maunoir's association of missionary priests. From its very beginning he had conducted the association so that it would produce a good and competent priesthood. For this reason he invariably brought the missionaries together twice each day for conferences. Actually these gatherings were review classes in dogmatic and moral theology, in casuistry, in sacramental rites, in preaching and catechetical methods for the teaching of humble people. The continual practice in mission activities afforded invaluable experience in the priestly offices of the confessional and the pulpit. The young priests learned by doing. In the exhilaration of accomplishment their confidence increased and their ambition grew to do greater things for God's glory and men's souls. As they mingled with the great crowds thronging the sermons, besieging the confessionals, marching and chanting in the processions, the fire of their zeal burned into brighter flames; here, truly they beheld "the fields white unto the harvest."

The quasi-monastic discipline in which Père Maunoir directed the missionaries, and which they so readily accepted, guaranteed solid development. The ascetical training was obtained by early rising, silence, frugal meals and numerous acts of obedience. Daily recitation of the Office in common, meditations, examinations of conscience, pious readings and spiritual conferences fostered the spirit of prayer, so essential to the priestly life. Working in close concord with thirty or forty priests for a month at a time, and repeating the the experience often, these Breton priests learned the necessity of living in unity with their confrères of the neighboring parishes that their united labors might gain greater and more efficacious good.

"Walking Seminaries", some one has called the missionary bands of Père Maunoir. No finer tribute could be paid them. The sad inadequacy of clerical training prior to the Reformation produced frightening numbers of ignorant and immoral priests. The Council of Trent prescribed the sovereign remedy when it ordered that each diocese erect a seminary to insure a supply of learned and good priests.[1] But a long time passed before the Tridentine directives were widely implemented; Brittany, like so many other lands, had no seminaries even in the first half of the seventeenth century. The Breton clergy, though better than most, were still far from properly trained. Père Maunoir's thousand virtuous and capable priests supplied for many of the deficiencies. It is not without significance that fully developed seminaries were established in Brittany just before the death of the Tad Mad, and also that they were founded by his missionaries.

It would be impossible to list the great missionaries among Père Maunoir's diocesan co-laborers. As examples a few may be mentioned: M. de Trémaria, the closest co-operator, of whom more later; M. De Goandour, "a model of pastors," who brought about in his parish of Inzinae a general conversion comparable with that obtained by the Curé of Ars; M. Tourmel, an eloquent preacher, called the "Breton Cicero"; Dom Jean Leuduger, already spoken of as the founder of the Daughters of the Holy Ghost and the chief missionary of the diocese of Saint-Brieuc, from whom St. Grignon de Montfort, the apostle of Vendée, received the tradition and the spirit of the Tad Mad.

[1] Before the Reformation there were no diocesan seminaries; that saving institution was invented by the Council of Trent.

The extension of the missions through the length and breadth of Brittany and their permanent continuance, were due, after Bl. Julien, to his priest assistants. Pastors, marvelling at the good accomplished in some strange parish where they had gone to help, brought the missionaries to their own parishes. Other pastors, unable themselves to bear the cost of a mission, induced the seigneurs of their districts to share the expenses so that such great blessings might come to their parishes. Others still on returning home joined themselves with some of the neighboring priests to give missions in their own cantons. These last did not separate entirely from Père Julien, for they stood always ready to rejoin him upon the receipt of his invitation. Thus originated the diocesan mission-bands, which have been down to the present day one of the vital factors in Breton Catholic life.

Of all his missionary priests the closest to Père Maunoir was M. de Trémaria, whose life forms one of the most striking episodes of the Breton Missions. [1] Nicholas de Saludem, Seigneur de Trémaria, was born in 1619 at his ancestral manor of Kérazan, not far from Pointe du Raz. At the age of twenty-five he was a counsellor of the Parlement of Rennes; [2] but after some years he resigned his office, retiring to the Chateau of Kérazan. He was twice widowed, and had two children. Unfortunately M. de Trémaria was a libertine enmeshed in the voluptuousness of the period, and had long abandoned the practice of religion. His mother, Marguerite de Kérazan, another St. Monica, never ceased praying, weeping and

[1] Père Maunoir wrote a manuscript life of M. de Trémaria. Recently the Abbé Corentin Parcheminou published a brief biography, *Monsieur de Trémaria,* Quimper, 1937.

[2] The Supreme Court of the Duchy of Brittany.

hoping for her son's conversion. More than once she brought Père Maunoir to the chateau of Kérazan to speak with her son. The priest pleaded in vain. The dissipated nobleman heard him out courteously enough, but made no change in his evil course.

At last in 1655, M. de Trémaria, satiated with his debaucheries, fell prey to remorse. One evening in the spring of that year, overwhelmed by despair he felt the urge to commit a most evil sin, the worst he had ever perpetrated. Probably it was a temptation to suicide, though it may have been a temptation to a sacrilegious smashing of his crucifix. As he was on the point of raising the weapon, he heard a voice cry out, "Strike, Strike." It came apparently from the crucifix. M. de Trémaria's eyes with anguish sought the corpus, and in that moment his heart was changed. He dropped the weapon from his hand, and he begged of God, "Lord what wilt Thou have me to do?" [1]

God's will was manifested shortly. Soon after the extraordinary occurrence Père Maunoir arrived at the Chateau of Kérazan, where he was to have lodgings during a nearby mission. On his way to the chateau he occupied himself with praying for the conversion of the seigneur; he had no inkling of the changed disposition of the latter. The holy missionary besought God that as He had taken Père Bernard in death, he would give him M. de Trémaria, converted and ordained a priest for his companion. There was nothing small in Père Julien's faith. What was his joy, on entering the chateau to learn of the conversion of M. de Trémaria! The first part of his

[1] The account of this incident is to be found in every life of Bl. Julien Maunoir, and also in Abbé Parcheminou's biography of M. de Trémaria.

prayer had been answered, but what of the second part? Would the seigneur become a priest and a missionary assistant? The sight of Père Maunoir, staff in hand and pack on back, setting out for the mission, decided M. de Trémaria. He hastened after the missionary and accompanied him to the services. As he watched and listened to the Tad Mad catechising and teaching the cantiques, the converted nobleman realized that here God was revealing to him his vocation. Without more ado he offered himself to Père Maunoir.

On the latter's decision the new recruit set off for Paris to prepare himself for the priesthood at an embryo seminary, situated on Rue Saint-Honoré. Here a group of young ecclesiastics voluntarily followed a strict life of study and prayer under the direction of Père Jean Bagot, S.J. [1] A tutor came each day to instruct M. de Trémaria in theology and pastoral duties. But the repentant nobleman sought more than technical knowledge; with intense earnestness he applied himself to mental prayer and penitential practices. The sufferings of the Savior had for him an especial appeal; he spent all his prayer time before the crucifix. At that school he learned in a short time more than books could have taught him. After three months sojourn at Rue Saint-Honoré, in June 1656, he was ordained a priest. Immediately he returned to Brittany.

M. de Trémaria entered his first assignment by the side of his master at the Pardon of Saint-Tugean, June 24. Père Maunoir electrified the great crowd with the announcement that their old neighbor, Seigneur de Trèmaria, was now a priest and that he would be hearing

[1] Later the group moved to the Rue du Bac, where from the community was born Les Missions Etrangères de Paris.

confessions that very night. The newly-ordained hesitated at the assignment; the last time he had conversed in Breton was when he was a child of eight, twenty-nine years before. But sacrificing his misgivings, he entered the confessional. Late into the night he heard the penitents, and most of the next day too. To his delighted surprise he found himself easily understanding the Breton peasants, and being as easily understood by them. For him ever afterwards this quick return of Breton was a moral miracle. Mightily encouraged the new missionary plunged into a whole round of missions and pardons, catechising, preaching and hearing confessions, and all in the ancient tongue.

For almost two decades M. de Trémaria served with Père Maunoir. After three years chronic illness greatly restricted his active co-operation. He found employment, though it really taxed his strength, in the chaplaincy of the Hospital of the Sick Poor at Carhaix; though whenever his shattered health permitted he was out on the actual missions. Many times he drew upon his fortune to bear the entire expenses of a mission; he always supported the general movement by his prayers and sufferings. When he did preach he was particularly effective discoursing on the sufferings of Christ upon the Cross. His burning words and his frail figure deeply stirred everyone, nobles and peasants alike. But his most eloquent sermon was the example of his virtues. None could but help contrasting the frivolous, soft exquisiteness of his former days with the present hard, even rude, existence of this seeker of souls. The greatest sinners knelt at his feet to confess crimes that they would never have dared to tell anyone else. After a painful period of complete invalidism, but comforted in his last hours by his master, Père Julien, M. de Trémaria died on June 23,

1674. It was just eighteen years to the day on which he had heard his first confession on the Breton Mission.

The most striking figures in the ranks of the missionaries were the Breton bishops. To the fisher-folk, the peasants and the bourgeoisie, even to the petite noblesse and the country vicaires, their espicopal shepherds were exalted persons of another plane, to be reverenced in distant awe. But now to behold their bishops hearing long lines of penitents, mingling with the throngs of simple people at the catechetical lessons, singing the cantiques in full voice, and humbly accepting the assignments of Père Maunoir: all that aroused wondering astonishment indeed, but also loving, and much deeper reverence.

The first among these bishops was Msgr. René du Louët of Quimper. In 1646, when he brought five priests with him to take part in the mission at Mûr, he occupied the confessional more than anyone else, joined in the catechetical questionings and preached the formal sermons. His successor, Msgr. François Coëtlogon, always a staunch supporter of Père Maunoir, used the seven missions of 1669 in the diocese of Quimper to make his pastoral visitation and to confer the sacrament of Confirmation. Msgr. Pierre de la Brousse of Léon presided over the missions at Commana and Riec in 1673. Msgr. Denis de la Borde of Saint-Brieuc obliged Père Maunoir to assign him a daily task at the mission of Trevé. He was a septuagenarian. Père Julien thus described the old hero: "They could not restrain their tears on seeing this illustrious and venerable bishop, white as a swan, going to the church early in the morning, and sitting on a bench which served as a confessional, where he heard without distinction all who presented themselves, and where, without any thought for the weakness of his great age, he remained as long as the youngest and the most robust of the missionaries. He administered Confirmation to his people, and truly his own faith, in addition to the Sacrament which he conferred, was most potent in strengthening the faithful in their belief. God be blest for giving such holy bishops to His Church of Brittany." [1]

None of the Breton bishops supported the missions more steadfastly than Msgr. Balthasar Grangier of Tréguier. From the day in 1656 when he brought Père Maunoir and his missionaries to his diocese until his death twenty-two years later, he was the constant helper of the movement. There is the record of his bearing the entire cost of the mission at Lannion in 1671; that meant paying the expenses of lodging and boarding some thirty priests for four weeks. It is likely that he repeatedly assumed the same expenses for other missions. He loved nothing more than to participate actively in the work; he took a special delight in presiding over the conferences of the assembled missionaries. When his assigned task was hearing confessions, he went to the box at four in the morning and, except for his Mass and meals, did not leave until eight at night.

A pleasant anecdote is related about this zealous shepherd during the first mission at Tréguier. The evening sermon was being preached by Père Julien in the graveyard which adjoined the cathedral, one of the grandest in Brittany yet not large enough to hold the throng. Msgr. Grangier was assisting at the sermon. Being fatigued by his many labors of the day and by the prolonged sermon, the bishop became drowsy and began to nod. Lest his people be disedified, he thought it best to retire to his palace nearby. As the windows of the

[1] Boschet, p. 327.

episcopal chamber opened on the graveyard, he resolved to listen to the words of the preacher from his bed. Drowsiness, however, conquered and before the end of the sermon his lordship was fast asleep. Père Maunoir descended from the pulpit, the crowd dispersed, but the bishop slept on. Next morning the father again mounted the pulpit for the first sermon; and the sound of his voice woke up the bishop. Believing that Père Julien had preached all through the night, he hurried to the window and bade him desist at once. When the error was made clear to him, Msgr. Grangier acknowledged his mistake; but he added: "My judgement may not be as unreasonable as it seems; such is Père Maunoir's zeal that he would preach the whole night through to save a single soul." Years later on receiving an interior intimation of Bishop Grangier's death, Père Julien broke into tears as he was informing his companion, Père Martin. The latter, astonished at this unusual display of feeling, inquired the reason for it. The venerable missionary answered: "Ah, our Lord wept for His friend Lazarus. I may well weep for this saintly bishop, the protector of our missions and a perfect shepherd of souls."

Women were important helpers of the apostolate of Bl. Julien Maunoir. Some were noble ladies, like the Duchesse de Brissac and Madame de Kérazan, who brought the missions to their estates or to the neighboring districts that their tenants and domestics might be better instructed in the Faith. More actively participating were the peasant women who shared the catechetical labors, explained the charts, taught the chants and prepared the children for Confession and Holy Communion. First among all of them was Jeanne Le Gall, single-minded, indefatigable and brave; though only an untutored country lass, she possessed an extraordinary gift for explaining the enigma charts. Then there were the three widows of Douarnenez, Marguerite Pulaouëc, Thomase Roland and Catherine Daniélou, zealous teachers of the children and the unlettered in the missions of the diocese of Quimper. And surely a mention is due to a poor orphan girl of Mûr. For twenty years she taught the catechism and the cantiques in the missions of the dioceses of Quimper and of Vannes, and each year she prepared more than four hundred children for their Holy Communion. Père Boschet gives a detailed and touching account of her; her childhood with its loneliness and destitution (once an officious priest drove the ragged, forlorn little thing away from a catechesis), her deep attachment to the missions, her exceptional gifts of prayer, and her later skill with women domestics, as she sat among them, calmly working her distaff and teaching them the cantiques.[1] The good man devotes a whole page to the saintly orphan, and fails to mention her name once.

On the prayers and expiatory sufferings of two mystics, Marie-Amice Picard and Catherine Daniélou, Bl. Julien Maunoir placed special reliance for drawing down God's blessings upon the Breton Missions. Marie-Amice Picard was born at Guiclan, in the diocese of Léon, February 2, 1599. From her childhood she was a virgin of singular holiness; she lived the last seventeen years of her life, an ecstatic, in the episcopal city of Saint-Pol-de-Léon, dying on Christmas morn, 1652. Catherine Daniélou was born at Quimper, 1616. Extreme poverty and the harshest treatment marked her whole childhood which culminated in a forced marriage with a brutal old man. Despite all the physical cruelties she continued to

[1] Boschet, p. 168, ff.

be a girl of deep piety. The death of her wretched husband left her a penniless widow forced to earn her livelihood as a servant. Her new condition was not much of an improvement, but she used it to turn many souls to God. Catherine too was an ecstatic. She died at Saint-Geun-de-Mûr, while on a pilgrimage to the tomb of St. Elouan, November 4, 1667.

Both mystics had much in common. They were of humble origin, poor and unlettered. For many years they had suffered the pains of the Sacred Passion and the agonies of the Martyrs. To these afflictions were added continual interior sufferings and, at least in the case of Catherine Daniélou, violent temptations and demoniacal assaults. Nor were they spared the bitterness of calumny and persecution. Yet they also found staunch defenders: bishops, doctors of theology and, above all, Bl. Julien Maunoir; he wrote their biographies in testimony of his appreciation. [1] Both these holy women endured patiently their cruel trials in expiation of grave sins and for the conversion of great sinners. Catherine Daniélou had the larger share in the apostolate of Père Maunoir. Only occasionally did he personally seek the spiritual aid of Marie-Amice Picard; but he directed the soul of Catherine Daniélou for thirteen years. He marked out for her a unique rôle: she was not only to pray for the missions,

[1] *La Vie de Marie-Amice Picard,* décédée à Saint-Pol-de-Léon, le 25 de Décembre, 1652, tirée de Procès verbaux faits par l'ordre de Messire Robert Cupiff, évesque de Léon, et dediée a Mgr. l'Illustrissime et Révérendissime Pierre de Labrousse, évesque et comte de Léon. Copies are at Rome, Paris and Quimper. *La Vie manuscrite de Catherine Daniélou,* par le P. Julien Maunoir de la Compagnie de Jésus, son directeur. Copies are at Rome and Quimper. Both manuscripts were in the nature of confidential reports to bishops, theologians and religious superiors, hence they were never published.

she was to give them a special impulse by her sufferings and her mystical knowledge. Père Julien brought the holy widow of Douarnenez into the full current of the missions. He consulted her about his works, projects, itineraries, devotions and converts, seeking her advice and accepting her revelations, particularly in the struggle against sorcery.

Such were his companions in arms, whom Bl. Julien Maunoir marshalled under the standard of the King of Heavenly Jerusalem, priests, religious, bishops, lay-folk and mystics. Their union made possible the tremendous missions, with their thirty thousand participants, given nine and ten times in a year. Laboring with their beloved Tad Mad they revitalized the faith of Brittany.

Chapter 10

THE STANDARD OF BABYLON

The Breton Missions were not without their share of contradictions. Opponents rose up against the movement in every year of Bl. Julien's apostolate. Some of the opposition was legitimate enough; some arose from honest misunderstanding; and some was the base product of jealousy. But one opposition there was, sinister, bitter and persistent, that unquestionably was spawned in Hell. Its malignancy is the reason why this chapter has been entitled "The Standard of Babylon." The expression comes straight from the great meditation of St. Ignatius Loyola's *Spiritual Exercises,* "The Two Standards", with its unforgettable contrast of Christ rallying the army of the good under His holy standard at Jerusalem and of Satan marshalling the legions of the wicked under his evil standard at Babylon.[1] Ever since the days of his novitiate when he made his first long retreat, Bl. Julien constantly meditated on "The Two Standards." As a dedicated warrior under the Standard of the Heavenly Jerusalem he expected that he would have to stand up to continual onslaughts of the worst forces ranged under the Standard of Babylon. Events proved that he was not mistaken.

The legitimate opposition, for the most part, came early in the mission movement and did not last long. There were initial difficulties with the Quimper Jesuits. The superior, harassed with problems of finance and personnel, did not welcome a project that deprived his faculty of a zealous worker. Some of the professors lamented a capable classicist wasting his talents on a barbaric language in an undertaking of whose success they were profoundly sceptical. Then some priests, Jesuits and seculars, disapproved of Père Maunoir's methods, which were too novel for their conservatism. Some objections were rather picayune, as the complaint about the priest in the role of Christ carrying the cross in the processions. Other objections were more reasonable; there was room for difference of opinion about certain practices of Père Maunoir. Thus some learned and good priests never approved of his plan for treating the adepts of diabolism, at least in all its details. However the early and very evident successes of the missions assured honest doubters and often turned them into enthusiastic co-operators.

There were priests in Brittany who disliked Père Maunoir intensely. They were very few in number, and

[1] Robert Rouquette in *l'Etude*, Juillet-Août, 1951, Paris, used this idea as the central note of his article on the beatification of Bl. Julien Maunoir, which he entitled, "Les Deux Etendards en Basse-Bretagne."

they stood in marked contrast with the overwhelming majority who ardently admired and loved their Tad Mad. The more than a thousand missionary co-operators loyally following Père Julien's directives, proved that. Narrow rigorism motivated some dissident priests, especially those who acrimoniously attacked the grand processions and the great general communions. Jealousy undoubtedly prompted some of the censorious clerics. Probably it was this type that caused the mission at Plougastel-Daoulas in 1644 to start off so poorly, despite the ending of a disastrous drought by the prayers of Père Maunoir and Père Bernard. One priest, ignorant if not jealous, assailed the missionaries as impostors and seducers; another branded them as sorcerers with power over good and bad weather; and a third warned that confession to the missionaries was itself a sin from which the Bishop alone could absolve. For four days not a soul entered the empty Church. Only when a stranger, who had gone to confession, went about proclaiming the kindness and virtue of the fathers, did the parishioners realize their error. This was the first, but not the only time, that the charge of sorcery was used to turn the people against Père Maunoir.

There were disgruntled priests who were ready to go far in their resentment, as an incident in 1649 evidenced. The people of Bothea, a parish of the diocese of Quimper, had requested their bishop for a mission, and Msgr. du Louët had sent them the missionaries. But the pastor, M. Etienne, who was very much opposed, protested violently against the undertaking. Unable to prevent the mission, he continued his opposition in various ways: in his own sermons he attacked the singing of the cantiques as an abuse; and one day, without warning, he substituted in the pulpit for Père Maunoir an unknown priest who denounced the missionaries as false prophets. One of his assistants had the effrontery to assail with an infamous calumny the priestly virtue of Père Julien. The maneuverings were all in vain, and the mission ended as a pronounced success. The obstinate cleric, however, was not yet done; he denounced to the Sorbonne [1] the exercises of the missions, especially the cantiques and the grand processions. He received the following reply: "We cannot condemn what the bishops have glorified by their approval." Finally when Msgr. du Louët summoned the recalcitrant pastor to Quimper to account for his conduct, he denounced his bishop to the Parlement of Brittany [2] for usurpation of authority. The court returned judgement in favor of Msgr. du Louët and authorized him to punish the contumacious priest.

On a few occasions the opposition of jealous ecclesiastics did triumph. In 1665 a priest succeeded in turning his bishop from his friendship and support of Bl. Julien Maunoir. The fact is mentioned with some detail by Fabri in his *Historia compendiata,* [3] though he omits the names of the priest and the bishop. Far worse was the victory of the unworthy pastor of Saint-Thurien, a pestilential spot, where priest and people lived in unspeakable scandal. For three days in 1646, Père Maunoir and Père Bernard struggled vainly to open a mission there against adamant resistance. Then, stirred up by their wretched shepherd, the debased peasants, heaping abuse upon the fathers, drove them from the parish. Not

[1] The Sorbonne was then the theological faculty of the University of Paris.

[2] The Parlement of Brittany was the High Court of Brittany. In the days of the French monarchy parlements were high courts, not legislative bodies. The legislative bodies were called "Estates".

[3] P. Fabri, *Historia compendiata, ad. ann.* 1665, pp. 73, 74.

so bad was the incident at Trégunc in 1670. There the priest and the people were so prejudiced against the mission that they denied all hospitality to Père Maunoir, Père Martin and ten missionary priests. But affairs took a better turn when, with the evident help of Providence, a place of lodging was at last obtained. After the first sermon of the mission, the hearts of the pastor and his flock were completely changed.

Evil-minded laymen sometimes proved themselves most stubborn opponents. One instance when Père Maunoir suffered painfully from such malevolence occurred at the iron forges of Rohan in 1646. He and a companion, probably venerable Père Thomas, were overtaken by nightfall while journeying on foot through the Forest of Quénécan. At a very late hour and quite exhausted they reached the iron forges of Rohan. Many men were working there but, being an irreligious lot, they offered no welcome to the weary priests. The superintendent rudely refused the fathers' simple request for a bed and even denied their plea for at least a little straw for a night's rest. The tired priests had to push on to the glass-works at the edge of the forest. But the same surly rebuffs awaited them at the glass-works. Though the night was far advanced the missionaries had to continue their plodding through a dark and rocky countryside until they crossed into Cornouailles, where they found rest at last at a Cistercian monastery. Père Julien had a similar experience again in 1657 at Tressignaux, a place notorious for disorders. When he and his missionaries arrived the inn-keeper refused absolutely to board or lodge them. Going through the village they rapped at each door for hospitality, but not a single house would take them in. They were forced to seek the shelter of an abandoned, windowless and doorless hovel for their first night's repose.

Slander was a most frequent form of opposition. Times without number the most shocking calumnies were circulated against Bl. Julien: he was denounced as an impostor, a sorcerer, a poisoner, an irresponsible innovator, a gullible fanatic, an evil-living priest. One can but imagine the pain such scandalous lies caused this holy, zealous man. The slanderers attacked his collaborators too, especially Catherine Daniélou, whom they ridiculed as "the saint of the Jesuits." Nor did the calumniators disseminate their lies among the common people only; they had the boldness to bring their false charges to Père Maunoir's superiors, his Provincials, and even to the Father General.

The accusations were so plausibly dressed up that on more than one occasion unfortunately they were successful. One of the provincials, Père de Lingendes, in 1650 withdrew Père Maunoir and Père Bernard for a time from the direction of Catherine Daniélou. Another provincial, Père Pinette, while on visitation at Quimper in 1672, was so impressed by the complaints against the conduct of the missions that he insisted on certain changes in one particular practice. To secure observance he personally warned Père Julien that he might remove him from his beloved Brittany and send him to Pontoise. What was the provincial's surprise when, a very short while later, he beheld the venerable missionary coming into his room, all dressed up for the road, travelling cloak, staff and breviary! The old priest knelt down and asked for his orders, affirming his readiness to depart for any place the provincial might send him. Père Pinette was moved to tears; quickly he raised Père Julien up, embraced him and conjured him to keep on in his apostolate through every canton in Brittany.

Personal attacks were but part of a larger war against the Breton Missions. Evil persons, notably profligate nobles, railed against the missions and heaped scorn upon the different exercises, which were so often open rebukes to their own vicious lives. They aimed their attacks especially at the great processions; mingling with the crowds of bystanders they loudly and contemptuously shouted insulting remarks, or they tried to drown out the cantiques by bawling their ribald songs. On at least one occasion a gang of dissolute scoundrels tried to break up the line of march. Libertines also tried to disrupt the open-air sermons. Thus at Mûr in 1645, while Père Maunoir was preaching to a large crowd in the square before the parish church, two nobles tried to silence him, demanding that he get out and give place to the dancers whom they had with them. When he refused they ordered two flute-players and the company of dancers to push into the crowd and begin. The shrill sound of the flutes and the boisterous clamor of the dancers, who kept bodly advancing right up to the pulpit, finally forced Père Maunoir to withdraw. The same tactics were used again at Loperhat in 1660, just as the great procession was about to get under way. But here the marchers clashed with the dancers. In the melee the flute-players tried to drag Père Maunoir from the steps of the calvary and intrude one of themselves in his place. The crowd foiled their outrageous design. For a moment the Tad Mad's life was in real danger; a dissolute nobleman, drew a rapier and threatened to transfix him to the cross. That was not the only time that an attempt was made to murder Bl. Julien. In 1647 at Merléac desperadoes, who had slain a former pastor, plotted the assassination of Père Maunoir and his two companions. They actually penetrated into his chamber, only to be halted in their tracks; it would seem perhaps miraculously. In 1656, as Père Julien was proceeding to a pardon at Mûr, [1] a band of ruffians planned to waylay him in an ambush and slay him. A fortunate change in his itinerary saved him. His would-be assassins after awaiting his coming in vain, vented their hatred of the Tad Mad by murdering a young man who fell into their hands as he was returning from participating in the pardon.

Far worse than the maneuverings of jealous clerics or the vituperations of profligate nobles were the sinister campaigns of the Satanists. These disciples of darkness nourished a perfect hatred for Bl. Julien Maunoir, and he on his part battled them to the very end. Diabolism, ancient almost as religion itself and still existent in the modern, sceptical world, was particularly virulent in the seventeenth century Europe; the anarchic forces unleashed in the religious revolution had produced widespread outbreaks of superstition and, often accompanying them, the evil practices of the adepts of the black art. Henri Joly in his *Life of St. John Eudes* presents the following description of this fearful scourge in eastern France (it could have been written about many other parts of Europe): " 'The civil and religious wars, the incessant marching and countermarching of troops, the repeated visitations of plagues and the ensuing famines, Luther's diatribes against the devil, the movement of ideas and emotions that came from other countries, had produced a profound moral shock. Anemic bodies, acted on by excited minds, formed most suitable material for attacks of hysteria.' On the other hand, marauders of all

[1] Pardon, a religious pilgrimage in Brittany, one feature of which is a great procession.

ranks of society, who were doubtless, more interested in believing in the devil than in God, dealt largely in what they called witchcraft. In this way they terrified their victims whom they further subjected to their cupidity or brutality: the general illusion could only serve to increase the audacity of the former and the terror of the latter." [1]

Brittany afforded a fertile field for this noxious growth, for many phases of its life were affected with pagan survivals. Catholic Brittany of the early Celtic apostles and of the Middle Ages never completely threw off the ancient Armorica of the Gaulish druids. Many souls, so strong in the faith as to be incapable of a single doubt on the principal points of doctrine, nevertheless indulged in a considerable amount of superstitious practices. Such practices might be dismissed as fairly innocuous; but, in addition, there were in Brittany, as everywhere else, real or supposed sorcerers who traded on the popular credulity. Probably they were not numerous; and most of them were either imposters or paranoiacs. But they reached down into lower regions of depravity where souls stagnated in evil. These last were the adepts of diabolism, the participants or directors of the iniquitous nocturnal assemblies, the so-called "Witches' Sabbaths", where God and the faith were formally renounced, the sacraments and the Mass parodied with horrible profanations and Satan worshipped with divine honors, all amidst indescribable abominations.

Undoubtedly many of these dealers with the devil were psychotics. Some were degraded victims of their

[1] Henri Joly's comment, in his *Life of Saint John Eudes,* London, 1932, p. 14, on Abbé F. Martin's *Histoire des Dioèses du Toul et du Verdun.*

own vicious courses; horrible are the depths of perversion to which depraved Christians can descend. There is a widely held opinion that many of the witches' sabbaths were merely blinds for criminal orgies. Quite probable, too, is the view that some of these nocturnal gatherings, always held with great secrecy in remote spots, were covers for subversive movements, in which a hard core of haters of God and of the existing order plotted against religion and the state, using the paraphernalia of diabolism as a mask and as a means of terrorizing their dupes into serving as minor agents of their sinister designs. However imaginary or real its Satanism was, the movement was completely evil in origin, conduct and purpose. The adepts were bound to be unrelenting foes of Bl. Julien Maunoir, prepared to assail him and his missions with every intimidation, calumny, violence, and with murder too.

In the beginning of his apostolate, at the very important meeting with Dom Le Nobletz at Le Conquet, Père Maunoir had been advised about these evil forces. The old patriarch shared with his young successor his own knowledge and experiences, presenting him with a book on the treatment of witchcraft, *Malleus Maleficorum,* [1] and assuring him that the book would help him greatly in bringing back a category of sinners as yet

[1] Herbert Thurston, S. J. in his article, "Witchcraft" in the *Catholic Encyclopedia,* Vol. XV, p. 675 ff., comments on this book: "Probably the most disastrous episode was the publication a year or two later (1485-6) by the same inquisitors (Henry Institoris and Jacob Springer) of the book, *Malleus Maleficorum,* 'The Hammer of the Witches'... There can be no doubt that the book, owing to its reproduction by the printing press, exercised great influence. It contains nothing new ... It was sensational in the stigma it attached to witchcraft as a worse crime than heresy and in its notable animus against the female sex."

unknown to him. Six years were to pass, however, before Père Maunoir would come into conflict with organized diabolism. During those years he seems to have encountered cases of possession, one, at least, at Dirinon in 1644. Possibly he may have had suspicions of deeper evils, although his biographers give no indication of such suspicions. They do state that during the period he had had no recourse to the book given him by Dom Michel.

It was in 1650 that Père Maunoir came to his conviction that there existed in Brittany a wide-spread diabolism. During a mission at Saint-Guen Père Bernard brought to him a case of one who seemed to be an adept of a nocturnal assembly. Père Julien was horrified at the disclosures of the individual, but fearing to act precipitously, he carried the matter to Msgr. du Louët, the bishop of the diocese. After consultation the bishop and the two Jesuits were convinced of the reality of the nocturnal assembly and of its evil. Père Maunoir resolved to probe the evil profoundly so that he might rescue unfortunate adepts and overthrow the empire of diabolism, "The Iniquity of the Mountain", [1] as he used to call it. Thus began Bl. Julien's long warfare with Satanism, a warfare that brought down upon him the bitterest opposition and the most hateful calumnies. After many years, in 1672, Père Maunoir composed an account of his experiences; it was written in Latin, for it was intended only as a report to the Father General of his order, not as a publication for popular consumption. In some instances, no doubt, Père Maunoir was over credulous; he was after all a man of his age. As regards the fact of diabolism he was certainly correct.

[1] This term was borrowed from the Venerable Bede, (*In Marc.* Lib. III, comment, cap. II.)

He had behind him the strongest authority: the Sacred Scriptures; the Fathers, such as St. Augustine; the theologians, notably St. Thomas Aquinas; many wise saints of his own day, St. Francis de Sales, St. John Eudes, St. Vincent de Paul; the penal prescriptions of canon law, and the liturgy of the Church with its rite of exorcism. The evil was there. The adepts of the sabbaths, whether deluded fools, imposed-upon-simpletons, or depraved debauchees, actually foreswore God, adored Satan, practiced unspeakable abominations, and were held in a vise of terror by the masters of the infernal sect. And even if not present in visible form, he, whom the Holy Gospels call the Prince of this World, was there too; for always is he at the heart of the mystery of evil, and the source of sin. To deliver poor unfortunates from this loathsome slavery and to bring them to the repentance of the secret confessional, that was Père Julien Maunoir's single purpose. He was a compassionate apostle, not a fanatical gatherer of human fagots for the witches' pyre.

It was in his effort to rescue the adepts that Père Maunoir developed his much discussed *Method*[1] for dealing with the "Iniquity of the Mountain." Experience in the confessional revealed to him how hard it was for these poor wretches to make an avowal of their sins. Their lips were closed by shame at their abominations, by apprehension of civil punishment, by terror at the

[1] Kerbiriou, *Les Missions Bretonnes,* p. 162: "It is given in detail in the *Latin Journal of the Missions*. There also exists a manuscript in French, taken from the *Journal* after the death of the Father, with the simple title, *The Mountain,* and the subtitle: 'Work of Père Maunoir of the Company of Jesus, who died in the odor of sanctity in the village of Plévin, a parish of the diocese of Quimper, which must be read and communicated only with the greatest prudence.' "

harm promised them by the unregenerate diabolists. To break down the wall of silence for these unfortunates and to help them make good and integral confessions, Père Julien drew up a questionnaire on the sins of the nocturnal assemblies, for the use of confessors in the confessional only. The interrogations were numerous and detailed, and the questioning was progressive to provide for cases where hesitant and partial admissions had to be brought to full declarations of the essential facts. This was the *Method.* [1] But there was more to it than a mere schedule of questions. There was much advice to confessors on how to ask the questions, when to ask them and when not to ask them. There was a wealth of counsel on how to encourage and assist the penitent in overcoming his mortification or his ignorance, with strong insistence on kindliness and discretion. Père Julien himself always applied the questioning with sympathy and understanding. Of course whatever was revealed was protected by the seal of confession.

The *Method* encountered considerable opposition, even from some of Père Maunoir's own Jesuit confreres. The objectors asserted that Père Julien was affected by romances and chimeras, and that his questionnaire had the effect of extracting from rude people avowals of purely imaginary details. Yet, for Père Julien Maunoir's sagacity there is ample testimony; his Jesuit superiors in the *Annual Letters of the Company* refer continually to him as a priest of good judgement, great prudence and wide experience, this in 1683 quite as well as in 1643.

[1] A lengthy analysis and evaluation of the *Method* will be found in Canon Kerbiriou's *Les Missions Bretonnes,* Brest (1935), Troisième Partie, Chapitre Quatrième: "Contre la Cabale: Le Directoire du Confesseur. Exposé et Critique."

Two bishops, in whose dioceses he conducted missions year after year, Msgr. Visdelou of Léon and Msgr. Grangier of Tréguier, both intelligent and solid men, strongly supported him through the controversy.

The *Method* was not for universal use, nor for indiscriminate use either. Père Maunoir would give it only to a very few learned and prudent confessors; in his life of Catherine Daniélou he states that for a long time only four missionaries had been entrusted with applying the *Method.* From those who were to be entrusted with it, Père Julien demanded much: practical prudence, first of all, then evident saintliness, profound humility, true zeal, lively faith and high ideals of the sacred ministry. He was most explicit in his cautions to those confessors. They were to use the *Method* with prudent reserve, and in some cases they were not to apply it at all. They were to familiarize themselves beforehand with local and personal conditions. They were to guard against too great haste in believing the statements of the penitents. They were always to inquire whether the incident actually took place, or was simply produced in a dream, or in the mixed-up imaginings of old age. Other missionaries, in diverse parts of France and without any previous knowledge of Père Maunoir's *Method,* declared, when they read it for the first time, that the crimes in its catalogue were what they themselves had encountered in the confessional.

The rector of the Collège of Quimper, [1] who had some doubts about the value of the *Method,* submitted it and his questionings to an old professor of theology, Père Pierre Colloët, S.J. This father was a Breton; on

[1] Probably this was Père Huby, who was rector from 1649-1652. Several of the catalogues of the college about this time are missing.

occasions he had assisted Père Maunoir in the missions and had used the *Method* in the confessional. Père Colloët reported that the *Method* had led to the results sought for by Père Maunoir, but that for himself he thought that the habitués were far from being as numerous as they pretended. It might be noted here that the Jesuit superiors allowed Père Maunoir to practise the *Method* and to impart it to others, seculars and religious.

The greatest approbation of the *Method* came in Paris in 1658. Several priests had denounced the questionnaire to Msgr. Grangier, Bishop of Tréguier, and demanded its condemnation. The bishop, not wishing to act without a hearing, called into conference Père Maunoir, M. de Trémaria and four other priests. After five days of discussion the objections were arranged into some twenty articles, which the bishop determined to submit with the *Method* itself to a tribunal of theologians at Paris. Msgr. Grangier declared that if the tribunal approved of the *Method* he would encourage its use in his diocese, but if the tribunal condemned it he would allow no further mention of it in Tréguier. The prelate, acompanied by M. de Trémaria, journeyed to Paris to submit personally the problem to the special tribunal. The composition of this body guaranteed its wisdom and impartiality. These judges were two bishops, Msgr. de Pamiers and Msgr. de Boulogne; five doctors of the Sorbonne, M. Ferret, Vicar-General of Paris, M. Bail, Sub-Penitentiary of Notre Dame, M. Boudon, Archdeacon of Evreux, M. Matsos and M. Renou; two Jesuits, Père Bagot and Père Hayneuve; and most important of all, St. Vincent de Paul. The tribunal spent three months in examining the *Method* and the objections, and finally announced its decision on February 2, 1658. It was an unanimous approval. Following the Paris approbation, the bishops of Tréguier, Léon and Quimper signed and sealed their own approval; M. de Kerlivio, the saintly Vicar-General of Vannes, adopted the *Method* for the use of his ministry; Msgr. Pallu, Bishop of Heliopolis, brought it to the Far East.

The closing paragraph of Canon Kerbiriou's treatment summarizes very well Bl. Julien Maunoir's conflicts with the powers of darkness:

> "What is the conclusion? It is that Maunoir played an active role in the struggle undertaken by popes, bishops, universities and parlements for the extermination of a scourge which was attacking society and religion. We owe to him the justice of not asking him to be what he could not have been, given the milieu and the times in which he lived. Even if diabolism were only a form of moral depravity, its dissolute and subversive practices constituted a grave peril. The remedy was not only in the judicial order, but also in the religious order, especially at a time when the Church had greater influence on souls than in our day and when many of the unfortunates were misled and duped victims whose consciences had felt the stirrings of remorse. Maunoir utilized his long experience with souls. He proposed the method of piety and compassion tending to a reconciliation with God, as against the method of terror in the secular courts of justice which pursued the blameworthy to punish them. In his plan the avowal was not followed by the horrible vision of corpses dangling from gibbets and of human bodies being devoured in flames. No loud and scandalous

publicity; only the judgement of the confessional and the guarantee of the sacramental secret. The culpable, or those who believed themselves such, were to be found only in those lower regions of life into which human justice cannot penetrate. In the concert of compassionate voices which were raised to bring back poor souls to God, the Breton apostle caused his own to be heard with an incontestable accent of pity. In this delicate question it will be permissible to repeat the completely spontaneous expression of the Bishop of Cornouailles, Msgr. de Coëtlogon, who had hastened to the Collège of Quimper for the disposal of the heart of the zealous missionary, shortly after his death, 'There is a heart that has perfectly hated the devil.' "[1]

[1] Kerbiriou, *Les Missions Bretonnes,* pp. 186-187.

The Heart of Bl. Julien.

Chapter 11

THE CHAMPION OF CHRIST

What type of man was this champion of Christ's Standard in Brittany? How did he appear to the throngs at the sermons and the grand processions? They observed a priest of medium height, vigorous in step and gesture, garbed in an old rusty-black soutane and, if it was a procession day, wearing an embroidered surplice. Quickly they were attracted by his distinguished countenance. His face was oval, framed by the locks of hair at the temples and by a short beard. His brow was broad and high, indicative of elevation and maturity of thought. His large, lively eyes, pure as a child's gazed on them with marked gentleness. His small, well-cut mouth was frequently smiling, affectionately and gravely. Almost always his countenance was animated, whether he was

Blessed Julien Maunoir, S.J.

(AN OLD PORTRAIT)

conversing or praying. Of the last Boschet reported: "When the father said the common prayers with the missionaries, there always appeared in his face a redoubling of fervor and the sensible marks of a secret pleasure which saints experience in their communication with God. . . When he came from the sacred ministries, his countenance was so illuminated that many, who spoke with him, felt in themselves the ardor that influenced him; and there were some who believed that they beheld him, on occasions, framed in a glowing light." [1]

Père Maunoir was at home everywhere in Brittany, and with all classes, noblesse, peasants and bourgeoisie. People were drawn to this priest, so noble in calling, so humble in demeanor. They soon experienced how consoling were his blessings and how sustaining were his counsels, and they quickly became convinced that his manifest ardor for Divine Love would surely enkindle their own. They found him gentle, gracious, happy in outlook, often gay in repartee, and accessible to every person, high or low. Small wonder that the Bretons reserved for him a unique title, "An Tad Mad," the Good Father.

Under Bl. Julien's winning externals vibrated a soul remarkable for right and sound judgement, exquisite good sense, lively and profound intelligence, naïve candor and strong heroism. Less rugged in character than his master, Dom Le Nobletz, he was more amiable and more attractive. Yet Père Maunoir was not so much brilliant as he was solid. He was always the patient pedagogue, teaching the deepest truths clearly and interestingly, the fruit of his student years' application to literature, philosophy and theology.

[1] Boschet, p. 440.

The Bretons remembered their Tad Mad most of all for his eloquence, especially in the great open air sermons. They never could forget those stirring scenes. High above, the white clouds stood in the blue sky; all about, the green and gold fields slumbered; and beyond, the darker green forests rose, stretching to the purple hills in the far distance. Often within view, the vast blue-green sea rolled and sparkled in the sunlight. Here in the churchyard amid the gravestones the tremendous crowd stood close-packed, every eye centered on the pulpit, set out a pace or two from the gray side of the ancient church so that the weather-beaten wall would serve as its sounding board. And in the pulpit, moving nervously and with rapid gesture, their Tad Mad was speaking out in strong voice, now teaching, now pleading, now denouncing, now exhorting, now raising his crucifix on high and pointing to it in impassioned appeal. Sometimes the great crowd was gripped in a vast silence—one could almost feel the stillness; sometimes it was swept up into great waves of sobs and cries, answering his pleas for repentance.

Père Maunoir did not seek originality in the subjects of his sermons; he preached almost exclusively on the customary mission topics: the Four Last Things, the Sacraments, the Love of God, the veneration of the Blessed Virgin and of the Saints, especially the Holy Ones of Brittany. His primary task was to instruct poor people. For that task, as has been noted, God had endowed him with a rare gift of teaching; no one ever explained with greater clarity the mysteries of Faith. When he exposed the temptations and the faults of each age and state, he spoke so pointedly that he seemed to have made a complete study of all the customs and morals of Brittany.

He held his auditor's attention by apt and interesting examples, vividly told, yet never with offense, for there was nothing of the vulgarian in Père Julien. With his deep knowledge of the human heart he knew all the paths that led to it; in consequence he was able to move emotions at will. Some one has said that he had even greater power to move than to instruct or to please. Few preachers ever stirred audiences so deeply; many times he had to stop in the midst of his discourse. And these outbursts were no merely passing emotional storms, as the durability of the Breton reform amply proved.

The durability of that reform was the seal upon the eloquence of Bl. Julien Maunoir. His pleadings transformed the ignorant and the libertines, the superstitious and the impious, the blasphemous and the avaricious, the slaves of passionate hatred and the abandoned wretches of drunkenness. The *Latin Journal* and the depositions given at the posthumous processes are replete with detailed instances. Frequently they state that after a month of Père Maunoir's mission instructions the ignorant knew their prayers perfectly and had acquired a satisfactory knowledge of the catechism. They tell of sinners who made the law of God the rule of their conduct, keenly studying the practice of their duties. They reveal that the formerly blasphemous, if oaths escaped their lips, voluntarily imposed penances upon themselves. They recount the acts of restitution and charity, given at the time of the missions, guaranteeing the future justice and mercy of the converts. They report how notorious and long-standing enemies were reconciled, hastening to embrace publicly in the streets. They gave examples of heroic sobriety in the victims of the drink evil. Many of the repentant converts begged the Tad Mad for remedies against relapses, so determined were they by his exhortations to break with their evil tendencies. The genuineness of the common reform was even more strikingly evidenced by its positive fruits: wide increase of family and public prayers, permanent revival of devotions to the Blessed Mother and to the Breton saints, and above all, a tremendous increase in the frequentation of the sacraments; this in an age of Jansenism.

One of the chief reasons for the success of Père Maunoir's apostolate was the miraculous favors he obtained from Heaven. Truly, Bl. Julien Maunoir was a thaumaturge; Père Poncet wrote in 1658 to Father General Goswin Nickel, "He works in the midst of miracles and prodigies." Since his whole Breton Mission movement was carried on in an atmosphere impregnated with a sensing of the miraculous, it would be a mistake, to say the least, to dismiss lightly this phase of his activities. The crowds thronged the sermons, the confessionals, the altar-rails and the great processions, because they were convinced that this holy priest, to whom they were listening, by whom they were being absolved, from whom they were receiving the Body of Jesus, and after whom they were marching and chanting, was endowed by God with the gift of miracles. Quite as strongly convinced were his priestly associates and his episcopal superiors.

Extraordinary are the number and the nature of the miracles attributed to him. Boschet, his first biographer, [1] whom Brémond labels a man of sense and caution, confessed his bewilderment at the wonders he encountered: "They sent me a copy of the journal which P. Maunoir

[1] Boschet's work appeared in 1697, fourteen years after Père Maunoir's death.

had written himself... and in addition a large volume about his miracles. In the last I found incidents so marvelous that I suspected the copyist of embellishing things to enhance the glory of the holy man." These and other memorials, quite as astonishing, impelled him to visit Brittany and to interview every surviving missionary priest who had collaborated with Père Maunoir. To facilitate his interrogatories he divided the extraordinary incidents into four categories: (1) conversions of certain most abandoned sinners, whom God had drawn from their disorders by means of apparitions of Christ, the Blessed Virgin, or the saints, or by the particular gift Père Julien had of knowing the secrets of conscience; (2) beneficent changes in the forces of nature: the stopping or suspension of rains, the ending of droughts, the appeasing of tempests, the calming of the seas; (3) prodigious results of the missions, e.g., entire villages converted and instructed in a short time by two or three missionaries; (4) cures of diseases, injuries and fevers. Boschet journeyed the length and breadth of Brittany, seeking out bishops, priests and learned persons among the surviving witnesses of so many miracles, questioning them with painstaking care on what they themselves had seen. So fearful was he of making an error that at the end he put aside the category of conversions, deferring his judgment to later decisions of more competent authorities. He accepted testimony on the other categories, though with some hesitancy.

Le Roux, thirty years later, displayed the same carefulness in gathering his collection of the virtues and miracles of Père Maunoir. His listing of the miracles attributed to Père Julien affords some idea of their scope and character: gift of prophecy; changes obtained in the forces of nature; cures of the blind, the mute, the lame, the paralytic, the insane; prevention of physical disasters. It should be noted that in the treatment of the sick Bl. Julien almost always applied to the victims relics or holy objects, or he invoked the intercession of the saints. He never intimated any personal power. Le Roux, a Breton missionary for many years, based his study on the processes instituted by the bishops of Brittany upon the death of Père Maunoir. Quite as remarkable as the miracles reported, was the large number of priests, nobles and common people who appeared at the tribunals to testify as eyewitnesses to the miracles of Père Maunoir.

What is to be made of this abundance of miracles? At this late date it is extremely difficult to distinguish in the mass of evidence between the authentic and the imaginative. Of course it is necessary to avoid credulity; many of the cures would not stand the examination of a serious medical bureau today, and a few are patently fantastic. Not all were accepted at the time by the missionaries, some of whom felt that Père Maunoir gave too attentive an ear to certain marvelous accounts. But on the other hand, it is just as necessary to avoid narrow rationalism. Numerous witnesses swore on oath that they had seen the rains stop at Père Maunoir's prayers, or that they had talked and walked with persons who were helpless invalids prior to the holy priest's blessings. Among these deponents were many learned and substantial people, worthy certainly of credence. One must be slow to dismiss such an assemblage of testimonies. The Church exercises the greatest strictness in accepting major miracles for beatification and canonization; but she permits the popular acceptance of hosts of minor miracles, as the chapels of her numerous shrines, filled with ex-votos, witness. Most saints, present-day as well as past, were wonder-workers in deeds, as St. John Baptist Vianney, or in invocation, as St. Thérèse of Lisieux. Writing on Bl. Julien Maunoir in *l'Etude* Robert Rouquette aptly remarks: "There are moments, those precisely when the great charismatic breathings of the apostolate are passing over the Church, when miracles are multiplied on the paths of most pure, very simple and very devoted men." [1] There were surely such moments in the Breton apostolate of Bl. Julien Maunoir.

It would be of little profit, in the limits of this present work, to narrate even a small number of these wonders. They were much the same: Père Maunoir praying, the heavy rains ceasing and the great procession starting on its way; the good father anointing a poor sufferer with a blessed object, invoking God's help, and then, the cured one up and about, leading a normal existence. One incident, perhaps more striking than the rest, deserves recounting; it is Père Julien's vision of the Battle of Southwold Bay, between the Anglo-French and the Dutch fleets, June 7, 1672. In the evening of that day, as he was preaching in the chapel of Douarnenez, Père Maunoir stopped suddenly, as a man inspired and envisioning surprising events. After a few minutes he made the whole congregation get down on their knees. He urged them to pray for the success of the French and English fleets, at that moment engaging the Dutch fleet; and he begged them especially to recommend to God the sailors from Douarnenez. Deeply moved himself he knelt in the pulpit as he led the prayers. Improvising a stanza in Breton verse on the helping power

[1] Rouquette, *l'Etude,* Juillet-Août, 1951, p. 53, "Les Deux Etendards en Basse-Bretagne."

of the Blessed Virgin, he chanted it and had the congregation chant it after him. At the conclusion of the hymn Père Maunoir arose and assured his hearers that up to that moment God had protected the sailors from Douarnenez and not one of them had been wounded. But he warned them that, since the danger still continued, they must keep asking God to protect their sailors unto the end. He resumed his sermon, though interrupting it several times to exhort all to augment their prayers; it was as though he were beholding the vicissitudes of the battle and the changing perils of their kinsmen. Some days later news came to the little fishing-village that on June 7 the French fleet of Vice-Admiral d'Estrées and the English fleet of the Duke of York had surprised and defeated the Dutch fleet of Admiral de Ruyter at Southwold Bay. Letters from sailors of Douarnenez soon followed bringing the good news that though they had been in the gravest perils, with many killed around them, not one sailor from their town was even wounded.

The abundance of visions in the Breton Missions offers a harder problem than the number of miracles. In extraordinary conversions, many of the converted asserted that the Blessed Mother, or the Saints, or the Holy Souls had appeared to them and prompted their repentance. Far greater caution is needed here, since the only witnesses are the asserters of the alleged visions. While actual apparitions are not to be ruled out completely, imaginative interpretations must be looked for in very many cases, especially when dealing with Celts to whom the Saints and the Holy Souls were so vitally real. These converts were simple souls, often illiterate or only semiliterate; hence they were people who had to receive their religious teaching by stories, parables, visual charts, or episodes portrayed in the great procession; their religious knowledge came to them through the medium of sight. When the grace of God changed them, they were apt to imagine, given their highly emotional state during the struggle, the presence of the Saints or of the Holy Souls. They were not consciously making fables, but rather translating the realities of interior grace. No doubt there was some contagion of related experiences; but there was also contagion of graces, of conversion and of the discovery of God.

Père Maunoir was circumspect in regard to visions. [1] His advice to his missionaries was neither to believe too easily nor reject too quickly, but to decide only after careful investigation. As for himself, so he remarked, he had regarded many of the visions, after examination, to be imaginary; but also he had judged a great number to be true. He had little time to probe extraordinary statements, since frequently they were reported to him during the height of a mission, just when crowds were besieging his confessional. His practice was to suspend judgment, but to profit by the good dispositions of the penitents, professing visions, to help them reform their lives. He blessed God who used their imagination to lead them to repentance. Without this merciful condescension, he doubted whether these sinners would have been converted. In certain difficult cases he obliged such penitents to come back to him for a more lesiurely examination. Père Maunoir was not as credulous as some of his critics have made him out.

What of the interior spirit of Bl. Julien Maunoir? First, above all else, he was a man of faith. Faith marked his childhood and his student days. At the start of his

[1] Boschet, p. 213.

religious life in the novitiate, he wrote a plan of faith which breathed, it would seem, a special inspiration of the Holy Spirit: "I will believe all that God has revealed in the Old Testament, and all that our Lord has revealed in the New Testament; I will believe in the traditions and decisions of the Church. In the presence of the whole celestial court, I will make profession of my faith; and, when there is question of confessing it before tyrants, armed with the power of God I will not fear the wrath of men at all; I will despise their tortures, and even death itself. Never will I entertain doubts in matters of faith, nor will I expose myself to the danger of losing it. I will avoid as far as I can conversation with heretics and I will not dispute with them at all. I will not read their books, except out of necessity, and only with permission of Superiors; and I will read them only on my knees, begging God to preserve me in all the purity of my faith." [1]

Père Maunoir pursued undeviatingly the accomplishment of that programme. Its spirit permeated his forty-two years of teaching and preaching through every diocese of Brittany. A veritable monument of the Catholic Faith was his catechism, *Quenteliou Christen,* which he also translated into French. And so too were his cantiques, especially those on the Apostles' Creed and on the Sacraments. In his daily conferences with the missionaries he was constantly refuting the errors of Calvinism; indeed for his priest assistants he had one unvarying rule, single-minded attachment to the decisions of the Church. Père Julien loved to declare that the Breton tongue had never proclaimed heresy. During a mission he was always leading the people in acts of faith, at the end of sermons, at the start of the period for confessions,

[1] Boschet, p. 414.

before and after Mass, before and after Holy Communion. His fervent accents vividly evidenced his own complete conviction.

From Père Maunoir's faith arose his abiding confidence. He wrote in his *Journal*: "I will place all my hope and all my confidence in God alone, and not in my prudence, in my spirit, in my vigilance, in my virtue, nor in any person whomsoever, except in so far as I regard all these as instruments which God employs for His glory. My confidence shall be equally firm in adversity as in prosperity. Even when it seems that all is lost, that God does not wish to hear me, that all things oppose my designs, yet nothing will be able to diminish my confidence; with that confidence I will undertake great things. I know by experience that in an instant God can bring about great changes. Therefore I will place myself in His arms in order that, by Himself or by those who hold His place, He may do with me all that will please Him." [1]

Père Julien's confidence explains his courage, his peace of mind and his continual gaiety, characteristics which so impressed his associates. The thirty priests of Cornouailles, all his co-laborers on the missions, who in 1714 signed a deposition concerning Bl. Julien Maunoir's sanctity, had this to say: "We always found him of an unalterable humor in good or in bad success; prosperity did not elevate him, and contradiction did not force him to lose courage; . . . He was firm in the execution of his plans, and full of confidence in the arm of the All-Powerful, who sustained him." [2] More striking even is the pastoral of the bishop of Quimper, Msgr. François de Coët-

[1] Le Roux, pp. 36, 37.

[2] The whole document with the name of the signatories is in Le Roux, pp. 73-77.

logon, issued in the year after Père Maunoir's death: "In the greatest fatigues, in the midst of persecutions, calumnies and even in danger of death, he was as calm as in his spiritual consolations. Indeed a similar tranquility of soul being, according to St. Ignatius, founder of the Company of Jesus, an infallible mark of sanctity, it is certain that Père Maunoir, the son of this great patriarch and his imitator, possessed eminently this august quality of a saint." [1]

The wellspring of Bl. Julien's faith was his tremendous love of God. He was occupied continually and often completely with the grandeur, the goodness, the mercy, the justice and the majesty of his Divine Master. Thus he made his early resolution:

> "I shall strive to fill myself so entirely with God that all my impulses will be for Him. Each day my first thought will be of God, my first breath will be for Him, my first desire to do His will, my first planning to work for His glory, my first care to please Him, my first regret for having offended Him, my first fear lest I displease Him, my first steps will be to Him and for Him. My first words upon awakening in the morning will be, 'Jesus, Mary and Joseph'; and I shall pronounce these words aloud that they may be the first that I hear. My first prayer will be that I may always love Him, but I shall pray as often as I can that He will derive from me and from my neighbor at every moment all the glory that He can." [2]

[1] Le Roux, p. 79.

[2] Boschet, pp. 418, 419, (How like the fervent outpouring of another holy Celt in *The Breastplate of Saint Patrick!* M.P.H.)

More than fifty prayer-filled and laborious years were the loving accomplishment of that resolution.

With all his ardor for the love of God Bl. Julien realized that he could never give his Divine Master sufficient marks of his affection. He would then enflame the hearts of the thousands and thousands of his Breton fellow countrymen; and so continually in the pulpit he preached with burning words the necessity of loving God more and more. Especially did he urge his hearers to contemplate the sufferings of Jesus; to help them he composed cantiques on the Sacred Passion and one very distinctive work, *Templ consecrat dar Bassion Jesus Christ.* He succeeded to the extent that he had shepherds and fishermen practicing mental prayer; these simple souls, as they guarded their flocks or sailed their boats, made oratories in the depths of their hearts where they spoke to themselves of the sufferings of their loving Savior.

Bl. Julien himself lived in constant union with God. He was continually praying, while he was trudging along the roads or resting in the fields. Even in the brief interludes of his confessional or pulpit labors, he kept repeating ejaculations or saying the Rosary. Wherever he was, he was absorbed in God. When on one occasion an officious priest complained about the practice of the missionaries reciting the Divine Office while walking through the streets, asserting that the noise of the passersby prevented the proper attention, Père Maunoir replied: "Does not the presence and the majesty of God to whom you pray make more of an impression on your spirit than the presence and tumult of men? Know that for the missionaries all places are proper for prayer. In my own case, by the divine mercy, I am as recollected in the street as in my room, and none of our exercises troubles the commerce of heart and thought which without ceasing I have with God." [1]

This remark had escaped Père Julien's lips, for he was extremely reticent about his own spiritual life. Yet it was in line with a confidence he made, shortly before his death, to a few intimate friends, among whom was Père Vincent Martin, his last Jesuit associate. Père Julien affirmed that God had bestowed upon him the grace of never losing sight of Him and of loving Him always with a conscious love, even in the midst of the greatest occupations. Père Martin expressed some astonishment at so extraordinary a favor; and the old missionary replied a little heatedly: "What! A man in love with a beautiful woman, who is only mortal, will carry everywhere the image of his beloved, and in the tumult of the world he will always be preoccupied with the memory of her, though perhaps she never gives him a thought, or she may even be unfaithful to him. And are you astonished that an eternal God, with all His infinite perfections, would make the same impression on me that is made on a worldly man by the frail charms of a pitiful creature, who will soon be the prey of death? Will you be surprised that I unceasingly love a God who loved me first and never stopped loving me, or that I think of Him as I carry out His orders, or as He imparts to me His greatest graces?" [2]

There are few reports of mystical experiences in the life of this workaday apostle. And here Bl. Julien Maunoir was like his brother Jesuit, St. Peter Canisius, whom he resembled in many ways. However in the part

[1] Boschet, p. 435.
[2] Boschet, p. 436.

of his *Journal* where he tells of the fruits of his prayer, he mentions certain intimate communications in his novitiate days, and he implies that God thus disposed him to work for his neighbor's salvation. There are also some scattered evidences of supernatural consolations flooding Père Julien's soul during the course of the missions, thus fortifying him in his exhausting fatigues. Dom Le Nobletz had promised his young disciple such solace, assuring him that a life filled with activity would not deprive him of the advantages of contemplation, and that it would be in the pulpit and in the confessional that God would bestow on him His most vivid illuminations.

Père Maunoir could not always conceal his mystical favors. M. l'Abbé de Kerméno, the founder of the Hospital Nuns of Lannion, and M. Garrec, the confessor of the Ursulines of Quimperlé, on different occasions, beheld a bright light encircling Pére Julien's head while he was making his thanksgiving after Mass. [1] The curé of Saint-Georges-de-Reintembault and several of his parishioners deposed that at the mission of 1682 during a sermon, they had seen a light shining over Père Maunoir's head. [2] The most striking instances reported were those which occurred in 1663 at Quimperlé, where the venerable missionary lay sick with so grave an illness that his life was despaired of. Mme. Coëtvan, the mother of the seneschal of the town, had the stricken father cared for in a room of her home. There during the administration of the holy Viaticum, Bl. Julien was raised in ecstacy and favored with heavenly communications. And more, as he confided to a charitable merchant who had volunteered to nurse him, on the previous night he had been

[1] Le Roux, pp. 94, 95.
[2] ibid., p. 95.

visited, first by St. Corentin who strengthened him, and then by the Blessed Mother who conversed with him for a long time. Twelve years later, when he and Père Martin were standing in that very room, Père Julien said to his companion: "Let us recite a Te Deum to thank God for the graces which He accorded me here." However he would not give his fellow Jesuit any inkling of what the graces were. [1]

Love for God necessarily begets love for men; and so the neighbor's salvation became the second passion of Bl. Julien Maunoir. In the very beginning of his religious life he planned thus for souls: "By the illuminations and graces which I receive from Heaven, I will regard men as God's children, as His friends and as His images, and as the price of the blood of our Savior Jesus Christ. So under these titles I will love them all, but I will love particularly those towards whom I feel the least inclination, such as the most unattractive of the poor, persons who are vile and despicable of themselves, or by their occupations. . . Base, interested, or purely natural reasons shall not be the motive of my charity." [2]

He realized these ideals continuously in the forty-two year apostolate that took him through the eight Breton dioceses from village to village, trudging along on foot, bearing a pack on his back and sharing the peasant's rough beef and black bread for his sustenance. Only in his very old age did he travel on horseback. Tramping the winter roads of seventeenth century Brittany meant hazardous experiences, and often terrible ones. But not even the worst conditions held back the Tad Mad in his

[1] ibid, 94.
[2] Le Roux., p. 47.

quest of souls.[1] For miles on end he sloshed through the mud, or slipped along the icy ruts, his body bent against the howling blasts, his hat and cloak drenched with rain or covered with snow. At the end of an exhausting journey, many a time, instead of seeking rest he entered a freezing church, ascended the pulpit and delivered his message of salvation. During the winter missions he arose long before daybreak and trudged through the damp fogs and the muddy streets to the church to say the first Mass and to give the first instruction. Then he betook himself to the confessional; and there, bathed in perspiration or chilled with cold, he sat for hours on its hard bench, receiving the burdens and sorrows of the unending stream of penitents. At least three times Père Maunoir was brought to death's door by pleurisy or pneumonia, resulting from his hearing confessions under such circumstances. To endure these freezing, benumbing hours, not only had he to despise the comforts of life and to brave fatal illness, but he had also to be absolutely convinced of how precious in the sight of God is a human soul, even of the grossest person. But with what understanding tenderness Père Julien received the poor peasants! The crowds around his confessional for hours on end emphasized that.

Père Maunoir preached in every sort of place: in cathedrals, in village churches, in town squares, in rural fields, in private dwellings, in hospitals and in prisons. He toiled all the day long, and often late into the night. Sometimes he was exhorting vast crowds; at other times he was pleading with a single soul, some poor afflicted

[1]Some of these details have been mentioned in a previous chapter, but they bear repetition here for the sake of the general picture of Blessed Julien.

one who had come to him, or whom he had sought out afar. On the highroads he was always conversing about God with the people he encountered, using a hundred strategems to reach their souls and never rebuffing anyone. To bring spiritual succor to remote and forgotten islanders he risked treacherous currents and cruel reefs. He gave his utmost effort when he pursued great sinners; for, they moved in the greatest danger, since they had offended God the most. Whenever he learned of a parish that was completely neglected, he broke through every barrier to bring there the message of God's love and forgiveness.

The salvation of souls which cost Jesus Christ so dearly was, perhaps, the most repeated topic of Père Maunoir's conferences to his missionary priests. He was continually seeking and suggesting to his associates newer and better methods of helping unfortunate sinners. One of his customs was to assemble in the beginning of every mission the clergy of all the parishes round about for the double purpose of discovering local evils and of animating the zeal of these priests for the spiritual welfare of their flocks. Sometimes his kindness in rescuing tortured souls extended beyond ordinary means. Père Le Roux gives a particular instance.[1] Bl. Julien was hearing confessions in the Jesuit church at Quimper, when he received an interior intimation that a sinner was hesitatingly approaching the church in an agony of indecision about confessing a certain grave sin. The father arose from the confessional, pushed his way through the throng of penitents and reached the poor sinner at the door. Taking the harrassed soul aside Père

[1] Le Roux, p. 49.

Julien revealed to him his knowledge of the painful quandary and successfully encouraged him to confess the sin.

The final test of holiness is humility. All his religious life Julien Maunoir consciously strove for a deep realization of this virtue. In his own opinion he was nothing and capable of nothing; all his achievements he attributed strictly, and gratefully, to God. He wrote once that he would rather die a thousand deaths than to take the least complacency in himself. [1] Failures and persecutions, no matter how unjust, he reckoned as the merited punishment of his sins. A zealous missionary who had assisted him for years could write: "The venerable father received a tribute of praise as a man of the world would receive an injury. He accepted an injury as the vainest worldling would welcome praise." [2] In order that his lowly opinion of himself would be real and practical, Père Julien always carried a crucifix on his person; one glance at Jesus, suffering and humiliated, confounded him and inspired him with sentiments of the deepest humility. Msgr. Grangier declared that what he admired in Père Maunoir was not so much his prodigies nor the fruits of his missions, marvelous as they were, but his meekness and his humility, which rendered him insensible to the acclamations and the veneration of the people. [3]

No one of the Breton bishops knew Bl. Julien more intimately than did Msgr. François Coëtlogon, Bishop of Quimper; hence the words of his pastoral, issued October 14, 1684, offer a true summary of Père Maunoir's holy character: "The harvests of holiness, which he produced

[1] Boschet, p. 411.
[2] ibid., p. 431.
[3] Boschet, p. 441.

The Crucifix of Bl. Julien Maunoir, S.J. preserved at Roz-Avel, Quimper.

in my diocese, and in many other dioceses of the province, by his singular talent for catechising, by his methods of preaching, by his devotion to hearing confessions and by his entirely heavenly life, are so admirable that he appeared to me with good reason to have merited the name of the Apostle of Brittany. If there were only question of the virtue and the perfection which he established among our priests, that fact alone would have been sufficient to assure him this holy title." [1]

[1] Le Roux, pp. 78-80, contains the entire pastoral, which was issued at the beginning of the inquiry into the sanctity of Père Julien Maunoir.

Chapter 12

TOWARDS THE CROWN

Thirty years of preaching and catechising, of composing cantiques and spiritual manuals, of assembling and directing great processions, of organizing and training large groups of priest-assistants, and Père Maunoir had established the Mission as an integral feature of Breton life. Ten years of life yet remained for the Tad Mad; but they brought to the aging apostle no diminution of labors. In fact during this decade Père Maunoir by introducing the Specialized Retreat brought the Breton Missions to completed form. It was also during this period that the old hero, aged sixty-nine, vigorously met and surmounted a perilous crisis that threatened to destroy his lifework.

For a long time now the foundations of Christian living had been so firmly secured by the missions that there was no longer the pressing need of inculcating only saving truths and essential devotions. The day had come for leading the generous-hearted to a more intensive dedication, for initiating devout souls in the ways of the interior life. Père Maunoir had given some thought to retreats for the laity, and was impressed by the opportunities they offered for the spiritual advancement of individuals. Mission sermons for the crowds had to be general in application; retreat meditations for small groups could be specifically pointed at clerics or laymen, nobles or bourgeois, peasants or artisans. Further, the retreat could complement the mission, solidifying conversions, inspiring priests to become missionary assistants, and producing an elite corps of chosen souls, ready to co-operate in the works of a parish mission.

Already, in 1663, a house of closed retreats had been founded at Vannes by the Vicar-General, M. de Kerlivio, with the co-operation of Père Huby, who acted as its director. It was a success from the very beginning, and before long groups of men, totalling 2,000 in a year, were following the Spiritual Exercises of St. Ignatius. Such results prompted Père Maunoir to plan a retreat-house at Quimper for the dioceses of Lower Brittany. There was room for a second house; Vannes was at a considerable distance and the language of its instruction was French. Père Julien selected a site in the neighborhood of the college. When his plans were fully formulated he approached the rector, Père Jegou, only to learn joyfully that the superior also had been thinking of a house of retreats for Quimper. Begging God's blessing the two Jesuits united their endeavors for the accomplishment of the task.

It proved a very difficult task, requiring four years of soliciting funds and of piecemeal construction before the good hopes were realized. There was much enthusiasm at the outset. One very wealthy gentleman promised to complete the whole project, but added a condition that the fathers support him in an affair that touched his personal honor. The fathers refused his offer, not wishing to confound heavenly interests with earthly ones; they preferred to put their trust in God and in the piety of the people of Quimper. A sum of 500 livres, the contribution of two pious souls, Mme. Brinnilie, of the family of Kerméno, and M. Picot, pastor of Plouguernéval, encouraged the rector to start the foundations in 1666; the first stone was laid by the bishop of Quimper, Msgr. Coëtlogon. Everyone, priests, nobles, townfolk, artisans and day laborers, sought to help, coming forward with money or materials for the building. But, as often happens, the first enthusiasm waned, and Père Jegou began to lose heart. Bl. Julien, however, would not give up. He rallied his downcast superior, exclaiming as he struck the table in forceful emphasis, "Do not be discouraged, mon Père, I promise you that you will get the money." Not long after the funds began to mount again. One contribution was large enough to pay for an entire wing; it was the gift of Mme. de Pratelas, one of the most generous benefactors of Père Maunoir and the Breton Missions. [1] The retreat-house, when it was completed, had eighty private rooms and several large dormitories, which with their double rows of beds could accommodate two hundred persons at a time.

[1] Besides her other benefactions Mme. de Pratelas purchased the house of Dom Le Nobletz at Douarnenez and made possible the erection there of the chapel of St. Michel, one of Père Maunoir's most desired projects.

Before the opening of the Quimper retreat-house Père Maunoir went to Vannes to seek the advice of Père Huby and M. de Kerlivio, and to observe the closed retreats in operation. He accepted all the methods of Vannes but one, the grouping of retreatants. At Vannes Père Huby assembled together all types, priests and laymen, nobles, bourgeois and peasants, for the same retreat; his idea was that the great numbers and the great variety would enkindle greater fervor. At Quimper Père Maunoir classified the retreatants according to condition and rank, giving each group a separate retreat; he felt that thus particular needs and problems would be more intimately and more effectively handled. With the Quimper retreat-house established, Père Julien returned to the missions, though he always maintained an active interest in this special venture which he himself had originated.

The marked success of the retreat-house inspired the Tad Mad to bring some of its advantages to the missions. Most of his people, because of their occupations or the distance to be traveled, found it impossible to go to Vannes or Quimper. Why not offer them the opportunity with a mission? Père Maunoir pondered the idea and resolved to try it at the mission of Lannion in January 1671. While the large main services were being conducted by some thirty priests at the church of Saint-Jean-du-Bally, Père Julien directed three retreats of groups of three hundred, one group each week, at the chapel of the Augustinians.

To help the retreatants in learning how to meditate, the subjects were taken from the Passion of our Lord; it was felt that the Passion would more readily inspire them with love for Him. The meditations were reduced to seven principal topics, one for each day: Sunday, the

Prayer and the Agony of the Garden; Monday, the Scourging; Tuesday, the Crowning with Thorns; Wednesday, the Condemnation to Death; Thursday, the Carrying of the Cross; Friday, the Crucifixion; Saturday, the Descent from the Cross. At the beginning of each meditation a missionary described the episode and then taught the retreatants how to form a mental picture of the incident and how to ponder in their hearts the thoughts and affections prompted by the sight of the agonizing Christ. M. de Trémaria, who was especially effective in preaching on the sufferings of the Savior, gave most of the discourses. It is highly possible that transparencies [1] were used to bring vividly before the eyes of the retreatants the events upon which they were meditating. Père Boschet makes no mention of them; but there is a constant tradition that they were employed in the eighteenth century mission-retreats. [2] Certainly transparencies were used at Vannes from 1663.

The experiment at Lannion proved an outstanding success. From then on every mission had its retreats, usually one a week. In the beginning there were objections that the mission-retreats would hurt the retreat houses, but experience soon proved that the two works actually complemented each other. The mission-retreats strongly impressed visitors to Brittany. Père Chaurand, a devoted missionary of Provence, expressed his admiration thus: "Each day of the retreat at eleven o'clock the exercitants, as they call them, are sent to take their dinner in the cemetery or elsewhere; in the evening they are

[1] Transparencies were either pictures on oiled paper, illuminated from behind, or primitive lantern-slides.

[2] *Les Exercises de la mission,* par Guillaume Nicolas, S.J., ms. p. 13-85. Archives of the library of the Jesuits of Quimper.

dismissed to go to the place where they are to sleep. It is marvelous to see all this crowd of laymen keeping silence like religious, not only while they are eating, but also on their way home to their sleeping quarters. After the retreat-masters have finished their work with the first band, they take on the second and the third and others still, during the whole mission. Père Maunoir, who is now seventy-five years old, directs all these works with as much keenness and energy as though he had only ten people to take care of, and with the strength and vigor which he had when he was forty years of age." [1]

The completion of the organization and the method of the Breton Missions did not bring retirement to the aging Père Maunoir; in each year of the evening of his life there were seven or eight great missions to be directed by him. And one of these years, 1675, witnessed the most painful trial of his apostolate, the Revolt against the Stamp Tax, a peasant insurrection that threatened to sweep away all the good that he had achieved. The rising was occasioned by the new taxes of Colbert, Louis XIV's great minister of finance. Hard put to meet the crushing expenses of the Grand Monarch's foreign wars, the minister proposed three imposts: a stamp on official documents, a stamp on tinware and a levy on tobacco. Local parlements, especially Brittany's, vehemently protested that ancient privileges were ignored, that the times were more than miserable, and that evils worse still were to be apprehended. Colbert remained adamant, ordering the immediate collection of the taxes and threatening the severest repression of any opposition.

[1] Letter of P. Chaurand to R.P. Galien, Provincial of the Lyons Province, February 1, 1682. *Documents inédits concernants la Com-Compagnie de Jésus,* published by P. Carayon, S.J., t. XXIII, Paris, Taranne, (1874-1886) p. 344.

Popular anger exploded, and a rebellion broke out at Bordeaux in March 1675. In a very short time ten provinces were aflame. In mid-April the insurrection swept into Upper Brittany, raging around Rennes and its environments. By the early summer the revolt was in full force in Lower Brittany, centering around Quimper. Père de Quermeydec, Rector of the Jesuit College, reported that 18,000 to 20,000 rebels, armed with muskets, guns, halberds and pitchforks, had forced nobles to dress in peasant garb and place themselves at the head of the insurgents. In the fury of the revolt some of the insurrectionists pushed far beyond opposition to taxes, reaching to a veritable communism, as the leveling demands in the *Code Paysan* of the rebels between Douarnenez and Concarneau revealed. The pastor of Plestin in Tréguier, M. Jacques Boëssy, wrote in the parish register in January, 1675: "The peasants believe that everything is permitted, all goods are common, and they do not spare even the ministers of the Church, pretending that they will slay some and will drive others from their parishes. 'O tempora, O mores!' May God and the King remedy these evils!"

Repentant peasants later told a Jesuit of Quimper that they believed that they had been bewitched and transported by a diabolical furor. But they also added that they had been provoked by the demands of the tax-collectors and by the evil treatment of their landlords. There was much justice in their complaints. The times were bad, the new and heavy taxes were ruinous and the exactions of the collectors were often insupportable. Generally the Breton noblesse and their peasantry lived in close cordiality; but there certainly were country squires in Brittany who treated their tenants with extreme harshness. Père Maunoir in his *Chemin assuré de pénitence* upbraided these oppressors. There is a further question which merits consideration: had the peasants been enflamed by subversive *provocateurs*? Right at the very beginning an ominous rumor swept through the country that the King was about to impose the gabelle. The gabelle, or the salt tax, was bad indeed; but "gabelle" had taken on a fearsome meaning for many of the peasantry; it stood for some unknown and terrible exaction. Immediately the governor of Brittany, Duke de Chaulnes, protested vehemently that this dreaded tax had never been contemplated; the Rennes Parlement issued a proclamation to the same effect to emphasize his denial. Nevertheless the rumor continued to spread. Then there were the communistic and anti-clerical demands of the rioting peasants. Such anarchic proposals could hardly be expected from friendly, simple-hearted and pious shepherds and fishermen. Were they authored by intriguers, possibly the sinister managers of the witches' sabbaths?

About the time the disaster struck Cornouailles, Père Maunoir had been called to conduct a mission at Plouguernével, only a few miles from Carhaix where the insurrection was in full fury. Any missionary would have been pardoned for drawing back, but Père Julien and his five assistant priests proceeded straight into the disturbed area. The inhabitants showed themselves sullen and hostile, persuaded somehow that the clergy were coming for no other purpose than to impose higher fees. The solemn high Mass, opening the mission, was just about to start when a crowd of armed rioters burst into the church, shouting loudly that the priests were going to raise the fees for baptism, marriages, and burials. Such a tumult arose that the officers of the Mass dared not leave the sacristy. With great difficulty the parish priest,

M. Picot, finally obtained silence. He assured the troubled gathering that the bishop had sent the missionaries for one purpose only, the good of their souls, and that there was no intention on the part of anyone of raising the fees. The rioters there and then demanded that the priests sign a pledge binding themselves not to seek any higher fees, and they pushed forward a notary armed with just such a document. The missionaries, making no difficulty, signed the document. Their action ended the tumult. They were unmolested and went through the Mass without further incidents. The same afternoon Père Maunoir assembled the children in the church for practice in singing the cantiques. A curious crowd gathered, soon filling the sacred edifice. Obdurate hearts softened as they listened to the young voices, and more so, as they recognized the lessons of the holy melodies. Here was Père Julien's opportunity. He pleaded most earnestly with the now more receptive auditors to return to their Christian duties. He was listened to, and the mission of Plouguernével was on its way to a remarkable success.

The insurrection persisted in the nearby countryside. Fearing that a personal visit might achieve little, Père Maunoir decided to bring the parishes of the vicinity into the mission. He advanced the great procession by eight days and invited all the people roundabout to participate. Crowds poured in from every hamlet. No Breton peasant could resist the living tableaus of the Savior's life, nor the mighty volume of the singing and the public praying. Once more Père Julien had his opportunity to plead for peace and for the abandonment of disorders. To insure the good resolutions he announced for the following Sunday the devotion most dear to Breton hearts, the general communion for the dead. This would mean confessions, with the opportunity for all to cleanse their souls, and Holy Communion with the gift of the Savior's strengthening graces for all. Everything turned out according to his planning, and peace was restored to the disturbed region.

As a true Breton in the hour of need, Père Julien thought to seek the help of the saints; above all of good Saint Anne. He assembled a pilgrimage of fervent souls and led them to Brittany's foremost shrine, Sainte-Anne-d'Auray, there to supplicate the "Grande-Mère" of all Bretons to rescue the dear land, which more than all others venerated her, from this fearful calamity. Then he led his pilgrims on to Vannes, to the tomb of St. Vincent Ferrer in the Cathedral of Saint Pierre. Kneeling before the reliquary of the great medieval apostle and the special guardian of Brittany, the Tad Mad and his pilgrims besought Saint Vincent once more to shield its people with his powerful protection. Père Maunoir, interiorly reassured at the shrine of his exemplar, returned with confident heart to his labors for peace.

He turned aside on his homeward journey to go to Port-Louis, where the Duke de Chaulnes was gathering troops for a punitive expedition into the disaffected areas. His purpose was to give the governor an account of his work in calming the storm and to offer to go along with the expedition to labor by spiritual means for pacification. Père Julien obtained his audience. The governor, listening to the results achieved at Plouguernével and learning of the pilgrimage, was quite impressed and readily accepted the missionary's offer. On August 24 the army started to move; and for six weeks the Duke de Chaulnes led his column through the South, the West and the North of Brittany, crushing the insurrection with the sternest severity. Summary courts were established and numbers of the revolters were hanged. Père Julien personally prepared these unfortunates for death, standing by them, consoling and strengthening them to the end. In every possible case he pleaded for mercy. They were his people; and he knew that they were not malicious. He knew that they were honest, credulous, simple peasants and laborers, crushed with heavy burdens, aroused against a phantom "gabelle", inflamed with drink and swept by mob fury into crimes of incendiarism. His repeated interventions with the governor saved many poor fellows from the gallows. One modern writer, though strongly condemnatory of the Duke de Chaulnes, has this to say of Bl. Julien: "In the midst of these sad scenes, it is a truly good fortune for us to meet that grand and touching figure of Père Maunoir, faithful to the most noble mission of the Catholic priesthood, which still blesses in the name of God when human justice has condemned, which saves what has been struck down and which causes life to blossom forth again even from death." [1]

On the departure of the king's troops from the duchy, Père Maunoir lost no time in recommencing the missions; now they were to be directed especially at repentance and consolation. He began at Pontivy, in the diocese of Vannes. This town had had a large share in the common afflictions; many of its peasants had been killed during the troubles and others had been executed. The response of the poor people, their piety

[1] de la Borderie, Arthur, *La Révolte du papier timbré.*, Saint-Brieuc, (1884) pp. 142, 147, 148.

and fervor, brought tears to the eyes of the missionaries. The same good fruits were gained in the mission of Plozévet, the last of that year of 1675, and in the eleven missions of the following year. The sad days of the Breton Revolt against the Stamp Tax passed into memory, but at no time in his apostolic career did Bl. Julien Maunoir merit more the loving appellation of the Tad Mad.

Chapter 13

HIGHROAD TO HEAVEN

The end of Père Maunoir's life-journey was coming into sight. Well past seventy he felt the infirmities of old age pressing upon him. His physical strength had noticeably declined; six missions in 1681 [1] and six in 1682 were all that he could manage, and then only by resting for weeks at a time to recuperate his failing powers. There was no diminution of his zeal; if anything, its ardor flamed more brightly. Père Chauraud of the Lyons province wrote to his Provincial, as was noted in the last

[1] One mission of 1681 merits special notice. It was given at the request of Mme. Marguerite d'Angennes, the saintly superioress of the Benedictine Convent of Saint Sulpice, not far from Rennes, in the parishes dependent on her convent. The principal services were held

chapter, that Père Maunoir, despite his seventy-five years, conducted a mission with the force and vigor of a man of forty. That, however, was the impression of a passing stranger. If Père Julien seemed especially solicitous for souls, if he preached with increased earnestness, it all indicated only too clearly his conviction that he was evangelizing this particular countryside for the last time. The people certainly sensed it. They flocked to his sermons in larger numbers; and they listened more intently than ever before, anxious to engrave his last words deeply in their hearts. They felt, as he felt, that it was his last farewell.

Bl. Julien seems to have had some intimation of the time and place of his death. He informed M. Boudon, Archdeacon of Evreux, when he met him during a short visit to Paris in 1681, that he would not be alive when the zealous prelate came to study his mission methods, but that then Père Martin would be directing the apostolic labors. In 1682 at Crozon, while preaching a Lenten course, the aging missionary collapsed. The pastor, Abbé de Coëtlogon, an old friend, begged Père Julien to give up his work and to spend his last days with him: "My good Father, if you are soon to die, die here. Leave to my parish the body which during life you mortified so much. We shall lovingly guard the precious deposit. It will be the best testimony of your affection that you can give us." The tired old priest only smiled and turned the request aside with a pleasantry. He knew that Crozon was not to be the place of his burial, and also that some

in the convent-church; the nuns chanted the cantiques and also taught them to the people. Four retreats were conducted, and in one of them a large number of ladies made an eight-day retreat within the enclosure. Evidently retreats for women were included in the Breton Missions.

months of laboring still remained. After Easter, persuaded that he had recovered sufficiently, Père Maunoir set out to give missions in the dioceses of Tréguier and Saint-Brieuc. But at Boubriac, in the Saint-Brieuc diocese, upon leaving the pulpit one day, he was so overcome with weakness and a severe attack of gout that his companions feared that his end was near. One of the missionary priests asked him if he would die at Boubriac. "No," replied Bl. Julien, "I shall not die here, but in the middle of the land of Saint Corentin." On another priest asking him where he wished to be interred, he murmured, "The tree will lie where it falls."

The last mission that Père Maunoir gave was at Scrignac, in the diocese of Quimper. Its parishioners, recalling a promise which he had made to them some years earlier that he would evangelize them once more before he died, were convinced that this was the last time they would see their Tad Mad. All day long they besieged his confessional; there was not a person in Scrignac but wished to confess to him and to receive his final counsel. Père Julien tried to hear them all. But his strength could not measure up to his charity, and he was forced to relinquish the work. After a few days of rest the unconquered apostle was again on the road, going to open a mission at Uzel, a parish of Saint-Brieuc. He reached the hamlet and was walking in its narrow street, when suddenly he stopped and said to his companion, Père Martin, "Let us return as quickly as possible to Cornouailles. It is necessary for us to go there; God has warned me." [1] Turning about, the two priests started

[1] This incident and all the others in the account of the death of Bl. Julien are taken from Boschet, pp. 370-383, and from Le Roux, pp. 26-31.

back to Plévin. Twice on the journey, weary and weak, the old missionary had to stop for rest. The first time was at Quillio, and there he blessed a holy Franciscan nun whom years before he had cured miraculously. The second time was at Plouguernével, and there he summoned up enough strength to preach his last sermon and to conduct his last catechesis. At length Plévin was reached. Père Julien was in such a state of utter exhaustion that he had to be put to bed at once in the house of the parish priest, M. Canant, one of his most devoted friends. Shortly he was seized with a fever and a violent pain in his side. Though no word of complaint escaped the sufferer, M. Canant and Père Martin became alarmed at his evident agony. On questioning him they concluded that his illness was a severe case of pneumonia with little hope of recovery. Next morning, when Père Julien was unable to arise for his Mass, their worst fears were confirmed. Sick as he was and in such need of consoling companionship, he yet insisted that Père Martin depart for their engagement at Plouyé. For him a mission must never be abandoned.

The news of the Tad Mad's grave illness spread rapidly over the whole of Lower Brittany. M. de Kerlouët, the governor of Carhaix, came at once to bring the sick priest to his chateau. Père Maunoir thanked him graciously, but declined his kindly offer. After the nobleman had departed, Père Julien observed to M. Canant that a poor religious ought to avoid grand mansions and that, having passed so much of his life with the missionary assistants, it was but fitting for him to terminate it in the house of one of them. The Bishop of Quimper dispatched one of his priests to inquire for the desires of his old friend. The veteran missionary had but one ruling desire, Heaven. For the time being his crucifix sufficed for him; "Leave me with the crucifix of our Lord, it is a good companion," he said. From all parts of Brittany, even the most remote, priests and laymen of every class hastened to Plévin. They wished to give one last mark of respect and gratitude to their Tad Mad. Some hoped for a parting word of counsel; all sought his final blessing. Père Julien received each visitor without distinction. To the laymen he spoke of God's justice and love, and of the care of their own salvation. To the priests he spoke of zeal for souls, urging them to join or to continue in the Breton Missions, assuring them that he knew of no priestly labor more holy or more useful. Père Julien was ever the apostle, even in the gathering shadows of death.

Mme. de Pratelas, the motherly patroness of the missions, hurried from Quimper, bringing with her the town's best physician, Doctor du Castel, and the Father Minister of the Jesuit Community, Père du Demaine. When the three arrived Père Maunoir was suffering the fourth attack of the fever. Doctor du Castel, upon examining the sick priest, could offer the watchers at the bedside no hope at all. Mme. de Pratelas was inconsolable and wept unrestrainedly. Her sobbing disconcerted Père Maunoir; and he said very firmly to her, "Pray to God, Madame." The good lady answered, "Yes, with your prayers joined to mine that God will restore your health." Bl. Julien, speaking once more with his accustomed gentleness, remarked in turn: "When God sent us into the world, Madame, He did not consult us; when He takes us back, He will not consult us either." The doctor could not but marvel at the calm courage of the aged missionary; no murmur escaped his lips in the cruel, unceasing pain, while his countenance manifested more of the ardor of divine love than of the fever that was devouring him.

Père du Demaine heard the dying priest's last confession, anointed him and brought him Holy Viaticum. Bl. Julien welcomed his sacramental Savior with transports of devotion; all present were sure that he was actually seeing the heavenly vision of his Divine Master. He lay silent for some moments in the rapture of his thanksgiving. Then he asked for a lighted candle; and when it was held in his hand he recited the profession of Faith and the promises of Baptism. Weak as he was, he pronounced the words with such animation that the attendants had to caution him to moderate his tones lest he increase the fever. He obeyed, calmly and quietly finishing the formulas. From then on he kept whispering pious ejaculations. Those at the bedside heard him softly repeating, "Jesus is my life, and I gain so much in dying," and "Jesus, author of my redemption, object of my love and my desires!" Sometimes he would speak to the Blessed Virgin, "O Mary, mother of grace, mother of mercy, defend us against the enemy of our souls, receive us at the hour of death."

Père Maunoir preserved his faculties almost to the end. Only in the evening preceding his death did his mind seem for a time to be affected. Once he said very distinctly to Père du Demaine and to M. Canant, "Give M. Le Nobletz a chair." Both priests supposed that his mind was wandering, so they made no move. He repeated his request, and M. Canant asked what he wished. Bl. Julien replied, "I pray you, give M. Le Nobletz a chair." Was his mind really wandering, or had the venerable patriarch come to strengthen his son for the last assault of the demon? A short while after Père Julien became strangely agitated. He begged Père du Demaine to sprinkle holy water on the bed, indicating one spot in particular. Quickly one of the priests presented his crucifix to him, saying, "Look, the Savior's Cross! Begone, Powers of Hell!" Bl. Julien seized the crucifix, kissed it most fervently and pressed it to his breast. His countenance cleared, and a holy calmness then appeared that remained until the end.

Père du Demaine asked the dying priest to bless him, M. Canant, M. de Coëtlogon and all the other missionary priests who were present. Père Julien complied, bestowing his benediction on each one of them and begging the Savior Himself to bless them and their works. The prayers for the dying were then said, with Père Maunoir joining in the responses clearly and distinctly. In the silence that followed, as the end approached, his whisperings of faith, hope and love multiplied, ceasing only when the power of speech had left him. A quarter of an hour later, about eight o'clock in the evening, he breathed his last. It was January 28, 1683. Père Julien Maunoir was in his seventy-seventh year. He had been a Jesuit for fifty-eight years, and he had consecrated fifty-three of them to the Breton Missions. His death was a gentle passing; the watchers hardly perceived it, so little change was there in the dead priest's countenance. When there was doubt no longer, those in the room came to the bedside and reverently kneeling down, kissed the hands of the Tad Mad. Then each one began to invoke him who was now, they felt certain, their apostle in Paradise.

At the very hour when Père Maunoir was dying, five miles away in the village of Montreff the parish-priest, M. Quillerou, was conversing with one of his parishioners, named Delen, outside their hilltopped village church. It was a sombre midwinter's night, and the two were standing in almost pitch darkness. Suddenly the granite wall of the church was illumined with a great brightness. The priest and his companion, greatly alarmed, feared that it was the reflection of some incendiary fire in the village below them. Anxiously they peered down; but no, all the houses lay in the cold darkness of the winter's night. Mystified, they scanned the horizon; their church, perched high on a south flank of the Montagnes Noires, commanded the whole region around Carhaix. Delen, who had climbed up onto the wall of the churchyard for a better view, called his pastor's attention to the eastern sky around Plévin; it was all aglow with a vivid lightsomeness. They watched wonderingly until they began to hear faintly the measured tolling bells of Plévin's church. M. Quillerou, who had visited Père Maunoir just the evening before, recognized that the bells were tolling the passing of his beloved friend. And the illumination, he now was convinced, was announcing the entry of Père Julien into Heaven. He and his parishioner knelt down and began to pray. A few minutes later the brightness disappeared, and the two found themselves again in the complete darkness of the night. Next morning all Montreff learned of the prodigy from their pastor and their fellow parishioner. Years afterwards M. Quillerou recounted the event and all its details to Père Le Roux; before his death he made a judicial declaration of it to the tribunal set up by the bishop of Quimper for the cause of Père Maunoir. [1]

When it had become certain that Père Julien's illness was fatal, Bishop de Coëtlogon, the canons of the

[1] Le Roux, pp. 30, 31.

cathedral of Saint Corentin and the rector of the Jesuit College, Père Paris, arranged for the interment of the body of Père Maunoir in the cathedral of Quimper and the depositing of his heart in the chapel of the College. Shortly after the decease Père du Demaine informed M. Canant of the agreement. At the same time he presented to the pastor of Plévin a letter of Msgr. de Coëtlogon which forbade, under pain of excommunication, opposition to the transference of the body to Quimper. In the morning a surgeon removed the heart, which was reverently enfolded in a silk cloth and deposited in a suitable place in the presbytery. The body was then clothed in sacerdotal vestments and offered for the viewing of the people.

In the meantime the news of Père Maunoir's death was spreading rapidly through the length and breadth of Brittany. Shortly countless bands of pilgrims were on the road for Plévin, hastening to look for the last time upon the countenance of their Tad Mad and to pay their heart-felt homage to his remains. The immense crowd that gathered took two days to file past the bier. Each person stopped for a moment to kiss the feet of the Blessed, the feet that had traversed their Brittany so many times, even to its remotest parts. The strongest precautions had to be taken to curb the avid relic-seekers. In consequence the good Breton peasants had to be content with touching their rosary-beads to the hands, the breviary, or the vestments of the Tad Mad. All the while they were doing so, these simple-hearted people kept addressing to him their desires and their prayers.

In the afternoon of the second day a rumor began to be circulated that Msgr. de Coëtlogon had ordered the interment of Père Maunoir's body in the cathedral of

Quimper. The Plévinois, aroused by the report, vehemently declared that no matter what had been decided they were going to keep the holy remains in their parochial church. Their friends from the neighboring villages quickly leagued themselves with them to prevent the removal. A heavy guard was posted for the night, and all agreed to come armed next morning to the churchyard.

Possibly the rumor started with the arrival of the vicar-general of the diocese, M. Callier, who did bring with him, though secretly, the bishop's formal order and an authorization to carry it out. But everything appeared tranquil that evening, and the prelate retired anticipating little trouble. Next morning, however, when he awoke he found the presbytery surrounded by a large crowd of armed peasants. He went out to them and explained his mission. The throng listened to him in sullen silence. M. Callier then tried to reason with them, but with no success; all he received were repeated shouts of refusal: "No, no, you shall not take our Tad Mad away from us." Frustrated the vicar-general decided to call in the civil authority, so he went to the château of the governor of the district, M. de Kerlouet, to enlist his support. But the governor, knowing from experience how dangerous it was to wound the feelings of the Bas-Bretons, refused to use force. He volunteered to try persuasion himself. Going back with M. Callier to the beleaguered presbytery, he exhorted the peasants with great earnestness to yield. His efforts were largely nullified by his wife who was strongly convinced that God had confided the body of His holy servant to the parish of Plévin. While her husband was speaking, Mme. de Kerlouet was moving among the peasants and urging them to remain firm in their determination. In the end the governor's pleadings proved no more effective than the vicar-general's reasonings. M. Callier had but one course left, the official announcement of the Bishop's command and of the penalty for contravening it. Reluctantly he ordered one of the missionary priests to read the document to the crowd. Possibly the peasants had little comprehension of the gravity of an excommunication, or they may have persuaded themselves that they could not be excommunicated for burying the dead. At any rate they were not deterred and they cried out in answer: "You may take away our lives, but you shall not take away from us the body of our Tad Mad."

M. Callier, in the face of such inflexible opposition, was at a loss what to do. Giving up for the moment any further action, he entered the church to say his Mass for the repose of the soul of Père Maunoir. While he was vesting a deputation from the crowd outside came to inform him that if the priests did not bring the body to the church and inter it very soon, the parishioners of Plévin would take it there and bury it themselves. M. de Kerlouet took M. Callier aside and advised him to content the people by going ahead with the burial, assuring him that in the night the body could be taken up and secretly transferred to Quimper. The vicar-general agreed and ordered the body brought into the church. He sang the Mass of Requiem himself and personally directed the ceremonies of interment. The body of Père Julien was deposited in the crypt of the de Kerlouets. M. Callier, later in life, often declared that from the time of the Mass he began to wonder if somehow God was not permitting the resistance of the peasants. He dismissed the idea of removing the body at night. The Plévinois, however, were taking no chances. That night they gained entrance into the church, though the door had been carefully locked after the burial ceremony.

They placed an extra large stone on the still open grave, and for the rest of the night stood guard heavily armed. Next morning, when the vicar-general entered the church and found the armed peasants, he gave up the contest.

During the day M. Callier returned to Quimper to inform the bishop and the canons of the contrary turn of affairs. With him went Père du Demaine, bearing Bl. Julien's heart. No effort was made by the peasants to deter the two priests. Msgr. de Coëtlogon, after listening to the vicar-general's report, decided to let matters rest as they were. Then he went straightway to the Jesuit college to venerate the heart of his beloved friend. When the Bishop had kissed the precious relic, he turned and made this remark to all present: "Here is the heart that hated the devil perfectly." A great public veneration, in which the entire city of Quimper participated, was soon held. At the conclusion of the solemn services the relic, encased in a heart shaped leaden receptacle, was placed in a small stone monument, within the sanctuary and in front of the tabernacle. It was a fitting spot, there before the altar where Bl. Julien Maunoir had offered the Holy Sacrifice a thousand times for his dear Bretons.

Msgr. de Coëtlogon was a great-souled prelate, who knew his people and loved them deeply, and so he inflicted no punishment for the incident at Plévin. Rather he allowed the solemn obsequies to be performed almost immediately in the village church. The services lasted through eight days and drew hundreds of priests and immense throngs of people. The climax was the funeral oration over the tomb of the Tad Mad on the last day. It was preached by one of the most eloquent of the priest-assistants, M. Falchier, the pastor of Cléden-Pohcr who

The Parish Church of Plévin,
in which is the tomb of Bl. Julien.

Oratory marking the spot where Bl. Julien died.

(ADJOINING THE PARISH CHURCH OF PLÉVIN.)

with confidence and enthusiasm proclaimed Père Julien Maunoir, "the father, the apostle, the savior of Lower Brittany." His words found undying echoes in the hearts of the Bretons. From that day down through almost three centuries in their churches, in their homes, in their fields, out on their fishing-vessels, everywhere, they have continued to chant *Allas! Allas! Bretonet*, the plaintive lament, composed for them by Père Martin, which carries as its refrain:

"Alas! Bretons! Alas!
Père Maunoir is dead!
Dead is your guiding torch!
Dead is your tender father!
Dead near Carhaix
As he foretold.
In Plévin's presbytery
He lies,
In the land of St. Corentin."

Chapter 14

THE VOICE OF THE PEOPLE

Two striking aspects of the veneration of Bl. Julien Maunoir are its extensiveness and its persistence. Directly upon his death the Bretons everywhere in the Duchy began revering the Tad Mad as a saint. Almost three centuries have passed, turbulent with recurring revolutions and intensive religious persecutions, yet the Breton people have never ceased invoking Père Julien as their heavenly intercessor. They were but following the lead of their shepherds. Even while the holy missionary lived Msgr. du Louët, bishop of Quimper, called him the visible angel of his diocese. Two bishops of Tréguier, Msgr. de la Barde and Msgr. Grangier, made similar statements; the former spoke of him as the man of God for Brittany, and the latter declared that since St. Vincent Ferrer no evangelical laborer had worked for the salvation of Brittany with as much success as Père Maunoir. Msgr. de Coëtlogon, in the year following Père Julien's demise, issued a pastoral letter to encourage investigation of his virtues and miracles. Its positive statements merit complete citation.

> "François de Coëtlogon, by the grace of God, Bishop of Quimper and Count of Cornouailles, to the faithful who shall read these presents, greetings in the Lord. To co-operate in the good design of making known the holy life of R. P. Julien Maunoir, of the Company of Jesus, I shall imitate St. John who said, in speaking of our Lord: *Quod vidimus oculis nostris, quod perspeximus. . . annuntiamus vobis. We shall proclaim to you what we have seen with our eyes.* I have been acquainted with R. Père for the last sixteen or seventeen years. What I have seen with my own eyes obliges me to render testimony to his illustrious virtues. I have always recognized that far from being guided by the spirit of the world, he was activated only by a spirit of goodness, of simplicity, of devotion and of continual submission. His doctrine, wisdom and prudence were those of an angel. He never appeared offended by anyone; nor did he offend anyone. In the most wearisome labors, in the midst of persecutions, calumnies and even in danger of death, he was as calm as in his spiritual devotions. Indeed, such a tranquility of heart is, according to St. Ignatius, the founder of the Company of Jesus, an infallible mark of sanctity. Certainly the son and imitator of the great patriarch possessed this august, saintly quality in an eminent

degree. God also favored him with special prodigious graces for the salvation of souls and for the health of the body. The sacred harvests which he gathered in my diocese and in some others of this province, by his particlar talent for catechising, by his method of preaching, by his devotion to the confessional and by his completely holy life, are so admirable that he appears to me with good reason to have merited the name of the apostle of Brittany. If it were a question only of the virtue and the perfection which he established among our priests, that alone would have justified his acquiring this beautiful title. Before the missions were instituted, too few of the priests preached and catechised in my diocese; but now a very large number, formed to preaching by his direction, are sought for everywhere and work successfully for the conquest of souls. This fact alone convinces me that the words of the Savior to His apostles are verified also in the person of P. Maunoir: *Posui vos ut eatis et fructum afferatis et fructus vester maneat, I have sent you to preach my word, and to produce fruits worthy of eternity*. Indeed, since his demise, the memory of his holy instructions and of his virtuous example augments the devotion of the people and the zeal of the clergy. *Domino cooperante et sermonem confirmante sequentibus signis,* God has co-operated through all Brittany in performing, through his charitable intercession, prodigies for the glory of His servant. No one can doubt these prodigies, for we have the testimony of an almost infinite number of witnesses and we have the juridical reports which our commissioners have made and are continually making to us.

> Given at Quimper in our episcopal palace, October 14, 1684. The great services which the deceased rendered to our diocese during the last forty-two years of his life, obliges us to offer, brief though it be, this true testimony to his blessed memory."[1]

The church at Plévin became a pilgrimage shrine and the scene of extraordinary cures. Just a few days after the obsequies of Père Maunoir, one of the best authenticated cures occurred; it was that of a deformed crippled boy, Jean Boisadam, the six year old son of Pierre Boisadam, a tailor of Carhaix. The lad bore a hump on his back and another on his chest; in addition his legs were so twisted by paralysis that it was impossible for him to walk or to stand. The child had lain helpless in bed for three years. Hoping for the aid of Père Maunoir the father went to his tomb to pray for the cure of his son. His petition was partially answered by the disappearance of the humps, a fact verified by the parents, several neighbors and the governor of Carhaix, M. de Kerlouet. The paralysis remained, and so the kindly governor had the crippled boy conveyed in his carriage to Plévin. During the Sunday high Mass, in the presence of a crowd that filled the church, Jean was placed upon the tomb of Père Maunoir. Before the eyes of the large congregation his whole body became animated, and his twisted limbs were straightened out. He stood up immediately, and without any support, walked around Bl. Julien's tomb. The amazed onlookers, unable to contain their joy, filled the church with cries thanking God for curing the boy and honoring their Tad Mad.[2]

[1] Boschet, pp. 466-468.

[2] Boschet, pp. 395-398; Le Roux, pp. 89-90; *Summarium super*

Jean Boisadam's cure made Bl. Julien's tomb a magnet drawing pilgrim throngs from every corner of Brittany. On the highroads one would frequently encounter wagons conveying desperately sick persons to Plévin, or more pathetic still parents trudging along, bearing afflicted children in their arms. Some followed the example of one noble lady and her husband who walked the last mile barefooted. Many a pilgrim was journeying as the proxy of some poor invalid too ill to be transported. In sickrooms all over Brittany, countless petitions for the help of the Tad Mad were sealed with the promise of pilgrimage to his tomb. Miraculous cures or at least the report of them with names, dates and places, reached such numbers that Boschet fourteen years after Père Maunoir's death, and Le Roux at thirty years, hesitated to summarize them for fear of being charged with credulousness.

The Breton folk were not bothered with such misgivings. They accepted the prodigies at the tomb of the Tad Mad and proclaimed them loudly and persistently. If their prayers had been answered in their own distant homes, at the first opportunity they journeyed to Plévin to return their thanks. The Bretons have always been a grateful people. Once the pilgrims had completed their fervent thanksgivings at the tomb, they made it a matter of duty to present themselves to the pastor of Plévin, who was an apostolic notary on the appointment of the bishop of Quimper, and to declare to him the fact of the cures, the nature of the sickness and the marvelous circumstances in which Père Maunoir had answered their petitions. As a consequence the parish archives of Plévin

signatura Commissionis Introductionis Causae, p. 65, n. V. de miraculis post obitum.

came to possess a large collection of documents and sworn depositions, available for the future cause of Bl. Julien. Msgr. de Coëtlogon remarked: "If we should have to cite popular testimonies to prove the heroic virtues of P. Julien Maunoir, we could have as many witnesses as Brittany counts inhabitants."

The cause for beatification received a decided impetus with the publication in 1697 of Boschet's *Le Parfait Missionnaire.* This account of the virtues and miracles of Père Maunoir induced the Estates of Brittany, assembled at Vitry, to supplicate the bishops of the province "to institute the verbal processes and to make the necessary inquiries, in the places where Père Maunoir had conducted his missions and in the localities around his tomb, about the miracles which God had operated through the intercession of the said Père Maunoir, in order at the proper time to arrive at the declaration of his sanctity and at his canonization."[1] The bishops judged it best for the time being to continue the collecting of depositions of those claiming cures. At length in 1714, at the request of Père Le Roux; Postulator of the Cause, Msgr. de Ploeuc, bishop of Quimper, and Msgr. Frétat de Boisseau, bishop of Saint-Brieuc, set up commissions for the processes of beatification. There were two commissions at Quimper: one on Père Maunoir's renown for virtue and sanctity, the other on the miracles obtained through his intervention. The commission of Saint-Brieuc sought information on the miracles only.

The sessions of the three commissions were crowded with eager witnesses, who gave an unusually large number of sworn depositions. Msgr. de Ploeuc wrote in his account to the Holy See: "The miracles and prodigies

[1] The entire document is given in Séjourné, II, pp. 399-400.

operated by the servant of God cease not to demonstrate how powerful is his intercession. Scarcely had we commenced the *informationes* [1] on one or other of the miracles than the report of twenty others no less certain, no less credible, came to us immediately from all sides." [2] In all this mass of testimonies perhaps the most moving was a long statement on the virtues and miracles of Père Maunoir, signed by thirty venerable old priests who had been his missionary companions. The document is too lengthy for reproduction here, and the signatures of those Breton curés and vicaires of long ago would mean little to present-day readers. But one signature deserves our attention; it is the one that reads, "Jean Leuduger, scholastique et chanoine de Saint Brieuc." M. Jean Leuduger was one of the saintliest priests in the Brittany of his times. He was the organizer and for many years the director of the missionary priests of Saint-Brieuc, in addition to being the official theologian and canonist for the cathedral chapter. He was also the founder of the Daughters of the Holy Ghost, the "White Sisters", a congregation of teaching and nursing sisters, well known in Brittany, England and the United States. Finally he was one of the inspirers of St. Louis Grignon de Montfort, to whom he communicated the missionary methods of Bl. Julien Maunoir.

The processes were finally completed. In sending them to Rome, each bishop emphasized two points: the universal affection of the Breton people for Père Maunoir, and the universal desire for his canonization. Thus wrote

[1] *Informationes,* investigations for the seeking of information as to sanctity and miracles.

[2] *Ex processu informat, Corisopit. Summar. super signatura Commissionis Introductonis Causae,* pp. 25, 26.

the bishop of Quimper: "... there is not a single person who does not hold him in veneration, and there is not a single person who does not pursue him with homage and prayer. All beg of you, Holy Father, to be pleased to proceed to his beatification and canonization." [1] The bishop of Saint-Brieuc similarly declared: "All Bretons possess for him an extraordinary devotion. They throng from all parts to his tomb; and if the common people are impressed so, no less are the highest personages of the province... they pray with intense ardor for his beatification and canonization." [2]

The findings of the commissions were made available for the people of Brittany and of France too in 1716, a little more than a year later, by the publication of Père Le Roux's *Recueil des Vertus et des Miracles du Révérend Père Julien Maunoir, dé la Campagnie de Jésus* (A Collection of the Virtues and the Miracles of the Reverend Father Julien Maunoir, of the Company of Jesus). The book was more than a compilation of depositions. It offered also the results of the author's personal inquiries during his thirty years on the Breton Mission, to which he had been assigned in 1687, three years after the death of Père Maunoir. A Breton speaker by birth, a French speaker by education, he conversed familarly with all classes of the duchy. He worked constantly with the priest assistants who had known Père Julien so intimately. Time and again he visited the places of Père Maunoir's apostolate; there and elsewhere he experienced the efficacious results of his predecessor's methods. And all the

[1] *Ex processu Sanbriocensi super miraculis. Summar. super signatura Commissionis Introductionis Causae.* p. 76.

[2] *Ex processu Sanbriocensi super miraculis. Summar. super signatura Commissionis Introductionis Causae.* p. 76.

time he was witnessing the vast popular devotion to the Tad Mad, and hearing of, possibly even beholding, the blessed favors attributed to Brittany's modern apostle. With reason Père Le Roux had been appointed the Postulator of the Cause. [1]

So spontaneous and so widespread was the movement for the beatification that there seemed to be every hope for its early realization. Yet two and a half centuries were to pass before the Bretons could address their Tad Mad with the title "Blessed." The long postponement was due to the crushing disasters which French Catholicism had to suffer during all those sad times. First there was the determined opposition of the Gallican legalists, who were powerful enough in the Parlement of Rennes in 1743 to obtain a decree prohibiting missions and retreats in Brittany. Then came the complete catastrophe of the suppression of the Society of Jesus in France in 1762, and in the whole Church in 1773. A generation later the bloody cataclysm of the French Revolution raged, with the ruthless liquidation of the Chouan counter-revolutionaries in Brittany. The first decades of the nineteenth century brought the almost complete preoccupations of the Napoleonic wars, and following them the long, slow recovery of the French Church, destitute of men and means. Most of that century witnessed the unrelenting assaults of the dedicated French anticlericals, culminating in their expulsion of all religious orders in the first years of the twentieth century. Finally there were the enormous devastations and the complete paralyses of the two World Wars.

[1] The official who collects for the Holy See information regarding the virtues and miracles of a proposed beatus or saint.

Despite all vicissitudes and disasters the people of Brittany persisted steadfastly in their veneration of the Tad Mad. Never was there a time when the pilgrims were not assembling at the tomb, except during the fearsome days of the Terror. Even then they came covertly. The revolutionists closed the church of Plévin and burned its precious archives, but not one of them dared lay a sacrilegious hand upon the venerated tomb. As soon as the churches were opened again Breton throngs were kneeling once more around the revered spot. In 1825 the Jesuits placed at the tomb a wooden statue of Père Maunoir, life-sized, painted in natural colors and carved in attitude of prayer. The people esteemed it highly, for it enabled them to picture their venerated apostle as being in their midst and still praying for them. Recently, on the occasion of the beatification, the old statue, considerably worn by time and the acquisitive piety of pilgrims, was replaced by a new wooden statue. This one represents Bl. Julien in the act of preaching; it summarizes, as it were, his apostolate. Bretons on their pilgrimages to Plévin always include a visit to the oratory which stands on the site of the presbytery in which their Tad Mad died. The oratory has been named happily Ty-Mamm-Doué. [1]

The people of Saint-Georges-de-Reintembault have their own memorials of their townsman. There is the house where he was born, at least the part that remained after a fire of long ago. An oratory has been located in this surviving section. Then there is the base of the old village calvary, where as a child he used to play at

[1] Ty-Mamm-Doué. "The House of the Mother of God," after the shrine of the Blessed Mother near Quimper, where Bl. Julien dedicated himself to the salvation of the Bretons. Cf. Chapter III, p. 47 ff.

The Tomb of Bl. Julien at Plévin.

(The statue has been recently replaced by a new one representing Bl. Julien preaching.)

preaching. But the object of the townspeople's greatest devotion is the mission cross which Père Maunoir erected during the great mission of 1662. In 1840 when a terrible epidemic swept Saint-Georges, striking down three hundred victims in the small village, the clergy led the people in procession to this cross. The scourge ceased before evening. [1] A similar pilgrimage, some years before, saved the nearby town of Saint-Jacques from destruction by fire. The conflagration raged so fiercely that the flames could be seen at Avranches, twelve miles away. While the men of Saint-Georges hastened to battle the flames, the women went in bare-footed procession to the mission cross of the Tad Mad. As they were finishing their prayers, the fire died down and was shortly afterwards extinguished. [2] Another mission cross of Père Maunoir is venerated at Dirinon; crippled children and those slow to walk are brought to it for cure. At Plouguernével the pulpit in which Père Julien preached his last sermon is held in special reverence.

The Jesuit residence at Quimper possessed the most valuable collection of relics. Most revered of all is the reliquary containing the heart of Bl. Julien. For two hundred and fifty years it had been kept in its place of deposit within the sanctuary of the college chapel, even after the Suppression when the institution became the Lycée of Quimper. In 1931 the precious relic was transferred to the present residence of the Jesuits, Ros-Avel, Rue de Rosmadec. Next is Père Maunoir's crucifix. It has had a wandering history: it was passed from one Jesuit to another until after the Suppression, was then guarded by nuns right through the Revolution, and was

[1] Séjourné, II, p. 344. The citation is from the parochial archives.
[2] Ibid., II, p. 344. (No date is given for the fire at Saint-Jacques).

finally restored to the Quimper Jesuits in 1838. The venerable crucifix is often brought to the bedside of the dying for the last kiss. Then there is his breviary, *Pars Hiemalis;*[1] though its old pages are yellowed and stained, it is in fairly good preservation. The volume is doubly dear to Bretons, for it first belonged to Dom Michel Le Nobletz and was given by him to his spiritual son. On the flyleaf is the following inscription: "Olim D. Michaelis Nobletz; at nunc collegii Corisis soc. Jesu. Hoc utebatur R.P. Manerius" (formerly D. Michel Nobletz's; but now belonging to the college of Quimper of the Society of Jesus. R.P. Maunoir used this book.) The last relic is a burse which Père Julien used for carrying the Blessed Sacrament to the sick; its linen texture and silk ornaments unfortunately are quite ravelled and worn with age.

Not far from the Jesuit residence at Quimper, just a short walk from the town, stands a very significant memorial of Bl. Julien, the ancient shrine of Ty-Mamm-Doué, where as a young scholastic he dedicated himself to the Breton Missions and prayed for the gift of the Breton language. Since his beatification it has become more than ever a popular center of pilgrimage.

But the most remarkable memorial of all is the affectionate loyalty of the common people of Brittany, so constant through three hundred years. Reverently they treasure any objects, crosses, medals, rosaries or pieces of linen cloth, which have been touched to the tomb of Bl. Julien or to the reliquary of his heart. In their homes they keep his portrait always in the place of honor. In every circumstance of life they put complete confidence

[1] *Pars Hiemalis* is the winter (hiems) volume of the Roman Breviary, there are four volumes, one for each season.

in his protection. On visiting a sick room they greet the invalid with "May God and the blessed Tad Mad bring you back your health." If death is approaching they say, "Recommend yourself to the blessed Tad Mad." Often times old people are heard to sigh: "When will the Tad Mad come to find me?" Their consoling words in the hour of bereavement are, "The Tad Mad has taken him." The poor beggar-man, on receiving his alms, thanks his benefactor, "May God and the blessed Tad Mad reward you and keep you from harm!" Even at the start of life mothers teach their little ones to say, "Tad Mad, pray for me."

One event all Bretons longed and prayed for, the quick coming of the day when the Church would raise their Tad Mad to her altars. In 1869 the bishops of Brittany, supported by their brethren of the French episcopate, petitioned the Holy See for the introduction of the cause. After the necessary preliminaries Pius IX in 1875 signed the favorable decision of the Congregation of Rites. The cause, however moved slowly; among other delaying forces was the chaos produced by two world wars. At length on March 6, 1949 Pius XII sanctioned the decree of the heroicity of the virtues of Julien Maunoir. Two years later, February 11, 1951, the Holy Father approved the two required miracles: one was the cure of a fracture at the base of the skull in the case of Mlle. Yvette Le Goff of Carhaix, which occurred June 11, 1921; The second was the cure of tuberculosis of the lungs in the case of Mme. Marie Gridou, which occurred at the tomb on January 13, 1926. At long last on Trinity Sunday, May 20, 1951, Père Julien Maunoir, S.J., missionary extraordinary and modern apostle of Brittany, was solemnly beatified. All Bretons pray that the day of the canonization of their Tad Mad be not distant.

APPENDIX I.

LIST OF THE MISSIONS PREACHED BY BL. JULIEN MAUNOIR, S.J. [1]

1640-1641

Quimper

Hospitals and prisons of Quimper
Parishes in the environ of Quimper
Ploaré
Saint-Hélène-de-Douarnenez
Pont-Croix
Pouldergat
Dependencies of Curlizon
Dependencies of Notre-dame-du-Juch
Dependencies of Saint-Jean-de-Tréboul

Saint-Pol-de-Léon

Isle of Ouessant
Isle of Molène

Quimper

Isle of Sein

1642

Quimper

Plounévez-du-Faou
Plounévez-Porzay
Plozévet

Dol

Isle of Bréhat
Lannevez
Kérity
Perros-Hamon
Perros-Guirec

Saint-Brieuc

Paimpol

Saint-Pol-de-Léon

Le Conquet
Isle of Ouessant
Isle of Molène

1643

Quimper

Quimper
Brasparts
Pleyben
Saint-Ségal
Audierne
Ty-Mamm-Doué
Cléden-Cap-Sizun
Plogoff
Penmarc'h
Plovan
Rostrenen

1644

Quimper

Quimper
Douarnenez

[1] As was noted in Chapter VII this list was made by Boschet in 1697, republished by Le Roux in 1715 and checked and republished by Séjourné in 1895. Boschet, pp. 471-482; Le Roux, pp. 227-240; Séjourné, II, pp. 239-368.

Plouhinec
Mahalon
Pont-Croix
Plozévet
Daoulas
Plougastel-Daoulas
Dirinon

1645

Quimper

Roscanvel
Hanvec and its dependency, Rumengol
Landerneau, (St. Thomas)
Loganna
Saint-Rivoal
Berrien
Scrignac
Bénodet

1646

Quimper

Quimper
Douarnenez
Ploaré
Pouldergat
Poullan
Curlizon
Langonnet
Saint Mayeux and its dependencies, Caruel and Vieux-Marché
Mûr-de-Bretagne and its dependency Saint Guen

Vannes

Cléguerec
Lignol

Quimper

Landeneau
Saint-Martin

Saint-Brieuc

Saint-Thelo

Quimper

Saint-Thurien
Locamand

1647

Quimper

Callac
Plusquellec and its dependency, Calanhel
Carnoët
Plourach
Neulliac and its dependency, Kergrist
Saint-Caradec
Merléac and its dependency, Le Quillio

1648

Quimper

Corlay
Le Haut-Corlay
Plussulien
Le Bodéo and its dependency, La Harmoye
Saint-Martin-des-Prés

Rennes

Saint-Georges-de-Reintembault
Mellé
Montault
Louvigné-du-Désert

Quimper

Fouesnant
Goulien
Plogoff
Cléden-Cap-Sizun

1649

Saint-Pol-de-Léon

Saint-Pol-de-Léon
Roscoff
Isle of Batz
Landerneau (Saint-Houardon)
Saint-Julien, a dependency of Ploudiry
Pencran-de-Notre-Dame, a dependency of Ploudiry
Plouzané and its dependency, Locmaria

Quimper

Landerneau (Saint-Thomas)
Plounévez-Quintin and its dependency, Trémargat
Bothoa and its dependency, Saint-Tréphine
Saint-Gildas, dependency of Vieux-Bourg

1650

Quimper

Saint-Guen, a dependency of Mûr
Mûr-de-Bretagne
Saint-Mayeux
Saint-Gilles-Pligeaux
Saint-Gilles-Vieux-Marché
Le Vieux-Bourg-Quintin
Saint-Gonnéry
Kerpert, dependency of Saint-Gilles-Pligeaux
Saint-Corentin, dependency of Carnoët

Saint-Pol-de-Léon

Plourin, near Morlaix

1651

Quimper

Ergué-Gabéric
Locamand
Tréméoc
Mûr and its dependency Saint-Guen
Saint-Suzanne
Merléac and its dependency, Le Quillio
Notre-Dame-de-Tormenou (Locronan)
Saint-Jean-de-Tréboul

1652

Quimper

Douarnenez
Ploaré
Saint-Nic
Pont-Croix
Beuzec-Cap-Sizun
Meilers
Poullan
Isle of Sein
Le Quillio, a dependency of Merléac
Saint-Elouan, in Saint-Guen
Cléden-Poher

Saint-Pol-de-Léon

Tréménac'h

1653

Quimper

Rostrenen
Kergrist-Moellou
Glomel
Sainte-Paule
Nizon
Saint-Trémeur (Carhaix)

Saint-Pol-de-Léon

Cléder
Goulven

1654

Quimper

Cuzon, in Kerfeunteun
Ergué-Armel
Plonéis
Tréogat
Crozon
Mûr
Pont-Croix
Saint-Martin-des-Prés
Merléac
Saint-Michel, a dependency of Glomel
Le Quillio
Tréogan

1655

Quimper

Plogastel-Saint-Germain
Pouldreuzic

Plovan
Lebaban
Cléden-Cap-Sizun
Plogoff
Laz
Saint-Goazec, a dependency of Laz
Châteauneuf
Leuhan
Coray
Douarnenez

1656

Saint-Pol-de-Léon

Le Conquet
Lochrist
Plougonvelin
Trébabu
Ploguin

Quimper

Douarnenez
Poullan
Isle of Sein
Plonéour-Lanvern
Tréogat

Tréguier

Tréguier

Saint-Brieuc

Plouha

Quimper

Saint-Tugean, in Primelin
Saint-Téis, or Déicole in Cléden
Saint-Philibert, Saint-Honoré in Plonéour
Plovan
Plomelin
Bodivit, in Plomelin
Plomodiern

1657

Quimper

Douarnenez

Tréguier

Louannec
Kermaria-Sulard, a dependency of Louannec
Tréguier
Notre-Dame-de-Coz-Yaudet
Bourbriac
Tressignaux
Bocqueho

Quimper

Pluguffan
Saint-Bihy, a dependency of Haut-Corlay
Kerlaz, in Plonévez-Porzay
Notre-Dame-du-Juch

1658

Saint-Brieuc

Plouha
Pléhédel
Pléguien

Tréguier

Notre-Dame-de-Coz-Yaudet

Quimper

Ploaré
Kernevel
Guengat
Pouldergat
Tréméoc
Kerlaz, a dependency of Plonévez-Porzay
Notre-Dame-du-Juch
Isle of Sein
Notre-Dame-du-Quillinen, a dependency of Briec

1659

Quimper

Perguet, now Bénodet

Tréguier

Plestin
Trémel

Quimper

Locronan
Plogonnec

Plonévez-Porzay
Saint-Caradec
Neulliac
Kergrist-Moëllou
Clehars
Plogoff
Cléden-Cap-Sizun
Le Moustoir, a dependency of Trébrivan

1660

Quimper

Douarnenez
Daoulas
Plougastel-Daoulas
Moëlan
La Faou
Rosnoën
Loperhet
Dirinon
Mûr
Saint-Guen
Saint-Connec, a dependency of Mûr
Haut-Corlay
Le Quillio
Vieux-Marché

1661

Quimper

Pouldergat
Poullan
Ploaré
Croixanvec
Saint-Gonnéry
Prison and hospital of Rennes
La Chapelle-Janson
La Guerche
La Bodéo
La Harmoye

1662

Quimper

Douarnenez
Bannalec
Le Tréhou
Trébivan
Plévin
Motreff

Rennes

Fougères
Saint-Georges-de-Reintembault

1663

Quimper

Kernevel
Carnoët
Plusquellec
Douarnenez
Saint-Thurien
Bonvel
Elliant
Saint-Martin-des-Bois

Saint-Pol-de-Léon

Isle of Batz

1664

Saint-Pol-de-Léon

Tréménac'h

Quimper

Pestivien
Saint-Martin
Bothoa
Sainte-Tréphine
Saint-Nicolas-du-Pélem
Douarnenez (Saint-Michel)

Vannes

Ploerdu
Caudan
Pluméliau
Plumergat
Teven

1665

Quimper

Quimperlé

Tréguier

Tonquédec

Quimper

Pleyben

Querrien
Douarnenez
Plozévet
Guiscriff
La Feuillée

Dol

La Bousaac

1666

Quimper

Le Faouët
Douarnenez
Scaër
Crozon
Langonnet

Rennes

Fougères et Saint-Georges

Quimper

Plomeur
Plozèvet

1667

Tréguier

Plourin, near Morlaix

Quimper

Roudouallec, a dependency of Gourin
Le Saint, a dependency of Gourin
Ploaré
Douarnenez
Kernevel
Melgven
Concarneau

1668

Quimper

Guiscriff
Mûr
Saint-Mayeux
Saint-Guen, a dependency of Mûr
Saint-Connec (Mur)
Neulliac

Saint-Pol-de-Léon

Brest
Tréménac'h
Plouguerneau
Kersaint
Landivisiau

Quimper

Poullaouen

1669

Quimper

Nevez
Esquibien, and its dependency, Audierne
Primelin, and its dependency, Saint-Tujean
Douarnenez
Riec
Merléac
Coray

Saint-Pol-de-Léon

Lesneven

Dol

Perros

1670

Quimper

Trégunc
Lanriec
Beuzec-Conq
Saint-Michel (Douarnenez)

Tréguier

Plourin, near Morlaix

Saint-Pol-de-Léon

Ploumoguer

Quimper

Moëlan
Langolen, a dependency of Briec

1671

Tréguier

Lannion

Quimper

Crozon
Camaret
Roscanvel
Le Quillio, a dependency of Merléac
Saint-Martin-des-Bois

1672

Quimper

Quimper
Pont-Croix
Landudec
Beuzec-Cap-Sizun
Mahalon
Tourch

Tréguier

Pédernec

Saint-Brieuc

Trévé

1673

Tréguier

Guincamp

Quimper

Glomel
Elliant and its dependencies, Rosporden, Saint-Yvi and Locmaria-an-hent

Saint-Brieuc

Plémy

Dol

Isle of Bréhat

Saint-Pol-de-Léon

Saint-Pol-de-Léon

1674

Tréguier

Morlaix, parish of Saint-Mathieu

Quimper

Landévennec
Telgruc
Carhaix

Tréguier

Pleumeur-Bodou
Plouaret

Dol

Locquenolé

1675

Saint-Pol-de-Léon

Landerneau
Cléder

Quimper

Châteaulin
Douarnenez
Plouguenével

MILITARY MISSIONS

Vannes

Pontivy

Quimper

Plozévet

1676

Quimper

Penmarc'h
Beuzec-Cap-Sizun
Plomeur
Treffiagat
Tréogat

Saint-Pol-de-Léon

Commana

Quimper

Pleyben

Vannes

Auray

Saint-Pol-de-Léon

Saint-Renan

Vannes

Caudan

Quimper

Riec

1677

Quimper

Kerlagatu
Plouhinec

Saint-Pol-de-Léon

Brest

Quimper

Plomodiern
Quimper
Locamand

Tréguier

Tréguier

Saint-Brieuc

Saint-Brieuc

1678

Dol

Isle of Bréhat

Saint-Brieuc

Lachèze, and its dependency, La Ferrière
Moncontour
Lamballe

Vannes

Locminé

Saint-Pol-de-Léon

Saint-Servais, dependency of Plounéventer
Lesneven

Tréguier

Pontrieux, dependency of Quemper-Guézenec

1679

Tréguier

Quemperven

Quimper

Pouldergat and its dependency, Pouldavy
Maël-Pestivien

Tréguier

Plestin
Ploujean

Vannes

Pontivy

Quimper

Locronan
Huelgoat and Locmaria, dependencies of Berrien
Cléden-Poher
Coray

1680

Quimper

Plounévez-Quintin

Saint-Pol-de-Léon

Lochrist, Le Conquet

Vannes

Rohan

Quimper

Pluguffan, chapel of the Moëliens in Plonévez-Porzay

1681

Tréguier

Pont-Melvez

Quimper

Ploaré and Douarnenez

Rennes

Abbey of Saint-Sulpice
Noyal
Saint-Georges-de-Reintembault

Dol

Saint-Georges-de-Grehaigne

1682-1683

Quimper

Crozon

Saint-Brieuc

Ybias
Paimpol

Tréguier

Bourbriac

Quimper

Plounévezel
Scrignac

APPENDIX II

THE ORDER OF PERSONAGES IN THE GREAT PROCESSION [1]

"The Father who is the superior of the mission marches first, always at the head, with a staff in his hand. The disciples, who are the children of the catechism class, follow him two by two.

The Natural Law

Adam
Abel
Cain and the other children of Adam, with the dress and implements of toilers of the soil
Seth
Enos
Cainan
Malaleel
Jared
Mathusael
Lamech
Noah

The Patriarchs

Sem
Arphaxad
Salé
Heber
Phaleb
Rehu
Sarug
Nachor
Thare
Abraham
Isaac
Jacob
Joseph

The Law Givers

Moses
Joshua
Gedeon
Heli
Samuel
David, penitent
Solomon

The Prophets

Isaias
Jeremias, with Baruch, his scribe
Ezechiel
Daniel
Osee
Joel
Amos
Abdias
Jonas
Micheas
Nahum
Habacuc
Sophonias
Aggaeus
Zacharias
Malachias
(Each prophet carries some distinctive object by which he can be recognized)

[1] This list is taken from *Exercises de la mission,* a manuscript folio, written by Guillaume Nicolas, pastor of Landudec, September 8, 1754, pp. 372, 373. The manuscript is in the library of the Jesuit residence at Quimper. The list is similar to the ones used by Père Maunoir.

The Hidden Life of Jesus Christ

Saint Joachim
Saint Anne
The Conception of the Virgin
The Nativity of the Virgin
The Presentation of the Virgin
The Annunciation of the Virgin
The Angel Gabriel
The Visitation
The Nativity of Jesus Christ
The Shepherds
The Adoration of the Three Kings
The Purification of the Virgin
The High Priest Simeon
The Flight into Egypt with Saint Joseph
The Angel Guardian
Herod
The Massacre of the Innocents
The Bereft Mothers, all dressed in black
The Return of the Infant Jesus from Egypt
The Child Jesus who Interrogates the doctors and answers their difficulties

The Active Life of Jesus

Saint John the Baptist, who preaches and baptizes

THE APOSTLES

Saint Peter
Saint Andrew, brother of St. Peter
Saint James
Saint John
Saint Philip
Saint Bartholomew
Saint Matthew
Saint Thomas
Saint James, son of Alpheus
Saint Simon
Saint Jude
Judas Iscariot, who was the traitor

The Suffering Life of Jesus Christ

The Angel with the Chalice
The Judges
Annas
Caiphas
Herod
Pilate
The Jews
The Carrying of the Cross
Magdalene
Simon Cyrene
Saint Nicodemus, with the three nails and the crown of thorns
Joseph of Arimathea, with the winding sheet
Our Lady of Pity
Two Assistants
The Three Marys with their ointment
Mary Magdalene
Mary of James
Mary Salome
The Women of Jerusalem
Saint Catherine of Siena
The Sisters of the Third Order
Mary of Egypt

The Glorious Life

The Queen of the Angels
The Three Theological Virtues
Faith
Hope
Charity
The Four Cardinal Virtues
Prudence
Justice
Temperance
Fortitude
The Queen of the Martyrs
Saint Ursula
Saint Catherine
Saint Barbara
Girls dressed in red

Saint Helen
Saint Frances
Saint Geneviève
The Queen of the Angels
Girls dressed in white
The Queen of Heaven

The First Retreat
The Second Retreat
The Third Retreat
The Eucharistic Life
The clergy, two by two
The Blessed Sacrament

Finally the people walk after the Blessed Sacrament, the men in front, followed by the girls and the women. Amen.

In each of the three Retreat groups, the men walk first, followed by the women. The marchers will chant only joyful cantiques, omitting those which deal with death, judgment, hell and sin, or cause scruples to anyone. A cross is to be carried on high at the head of the children, and in the same way a cross is to be carried at the head of each Retreat group."

APPENDIX III.

DESCRIPTION OF THE CHART OF THE HEARTS.[1]

The *Chart of the Hearts* is a quite complicated affair; its very complexity would indicate audiences capable of following a continued symbolism. There are thirty squares, arranged six across the chart; in all but one the single motif is a heart, and each separate heart contains, or is surrounded by, numerous symbolical figures. The interpretation follows in this order:

"At the top of the chart appears, in Greek and in Latin, the ancient device, 'KNOW THYSELF'. Directly beneath runs the title: 'A Daily Exercise For All Christian Men Who Desire to Reach Eternal Life.' Then follow three series of squares, each ten in number.[2]

Square One of the first series gives the vision of God as the last end of man. Above is the Eternal Father, crowned with glory, and with Him the nine choirs of angels. Paradise is symbolized by a circle, the arcs of which have varied colors to show how star differs from star in glory. At the bottom is a gate, the several colors of which represent the different virtues; the key of this gate is the love of God.

Square Two is almost completely filled with a ladder, to signify the labor of climbing to the attainment of the full enjoyment of God. Beneath the ladder is an oratory to teach that prayer must accompany all efforts of the soul. The foot of the ladder rests on two bases, the written word of God and the tradition of the Church. On each rung are symbolic numbers: 72 (disciples of Christ), 3 (theological virtues), 4 (cardinal virtues), 10 (commandments), 7 (sacraments), 7 (gifts of the Holy Ghost), 12 (fruits of the Holy Ghost), 8 (beatitudes), 14 (works of mercy), 5 (precepts of the Church). On the eleventh and

[1] Cf. p. 148. This explanation of the *Chart of the Hearts* is taken from a film-lecture, author not noted, published in Paris and first given at Quimper, October 2, 1951. A more extensive explanation may be found in H. Le Gouvello's, *Le Vénérable Michel Le Nobletz;* (Paris 1898) pp. 204-205.

[2] Actually there are ten squares in the first series, twelve in the second and eight in the third. (M.P.H.)

twelfth rungs are placed two words, LABOR and LOVE, to emphasize the necessity of both in a zealous life.

Square Three signifies by one of the uprights of the ladder that the knowledge of God is obtained by the twelve articles of Faith.

Square Four signifies by the other upright the importance of recollection in God. The heart of man is the center of a turning wheel, the rays of which indicate the ten ways of keeping the recollection of God.

Square Five presents a little heart included within a bigger one, to symbolize our union with the divine will, the effects of which are represented by four circles in the lower part.

Square Six gives a series of concentric circles surrounding the heart. They are good resolutions to maintain this union; such as reflections on misfortunes, confessions etc.

Square Seven depicts the fortress of the heart, surrounded by two walls, and defended by four corps of guards and four sentinels.

Square Eight shows the heart ornamented with all the virtues.

Square Nine shows a forge, where arms are made for the defense of the heart. The forge's flame is nourished by two considerations, the goodness of God and the ingratitude of men.

Square Ten has a twelve-hour clock, marking the Christian's daily exercises. In the center a hand attached to the heart recalls that exterior works should be in accord with the heart.

The second series of squares contains twelve sections.

Square One has the figure of a man, gashed, disfigured and blackened; it is a soul burdened with original sin.

Square Two symbolizes the soul after Baptism; the Holy Ghost is dwelling in the center of a heart, which is ornamented with beautiful tapestries, the infused virtues.

Square Three has for its subject, temptations; the world, the devil and the flesh besiege the heart with their snares and seek to enter it.

Square Four depicts the soul that has yielded to temptation; the heart is engraved with the vices and sins consented to.

Square Five shows the heart possessed by the devil; it is filled with vileness, represented by frogs, serpents and other repellent beasts.

Square Six signifies the plight of the heart occupied by Satan; it is locked and at its closed door our Lord must stand begging admission.

Square Seven gives the entry of the Savior into the heart, which He inspects with a lantern to see the damage.

Square Eight describes the purgation; He sweeps the heart of all the vices which had been stamped upon it.

Square Nine portrays the Master cleaning the heart by the aid of His sacraments and by the virtue of His Passion.

Square Ten presents the heart washed clean; it is adorned with love of the Cross and of the Law.

Square Eleven shows the heart ravished by the love of God and the contemplation of His benefactions.

Square Twelve places the heart on the summit of spiritual life; our Savior is reposing in the heart that is adorned with decorations, the Christian virtues.

The third series of squares contains eight squares and deals with the seven deadly sins. In each square there is an animal figure to symbolize the vice.

Square One depicts Envy; a woman eating the heart of her neighbor and carrying a death-head on the point of a sword. A dog's head is the symbol.

Square Two is for Avarice; an old man with his back turned towards the Cross and gazing intently on his purse. A frog is the symbol.

Square Three treats of Luxury; a man and a woman plan lustful action. The head of a he-goat is the symbol.

Square Four portrays Pride; a woman richly dressed with a mirror in her hand. A strutting peacock is the symbol.

Square Five deals with Gluttony; a man seated at a table, with a glass in his hand. The head of a hog is the symbol.

Square Six shows Slothfulness; a woman uninterestedly holding a closed book. An ass is the symbol.

Square Seven represents Anger; a crazed man brandishing a dagger. The symbol is a wolf.

Square Eight is a summary; it pictures the sinner, walking on all fours, ridden by the devil and bearing two baskets filled with Capital Sins."

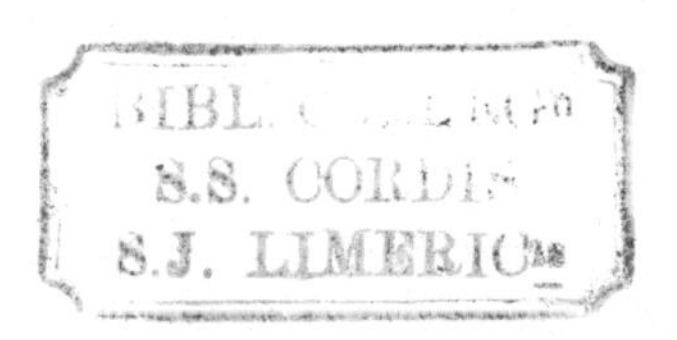

APPENDIX IV

THE WRITINGS OF BL. JULIEN MAUNOIR, S.J.

Printed works: [1]

I. *Canticou spirituel* . . . "these are spiritual cantiques and instructions profitable for learning the road which leads to Paradise." This work, described in Chapter VIII, "Charts, Chants, and Chapters," went through six editions and several reprintings during the author's lifetime."

II. *Ar Vuhez Gristen* (The Christian Life), attributed in part to Père Maunoir.

III. *Ar Vuhez Sant Caurintin,* a life of Saint Corentin, in 766 Breton verses. A Latin life of the saint has been attributed to Père Maunoir, but no trace of it has been found.

IV. Breton Cantiques in honor of Saint Elouan.

V. *An Templ consacret dar Bassion Jesus Christ,* "erected in the heart of the devout Christian," composed in Breton verse and prose. This volume includes some smaller works, written at various times: *The Catechism of the Prayer of the Heart, according to the Exercises of Saint Ignatius; The Seven Stations,* or *The Seven Days of the Week Consecrated to the Passion;* and *Cantiques on the Passion.*

VI. *Le Sacré Collège de Jésus.* This work was intended to help French-speaking priests in instructing and guiding their Breton-speaking flocks. The subtitle reads: "graded into five classes, wherein Christian lessons are taught in the Amorican language, [2] with three keys to enter therein, a *Dictionary,* a *Grammar* and a *Syntax* in the same language, composed by Reverend P. Julien Maunoir of the Company of Jesus, by the order of Monseigneur de Cornouailles."

VII. *Chemin assuré de pénitence,* "useful for penitents and confessors in preparing all sorts of confessions, general as well as particular, with a directory for confessors, corrected and augmented with the principal duties of a good ecclesiastic." If there ever was a Breton edition, it has not been discovered.

VIII. *Abrégé de la science du salut,* "proper for being taught in parish churches, chapels and homes, with some spiritual cantiques,

[1] Subtitles are translated into English to give the meaning and scope of the works.

[2] The first part of this book *Christian Lessons* was published under the title, *Catechisme de la mission.*

to be sung at catecheses, on the principal points of Christian Doctrine." There was a Breton edition, *An abrege eus an Doctrin Christen*.

Manuscript Works:

I. *Journal latin de missions, par P. Julien Maunoir, Ière décade de 1640 a 1650.* The original is in the Roman archives of the Society of Jesus; there are two copies, one in the diocesan archives of Quimper and one in the Jesuit residence at Quimper. A summary of the first three decades, *Analyse des trois premières décades, 1640 a 1670*, was made near the close of the seventeenth century; but it has been lost. There are numerous and long quotations from the *Journal* in the works of Boschet and La Roux. Here must be added the *Montagne, seu de Magis*, which contained Père Maunoir's method for hearing the confessions of alleged sorcerers; it was an excerpt from the *Journal* and appeared in French in 1650.

II. *La Vie du M. le Nobletz*, "priest, missionary, containing the idea of a perfect secular priest." A copy is in the diocesan archives of Quimper; another is in the Jesuit residence at Quimper.

III. *La Vie manuscrite du Père Pierre Bernard de la Compagnie de Jésus.* This has been lost.

IV. *La Vie manuscrite de Catherine Daniélou, par le P. Julien Maunoir, de la Compagnie de Jésus, son directeur.* There is a copy in the Jesuit residence at Quimper.

V. *La Vie manuscrite de Marie-Amice Picard*, "deceased at Saint-Pol-de-Léon, December 26, 1652, drawn from verbal processes made on the order of Messire Robert Cupiff, Bishop of Léon, and dedicated to Monseigneur, the Most Illustrious and the Most Reverend, Pierre de Labrousse, Bishop and Count of Léon." There was a copy in the former Jesuit college of Paris, l'Ecole Saint-Geneviève, and there is an abridgment in the Jesuit archives of the Paris Province.

VI. *Chef-d'oeuvre de la grâce de Jésus-Christ crucifié dans la vocation, conversion et fidélité constante jusqu'a la mort de M. de Trémaria, prêtre séculier et missionaire.* That is a biography of M. de Trémaria. The first part is in the departmental archives of Finistère, the second part is in the Kerdanet Library of Lesneven. There is a complete copy in the diocesan archives of Quimper.

BIBLIOGRAPHY

Acta Apostolicae Sedis, Vol. XLI. Roma, 1949.
"Decretum de virtutibus pro ejus (J.M.) beatificatione," p. 474.

Acta Apostolicae Sedis, Vol. XLIII. Roma, 1951.
"Decretum de miraculis," p. 178.
"Decretum de tuto," p. 225.
"Decretum pro eius beatificatione; recensio vitae et actorum," pp. 428, 430.
"Beatus renuntiatur," p. 431.
"Ejus virtutes B.P. exaltat," (in French) p. 437.

Acta Sanctae Sedis, Vol. VIII. (Date of document, 1875). Roma, 1908. Decree for proceeding to the cause of the Ven. Servant of God, P. Julien Maunoir, S.J.

Biographie Générale, t. XXXIV. Paris, 1869.
"Julien Maunoir," pp. 365, 366.

Boschet, Antoine, S.J., *Le Parfait Missionnaire ou La Vie du R.P. Julien Maunoir, S.J.,* seconde edition, revue et corrigeé, Lyon, 1834.

Brémond, Henri, *Histoire Littéraire du Sentiment Religieux en France.* Paris, 1926, t. V., Le Conquete Mystique, c. 2, "Jean Rigoleuc, Julien Maunoir et les Missions Bretonnes," pp. 66-118.

Brucker, Joseph, S.J., *La Compagnie de Jésus, Esquisses de son Institut et de son Histoire,* 1521-1773, Paris, 1919.

de la Chevasnerie, R. M., S.J., *Le "Tad Mad". Vie du Bienheureux* Père Maunoir, S.J., Dinard, 1951.

Duchesne, Msgr. L.M.O., *Fastes Episcopaux de l'Ancienne Gaul.* 3 vols. Paris, 1907-1915.

Fouqueray, Henri, S.J., *Histoire de la Compagnie de Jésus en France,* t. IV. Paris, 1925.

Gense, James H., S. J., Feast Days in the Jesuit Calendar, Bombay, 1954. "January 28, Blessed Julien Maunoir, Apostle of Brittany (1606-1682)."

Gougaud, Louis, O.S.B., *Christianity in Celtic Lands,* translated by Maud Joynt, London, 1932.

——— *Gaelic Pioneers of Christianity;* The work and influence of Irish monks and saints in continental Europe (VIth-XIIth cent.). Dublin, 1932, translated by Victor Collins.

Harney, Martin P., S.J. *The Jesuits in History,* New York, 1941.

d'Hérouville, H.A., S.J., *Le Vincent Ferrier du XVIIe Siecle, Le Vénérable Julien Maunoir,* Paris, Quimper, 1932.

——— *Une Vocation d'Apotre, La Jeunesse du Vénérable Julien Maunoir,* Saint Brieuc, 1931.

——— Woodstock Letters, Vol. LX, 1931, "Vénérable Julien Maunoir, S.J., a Pilgrimage to his Birthplace and Grave."

——— *Annales de Bretagne,* XL, pp. 271-283. "Julien Maunoir, Escrivain, Grammarien et Poete," Rennes, Paris, 1932, 1933.
Kerbiriou, Chanoine Louis, *Les Missions Bretonnes,* nouvelle édition, Brest, 1935.
——— *L'attitude du Père Maunoir a l'égard des états mystiques,* mss. Quimper, 1951.
Lavisse, Ernest, *Histoire de France,* Vols. VI and VII. Paris, 1911.
Le Berre, Mlle. Marthe, *Un Grand Missionnaire Breton, Le Bienheureux Père Maunoir.* 3ème édition. Rennes, 1951.
Le Gouvello, Hippolyte, *Le Vénérable Michel Le Nobletz.* Paris, 1898.
Le Roux, Guillaume, S.J., *Recueil des Vertus et des Miracles du R.P. Julien Maunoir, S.J.,* nouvelle édition, Saint-Brieuc, 1848.
Maurette, Fernand, *Toute France.* Paris, 1933. "La Bretagne". pp. 169-188.
Parcheminou, Corentin, *Monsieur de Trémaria.* Priziac. near Langonnet, 1937.
Patrignani, Giuseppe, S.J., *Menologio di Pie Memorie d'alcuni Religioso della Compagnia di Gesu.* Vol. I. Venice, 1730, "Giulio Maunoir."
de Rochemonteix, Camille, S.J., *Un Collège des Jésuites aux XVIIe et XVIIIe Siècles, Le Collège Henri IV de La Flèche. t. I. Le Mans,* 1889.
Roquette, Robert, *Etudes,* t. 270, Juillet-Août-Septembre, 1951. Paris. *"Les 'Deux Etendards' en Basse-Bretagne, Le Bienheureux Julien Maunoir* (1606-1683)".
Séjourné, Xavier-August, S.J., *Histoire du Vénérable Serviteur de Dieu, Julien Maunoir, S.J.,* Paris-Poitiers, 1895.
Sommervogel, Charles, S.J., *Bibliothèque de la Compagnie de Jésus,* t. V. pp. 752-756, Bruxelles-Paris, 1894. "Julien Maunoir." List of published works, wth their various editions, and of unpublished manuscripts.
de Tonquedec, Joseph, S.J., *Le Bienheureux Père Maunoir et le Clergé Breton,* Quimper, 1951.
Thurston, Herbert, S.J. and Attwater, Donald, *Butler's Lives of the Saints.* Vol. I. New York, 1956. "Bl. Julien Maunoir, Jan. 29."
Uguen, Chanoine J.M., *Buhez an Tad Julian Maner, Jezuist, Misioner Breiz,* Le Mans, 1933.

DAUGHTERS OF ST. PAUL,

In Massachusetts
50 St. Paul's Avenue
Jamaica Plain,
Boston 30, *Mass.*
172 Tremont St.,
Boston 11, *Mass.*
381 Dorchester St.
So. Boston 27, *Mass.*
325 Main St.
Fitchburg, Mass.

In New York
78 Fort Place,
Staten Island 1, *N.Y.*
39 Erie St.,
Buffalo 2, *N.Y.*
625 East 187th Street
Bronx, N.Y.

In Connecticut
202 Fairfield Ave.,
Bridgeport, Conn.

In Ohio
141 West Rayen Ave.,
Youngstown 3, *Ohio*
Cleveland, Ohio

In Texas
114 East Main Plaza,
San Antonio 5, *Texas*

In California
1570 Fifth Ave.,
San Diego 1, *Calif.*

In Florida
2700 Biscayne Blvd.
Miami 37, *Florida*

In Louisiana
86 Bolton Ave.,
Alexandria, La.

In Canada
8885 Blvd. Lacordaire,
St. Leonard Deport-Maurice,
Montreal, Canada
1063 St. Clair Ave. West,
Toronto, Canada

In England
29 Beauchamp Place,
London, S.W. 3, *England*

In Africa
Box 4392
Kampala, Uganda

In India
Water Field Road Extension,
Plot N. 143,
Bandra, India

In Philippine Islands
No. 326 Lipa City,
Philippine Islands

In Australia
58 Abbotsford Rd.,
Homebush N.S.W., *Australia*

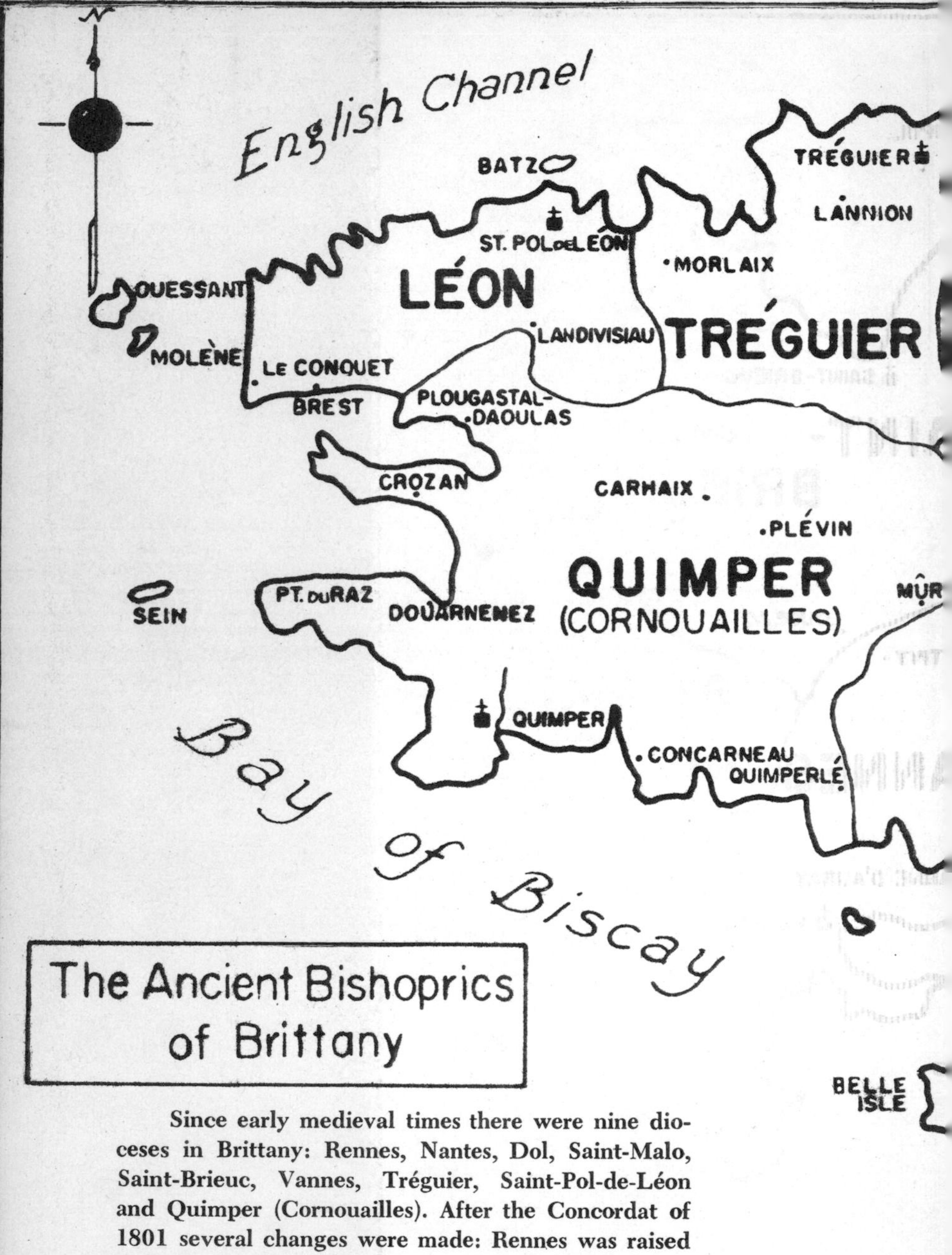

The Ancient Bishoprics of Brittany

Since early medieval times there were nine dioceses in Brittany: Rennes, Nantes, Dol, Saint-Malo, Saint-Brieuc, Vannes, Tréguier, Saint-Pol-de-Léon and Quimper (Cornouailles). After the Concordat of 1801 several changes were made: Rennes was raised to an archdiocese; Saint-Brieuc, Vannes and Quimper were suppressed and divided among the first four dioceses; Nantes was constituted a suffragan see of the Archdiocese of Tours.